Words of
Fire and Faith

I0894226

Words of Fire and Faith

Lee Lozowick

Edited by M. Young

HOHM PRESS
Chino Valley, AZ

Cover design by Zac Parker, Kadak Graphics

Interior design by Becky Fulker, Kubera Book Design

ISBN: 978-1-935387-35-0

Library of Congress Cataloging-in-Publication Data
(Application submitted)

Hohm Press
P.O. Box 4410
Chino Valley, AZ 86323
800-381-2700
http://www.hohmpress.com

For the Lineage and Legacy of the Beggar Saints

Swami Ramdas
Yogi Ramsuratkumar
Anjaneya Khepa Lee

and for the "Sahaj Vision," wherever it may live

The guru's arms are open wide. His heart is open wider. His treasury, overflowing with gold and other precious substances, is not only unguarded but is at the center of his world, unmistakable and unmissable. Whatcha waitin' for?

Lee Lozowick
June 2009

Contents

Preface xi
Foreword by Llewellyn Vaughan-Lee xiii
Foreword by Traktung Yeshe Dorje xvii
Introduction xix

Everything Is For The Best 1
Every Act of Dignity 4
Remember to Practice 6
To Speak without Compromise 9
Dignity 12
Get with the Program 16
Sahaj Vision 20
Spiritual Slavery 24
I Will Not Slow Down 29
The Will of God 33
The Big Clean Up 37
We Are Looking for Saints 41
Receiving What the Guru Gives 45
Precision in Practice 52
Transforming Every Obstacle 57
Seeing the Guru 62
The Higher Practice 67
To Die Longing 73
Overflowing with Knowledge 79
Faith 85

What Is an Ashram? 91
A Small Rant 96
To Grow into Devotees 99
A Far Deeper Work 104
Faith and Surrender 109
Who Will Make the Gesture? 114
What Is It That I Trust in You? 119
Sanctuary 124
Being Straightened 129
The Spirit of the Law 136
The Refusal 143
On the Gospel of Judas 149
Vanity, Pride, Lust 154
"Not What Should Be, but What Is" 160
Yes 164
Legacy 168
Doing the Best We Can 171
Field Attention 173
Know Yourself 177
Good Enough is Good Enough 182
Enlightened Community 186
Enlightened Duality 190
We Are at War 194
The Guru's Blessing 197
Sacred Objects 201
Do Your Part 205
Graceful Benediction 208

Holy Help 211
It's All One 215
Be True to Your Word 218
Radical Change 222
This Tender and Sweet Alchemy 225
"Delicate Impartial Love" 229
An Alchemy of Consciousness 233
Live and Learn 235
Live and Learn II 240
Be Different 243
A Chance to Move 245
Who Is the Guru? 247
Something to Look Forward To 250
Timing Is Everything 253
A Total Unknown 256
Who Do You Say I Am? 260
There Is Always Another Chamber 264

Afterword 266

Preface

From 2008 to November 2010, Lee Lozowick lived fully in the midst of an illness that impeded his ability to speak; during that time he handwrote his formal teaching addresses. A few of these "words of fire and faith"—as he called them—were originally edited and published, at his request, in the form of small booklets. In the two years since his *mahasamadhi* in November 2010, it has become apparent that Lee's last written instructions to his own students are a treasure trove that may be of great value to aspirants and practitioners of all traditions on the Path.

The rich, multivalent essays of this book invoke the powerful transmission of Lee's communication during a time when his "view from the edge" was extraordinarily vivid and clear. The essays convey the author's tenderness, fire, absolute certainty, and clarity—and perhaps most of all, his abandon and faith in the "Sahaj Vision" (as he calls it in these pages) of Surrender to the Divine Will. Lee pours out pith teachings with the same sense of humor, straightforward practicality, affection, generosity and ruthless or sweet compassion that shaped his work with students since 1975.

In the process of editing, Lee's inimitable style of writing has been kept in place as much as possible, as has his intimate, conversational tone and his free-wheeling use of the street-wise vernacular that is commonly found in contemporary conversation. Lee used capitalizations in a way that appears random but was quite intentional; he oftentimes capitalized words such as sangha, dharma, guru, ashram, practice, or spiritual master, while at other times these words appeared in his handwritten originals in the lower case; with minor exceptions, these have been left as he wrote them. His inspired, spontaneous use of metaphors and *sandhya bhasa,* or twilight language, which comes so naturally to the Bauls, is left intact for the reader to discern its various levels of meaning. At the end of each essay appear the sanskrit words राम राम (ram, ram) were handwritten by Lee.

Following the trail of any essay, one may be touched by the vibrant incandescence of a gifted teacher who faced life and death with fire and faith, without compromise or backing down; in another turn of the page, Lee writes as a spiritual practitioner within the human predicament. He speaks to essential, universal themes: self-honesty, cultivating attention, sanctuary, working with vanity, pride, lust, enlightened culture, reality as it is, faith, grace, divine ravishment, and the relationship with the Beloved.

In the pages that follow, Lee's insight and his burning love flow into us and uplift the heart. His essays may offer a particular help for those who are confronting their own mortality and seek to practice with a profound degree of refined awareness and grace, as he did, up to the moment and transition of bodily death. They are offered to all wayfarers on the Path, and to devotees, students, and friends of Khepa Lee, the heart son of Yogi Ramsuratkumar.

M. Young
February 24, 2013
Triveni Ashram

Foreword

Llewellyn Vaughan-Lee

What is the real nature of spiritual work? Is it becoming free from the ego and its illusions, from our sense of a separate self? Is it experiencing, if only for an instant, the greater consciousness of our divine nature, its qualities of peace, love, and bliss? Is it being open to the emptiness that is the essence of the Universe, or simply learning how to live with compassion and loving kindness? These are just words for a Love that calls and draws us to Itself, for a journey that has no name.

My friendship with Lee Lozowick developed over a number of years, when he would come with some students and we would sit and talk, share stories of this journey. He would mostly be in silence whilst others talked, as if expressing how little could be really said. And then we would have a lunch of homemade bread and cheese, and apple cake with whipped cream. There would be laughter and the enjoyment of friendship and simple food, before our ways would part again and he would drive off, taking his students on another stage of this journey.

These writings come from a time when Lee was already experiencing the transformative effect of cancer. I wonder—after life's ultimate transformation, when the caterpillar finally becomes a butterfly—how Lee sees spiritual work from where he is now? How does this thread of the soul's longing appear from the other side, how does love feel on this further shore? Every journey takes us here, and some would say our journey through this world is just a preparation for this crossing. Who leaves the shore and who arrives at this place of pure light, where we no longer see through a glass darkly, but know even as we are known? And what is left of a lifetime's struggle, of the stories by which we define our self? Or have we learnt to leave these stories, these struggles, at the water's edge?

There is a basic misconception in the West that the spiritual journey is about us, that it is our journey, our transformation. But the real devotee, the real wayfarer, knows that it is never about us, about the "I" who sets out on the journey. We may think that we are doing the practice, and yes, we need to have this intention, we have to engage in the work. But the real traveller on the path is the secret substance within the heart, the essence of our being. It is this divine core of our self that is transformed, that is merged, that realizes our deepest oneness. On this journey the "I'" is left behind, just a bystander to the real work of the soul. We may recite our mantra, sit in meditation, but this is just the outer covering for the deeper mystery that takes place within us.

Little can be said of the real journey of the soul, of the real work of transformation. It is lived through heartache, tears and silence, as well as the simple sharing of a cup of tea and laughter among friends. It is the real fragrance that is under what we call "spiritual practice," mysterious and wonderful, and always calling us to go further, deeper. In the pages that follow you will find traces of this living and dying, a scent of something else that belongs to what is Real. It shows that someone has passed this way on their own journey and left footsteps in the sand for us to follow to the water's edge. Maybe there is a boat waiting, or maybe we are left to swim until we too drown in the great unknown.

And yet something does remain, especially when someone has lived and loved and known the truth of what is Real. It is like a promise fulfilled, a call that is answered. It belongs to the essence of what it means to be a human being. Allow it to touch you, to reach inside and mirror yourself back to yourself. Allow yourself to be a part of this most mysterious work:

Strive to become the true human being:
one who knows love, one who knows pain.
Be full, be humble, be utterly silent,
be the bowl of wine passed from hand to hand.

Al-Ansâri

Foreword

Traktung Yeshe Dorje

Is not my word like fire and like a hammer that breaks rock into pieces?

Jeremiah 23:29

Sitting down to write a few words for this book of Lee's gems, I am reminded of Rebbe Israel the Maggid of Kozhenitz, who in his illness was so weak, so emaciated, that he had to be carried to services and yet . . . and yet . . . his words carried the fire of prayer and transformation. Lee's disease ravaged his body and caused his heart to shine ever brighter. I am also reminded of St. John of the Cross, alone in his cell, beaten multiple times weekly by the guards, and in this condition he found the honing of divine love into unbreakable power. Lee's disease beat his body regularly, and yet his Love became honed in compassion's thrust toward communication expressed in these writings.

Last week I had a dream of Lee. At four a.m. his voice was strong and unharmed by the disease which had ravaged his body. On waking I remembered the voice and inflection perfectly, "Sometimes philosophers ask 'Why something rather than nothing?' but The Lover knows the answer to this pseudo question before the words have left the philosophers' lips."

It is said that when the great Tzadik Elimmelek of Lizensk died, his last will and testament left Rebbe Medie his brain, Rebbe Yehoshua Heschel his tongue, Rebbe Yaakov Yitzhak his sight and Rebbe Israel his heart. Rebbe Israel was the Heart of his Generation, a candle that burned . . . the very body burned bright so that others might come to address God with familiarity, as he did. Lee was such a candle. Those who were with him at the end have spoken to me about the brightness with which he burned to the last.

These words are fire. They are Love, but often that Love burns and hammers. This hammering power, that cannot bear the abiding ignorance of others, is the greatest compassion. These words are the fire of love and a hammer of compassion. They tell us again and again as Rebbe Israel said, "Every man must free himself of Egypt every day."

These words unmake untruth. They unreason form. They untangle, with terrible delicacy, the filaments of flesh and thought and, in their great work of unmaking, they reveal the bright angle of Love.

With deep respect and affection for my friend Lee,

Traktung Yeshe Dorje

Written down on Wednesday, February 14, 2013, the parinirvana of Milarepa.

Introduction

A View From the Edge

As one infinitesimal speck in a moving Universe, we go along our way until, sooner or later, the desire to evolve consciously wells up within. In that moment, it is said, we encounter the *dharma*, or great universal law, but only dimly do we grasp the truth that the seeds of *satchidananda*—innocence, truth, bliss, beauty, being—are already present within us and waiting to blossom as God's graceful gift. The eternal Way opens up and takes us into its Great Process of Divine Evolution, but even so, to realize the treasure of the Path we will inevitably need help of a divine nature—and so, it is the guru who teaches and guides us, and who ultimately transmits Grace to us.

In the Indian traditions, the vital role of the guru has been embraced from antiquity, whereas in the fledgling West, we are often confused and tentative about the guru function, if not highly opposed to it—largely due to the fact that the guru does not promote the common agreement of the dominant paradigm on our planet. In fact, the guru transcends nationality, race, sex, culture, politics, and religions to live at the tangent point, the borderline between the known and the unknown, at the edge of the Great Mystery. In the inevitable collision between the infinite reality of being and the limited, egoic psychological view, the guru is often the focus of unconscious projections, assumptions, and expectations that are rooted in cultural and religious dogmas, creeds, and conventions; such psychological dynamics form an effective barrier against the guru's transmission of Grace. While the guru constantly communicates his or her "view from the edge" in action, word, and deed, the practitioner on the eternal Way must come to terms with suffering, illusory identification, conflict, and struggle.

At some point, the guru's function of dispelling illusions interacts alchemically with the seeker's false identity; for many this is experienced as a pitched battle between egoic identification and the divine vision of reality as it is. Ego is not soothed and placated but incited and initiated into a process of its own undoing, for sooner or later, in order to discover the truth of being, ego must cease domination and take its proper place as a servant of Life. The action of this drama becomes extremely powerful as the advent of the guru's death comes into view. It is a time when latent seeds of karma may begin to ripen and unfinished business takes on an urgency previously unknown, which naturally churns up powerful primal emotions that present a complex, rich field for the work of *sadhana.*

A great epiphany of this struggle occurs at the moment of the guru's bodily death or transition (*mahasamadhi* in the Hindu tradition and *parinirvana* in the Buddhist tradition); a vast wave of spiritual power is released from the awakened being of the guru, which blesses and influences infinite fields of being and worlds upon worlds. Here on the earth plane amongst the friends, family, and devotees of the master, this event is experienced like a supernal sunrise that dispels darkness—it is the advent of an unimaginable opening, an aperture or fissure between the subtle and gross worlds through which flows a river of grace and mercy, invoking love, radical insight, clarity, gratitude, awe and wonder in great measure.

The essays of this book were originally handwritten by Lee Lozowick during the time when he traversed a path taken by masters, teachers, and holy madmen over the millennium, in which he used his own life as the means through which he guided others. Simultaneously, as a practitioner and devotee of his own master, Yogi Ramsuratkumar, and as a human being and wayfarer facing death, Lee's provocative insistence upon living fully in the fire of transformation rings true on every page of this book. In it, he tells us that without a firm foundation on the Path, we cannot ride the waves of inexorable circumstance and the inevitable changes brought on by dying and death—the final moment in which we may actualize the spiritual potential of our humanity in this lifetime.

As Sushila Blackman writes in her memorable book, *Graceful Exits—How Great Beings Die,* the master, guru, or accomplished yogi does not die by any of our expectations, demands, or wishes. At this crucial and potent time, the master makes the communication that is unique to himself or herself. Such a one demonstrates his or her realization of the Supreme Reality in whatever way is the natural dharma of that individual being (*svadharma*).

Studying the lives of great teachers, we find that each one goes through specific phases within life's natural evolution; in these phases, while the essential transmission remains changeless, the form or style of the human teacher evolves to meet the demand of change. Lee Lozowick had a rare ability to live and transmit the Divine across the spectrum of life's experience. To use his words, Lee was "adept at navigating the dream," a talent or gift that took expression in his teaching work, which metamorphed many times over thirty-five years. During his last years Lee was engaged in an extreme *tapasya* or radical discipline that honed his body and being into a state of vulnerability and illumined clarity; as he said during his last months, "I have no buffers left." It was in this naked state of awakened awareness, honed to a fine point and delivered to those around him in the potency of each moment, that Lee began to work with his students with an untamed mercy that was conveyed directly, eye to eye and heart to heart. It is this mood of spiritual intimacy that touches the reader deeply in these pages, in which the author levies fierce challenges to our illusions even as he simultaneously asserts, "I have faith in you."

As his communication flowed from heartbreak to a pristine, uncompromised awareness of the primordial underpinnings of each moment, Lee wrote candidly in his essays about his spontaneous responses to students, expressing his intense dislike of this phase of his work. His naturally *sattvic,* gentle, and peace-loving disposition made this turn of the teaching particularly unpleasant for him; it seemed that this divine mandate to be true to his function as teacher was the actual ordeal for Lee, not the illness that appeared as the cause of his bodily death.

The story of Lee's journey has its origins in 1975, when he was translated from the ordinary sleeping state to an awakened state of being; it is a bold and tender tale in which, for the purposes of this book, we make our entry point in more recent times, when its last phase began. In late January 2008 Lee Lozowick returned from his last trip to India, the mother land of his lineage, teaching, and the spiritual way he established in the West—a lifetime work that Yogi Ramsuratkumar often called "Lee's mission." It was a powerful journey, beginning for Lee in Tiruvannamalai, Tamil Nadu, where he had spent so many intimate hours with his master, Yogi Ramsuratkumar, over the decades. Now, Lee made the last of many pilgrimages to the Yogi Ramsuratkumar Ashram, location of his master's samadhi shrine; there he visited with his beloved *gurubhais,* Ma Devaki and Vijayalakshmi Ma, the devoted attendants of Yogi Ramsuratkumar who have lived on His ashram since the *mahasamadhi* of the revered south Indian saint in 2001.

Before heading toward his final destination—Bengal, the home of the Bauls—he then traveled with his core group and a few students to Mumbai and Gujarat, where he visited friends. Arriving in Kolkata, Lee was met at the airport by a large traveling party of students, both musicians and non-musicians, and his hosts, Purna Das Baul and his son, Dibyendu Das. Purna Das and Dibyendu had visited Lee at his ashram in Arizona twice in recent years, and for this trip had arranged performance venues for Lee and his band SHRI in Kolkata, ranging from *kendras* (schools), community centers, and hospitals, to night clubs, folk centers, and open-air music arenas. As we had so many times before, we followed Lee through a labyrinth of music, gigs, and rock & roll—but at this unique time in the Bengali landscape, with Indian audiences rather than the familiar westerners of Lee's European and American tours, and at times collaborating onstage with the Bengali Bauls.

Another important meeting occurred during this trip: Lee was joyfully reunited with his old friend, Sanatan Das Baul, the first of the Bengali Bauls to recognize Lee as a Baul guru and *khepa* in the West, and his sons, Vishvanath and Vasudev, all of whom had known Lee since 1991. Arriving with his entire clan, Sanatan introduced Parvathy Baul to Lee as "my spiritual daughter," and in a their two days together, Bauls both East and West sang, danced, and invoked the ecstatic *bhava* of adoration.

Since the 1986 inception of Lee's bands, in which his dharma lyrics were put to rock & roll music, he had chosen to perform incognito for Western audiences—not as a spiritual teacher but simply as a singer in the band. This was a particular form of invisibility that served his work for many years, but in Mother India, home of his lineage, it was a different matter; at last Lee openly declared, "I have a guru. His name is Yogi Ramsuratkumar," or, introducing his song *I'm Yours,* he announced, "This song is for my guru…no one can light up my life like my guru…" It was a moment of significance that carried with it an inexplicable sense of completion. In fact, Lee and his students were at a crossroad—poised at a turning point into a new phase, cycle, or even a completely new dimension of the master's *lila* in this lifetime.

Throughout this trip, Lee wore a wool scarf wrapped around his neck in the chill Bengali weather as a protection for his throat, which was painfully sore. (In fact, his three-foot-long dreadlocks had been shorn in the spring of 2008 in an effort to ease the chronic soreness of Lee's throat.) Disregarding discomfort as usual, Lee continued to sing with his band and keep a grueling travel schedule through the landscape of Bengal, making long pilgrimage treks in a bus with a large group of students to places sacred to the Bauls: Shanti Niketan, Joydeb (Jayadeva), and Tarapith. He knew that upon his return to the U.S. he would see a doctor about the persistent condition of his throat, which had been sore for two years.

Back in the states in mid-February, Lee received a diagnosis of cancer of the mouth and tongue; he immediately entered into a disciplined regime based on natural healing methods, and it is here that the essays of this book begin. On February 19, 2008 Lee walked into his weekly Sunday night darshan to deliver the news in a poignant and straightforward address to his students. On this evening Lee was still speaking, although he kept his heartfelt and intimate address short and to the point. The small darshan hall at Lee's ashram in Prescott, Arizona was filled to capacity with mostly American students, who received his stunning message with varying degrees of shock, surprise, heartbreak, sorrow, or the hard-won acceptance or equanimity born from years on the Path. Truly it was a pivotal moment and ensuing time period in which Lee's students were called to practice the teaching with much greater intention and clarity.

The brief talk given by Lee that night has been included in this collection because it was the definitive moment of departure from life as we had known it with our guru. Lee's "little health lila," as he often called it, began to unfold, and along with it, the phase of his teaching that occurred during his last years. From that moment on, Lee immediately made it clear to students, family, and friends that he would not slow down for any reason, nor would he engage any form of allopathic medicine, even though his doctor had told him that there was a ninety percent cure rate for this form of cancer with chemotherapy and radiation. Sure that he could cure the quiet, unassuming but inexplicable gentleman with such piercing blue eyes who sat before him, the doctor had been shocked, deeply concerned, and upset when Lee declined the outlined treatment plan. He even wrote a personal letter to Lee, imploring him to engage the recommended treatment.

As much as Lee expressed the human qualities of love, commitment, and care in the human realm with family and friends, at the same time, death meant nothing to him—it was nothing more than "changing clothes," or "walking from one room to the next," as he once said. He asserted time and again that his health, in fact his life and death, were in the hands of his Father Yogi

Ramsuratkumar—not in the hands of modern technology, doctors, and scientists. The certainty and integrity with which Lee walked this radical path was the sign and seal of a great yogi, who practiced and lived fully the *sahaj* (spontaneous, innate) way of his realization of Spiritual Slavery, or radical Surrender to the Will of God—teachings that are beautifully illuminated in the coming pages.

In order to support the healing process and minimize stress on his throat, the next week Lee began to handwrite his weekly darshan addresses. From February through May 2008 this form of communication continued; under the care of his devoted student and long-time healer, Lalitha, Lee's throat and voice improved to such an extent that he not only resumed speaking publicly but he also sang on tour in Europe with his bands, the Lee Lozowick Project and SHRI, during the summer of 2008.

In May of 2008 he traveled to Montana, to the ashram of his student, Purna Steinitz, where Lee recorded his last CD: *Tongue of Poison, Soul of Love.* As the album title seemed to indicate, the songs were highly autobiographical in nature; combined with the soul-stirring grace and grit of Lee's voice, so richly nuanced yet thick with the impediment of his illness, they were a moving tribute to his unwavering, one-pointed commitment to the transformational possibility of his students and his intention to teach come rain or shine.

Lee returned to Arizona in the fall of 2008 after a full summer—two band tours and his usual travel, seminar, and ashram schedule of teachings—clearly a bit worse for all the wear on his physical form. For the next year he persevered in his chosen path of natural protocols for healing. While his health demanded a progressively more purified and austere diet, throughout 2009 he tenaciously continued every aspect of his usual schedule, including speaking engagements, traveling, and touring with bands. Lee insisted that his students and everyone around him remain optimistic about the possibility of a total recovery. He refused to entertain any form of speculation about his health and continued to affirm, "I'm optimistic. It's all in the hands of Yogi Ramsuratkumar."

By late November 2009, Lee's physical condition required a return to writing discourses for his weekly darshan or for seminars he would continue to give in Europe throughout the summer of 2010. As the writer himself walked the razor's edge of his last months with awakened dignity, grace, and an unflagging passion for the transformational Path, so are his "words of fire and faith," as he called them, alive with an inner flame that burns away our murky preoccupation with the drama of a separate self, steeped in the vagaries and hell realms of *dukkha*, or suffering.

In the last year of his physical lifetime, and particularly in the last six months, Lee's speech became more difficult to understand. It was during this time that he asked his core group (also known as the Cadre and referred to by Lee as "my Valkyries" and "my spokeswomen" in these essays), to participate in his teaching work by repeating everything he said in order to clarify his spoken communications, both in formal circumstances and in the flow of informal day-to-day interactions. He initiated this new dimension of collaboration with these four long-time female students—who had served as the "frame" around the master for many years—in May 2010 at Sat Loka Ashram in Montana. In an essay written later in the summer of 2010, Lee reflected on this specific task of "translating Lee" into his own language, its difficulties and the commitment it required. From May through November 2010, his core group sat on the floor beside his dais during darshans or seminars as they always had, but now with the added job of translating for him. In addition, Lee often instructed them—sometimes simply by pointed gesture—to assist him by offering answers to the questions of his students.

Always prolific in his use of the "word," both written and spoken, Lee had spent a lifetime enthusiastically engaging the dharma with his students. For decades he had addressed his students in discourses that were oftentimes, as he writes, "entertainment"—serious teachings kept light and palatable with Lee's stream-of-consciousness monologues, peppered with humor or served up in spontaneous comedic theatre, causing us to smile, grin, and simply enjoy his company, even when the most ego-deadly or provocative teachings were given. Now he was working at a deeper level and with a new intensity. As Lee arrived in France in late May 2010, what a surprise it was for many to encounter the "high volume dharma" of Lee's last months.[1] His mood was sweet and loving but also irascible and volatile; his interactions were often brisk and impatient, going straight to the point, direct almost beyond bearing. Most impacting of all was the fact that he had aged, as he candidly stated, ten years in the past one year. He seemed to be in an accelerated process of alchemical transformation, and he was determined to make the blessings of that state available to his students.

In July 2010, giving teachings in the south of France at the ashram of his dear friend Arnaud Desjardins, Lee wrote an introduction for his seven-day teaching program, excerpted here:

Bonjour*! It is difficult to express how happy I am to be here again! This year will be different, won't it? No more answers that last a whole hour—*quelle dommage! *I'll have to write my answers, which I've never done before. It should be interesting—and I hope not too difficult for you. I have something to ask of you, if you please. I have cancer. I'm not three years old. I'm not dying. I'm not a paralytic. I'm not infirm. Please don't treat me as if I were an infirm person, a baby, or someone who is about to die! People have a tendency to suppose that because I'm fighting an illness, I'm too stupid to be able to reply to simple questions, or to ask for what I want, or to add something!*

In fact I could say that cancer has no effect from a certain point of view. Although I may have lost my vocal capacity, I have not lost my clarity,

---

1 "High volume dharma" is a phrase introduced by Traktung Dorje Rinpoche, referring to the greatest sacrifice a teacher can make in terms of a teaching style that is highly confrontive and often caustic.

intelligence, dignity, or power. So please, give me space to breathe! I don't need your help to stand up, sit down, or go to the toilet. Thank you! The bad news is that my capacity for external communication is challenged; at the same time, this is also the good news, because while I am not able to converse at the gross outer level, what is in the interior—in the depths of my heart—is actually able to speak much more strongly. In any case, that is what people tell me. The teaching is transmitted with greater force and visceral clarity than ever. Hallelujah! And the Grace and Benediction of the two lineages—mine and Arnaud's—are more evident than ever. Hallelujah!

Lee began to use every means available to him to reach us, including dramatic or pointed physical gestures and the heroic use of his already beleaguered voice to speak directly to others. With his core group acting as intermediaries who assisted by repeating, with as much exactitude as they could muster in any given moment, everything that he said, Lee forged ahead at a time when most people would have retired into the sanctuary that is possible in the last weeks and months of life. The summer of 2010 goes down in the history of Lee's teaching work as an epic swan song in which he emanated a searing radiance not unlike the furious light of a dying sun. In constant interactions with students, Lee walked a razor's edge between love, mercy, praise and insult, shock, raw outrageous provocation and intense intervention—as he called it, "spiritual surgery."

As Lee tells us with straightforward sincerity in his essays, this was not always a pretty sight; it was often very painful to endure on both sides and churned up intense emotions and profound feelings as we were shaken to the core by the depth and power of Lee's communications to us—an experience made all the more poignant and precious as we realized what Lee was willing to endure on the behalf of his students.

In fact what Lee was doing was a kind of guerilla theatre—or guerilla warfare, depending on the view of ego in the moment. He threw his entire being—body and soul—into visceral, at times alarming confrontations in which he mimed, gesticulated, shouted in a brutal disregard for his throat and voice, cajoled, danced, sang, sweetly enjoined or begged his students to pierce through the blinders to see the truth of those motivations and unconscious designs that are our barriers to the realization of Reality. While he was often harshly critical of himself for being hard on his students, at one point he referred to this phase of his work as this "sweet and tender alchemy," a humble statement that merely hinted at the depths we could intuit: an alchemy of multidimensional and far reaching effects, from the eminently practical and useful to the supremely transcendental.

In the midst of all this, Lee was also training his students and friends in how to live fully and powerfully in the pinpoint of the present moment without assuming anything about the future. He refused to allow (much less suffer) any form of expectations, assumptions, worries, guesses, prophetic pondering, or projections of fears on his state of health, his life or his death at a future time. Lee's actions shouted, "Not dead yet! Therefore fully live..." He insisted that we embrace his context: Lee's physical illness and potential death was simply not a problem for him, and it shouldn't be for us either! He was helping us to build a foundation of wisdom that allowed us to work in a positive, powerful way within the experience of breakdown, sorrow or fear and even calamity. We were having the direct experience of an individual who was wrestling with a physical illness, not as a wounded victim of life or half a person, but as a complete and powerful individual. As Lee would state, "The Work never stops..." Transformation occurs, if we open our minds and hearts, regardless of the circumstance in which we find ourselves. Lee's embodiment of the Baul *sahaj manus*—the innate nobility and divinity of the natural, awakened human being—begged for a reciprocal response of dignity, honor, trust, and faith, a higher calling to allow the true teaching to take root in each of us at a cellular level.

In this book the reader enters the teacher's world and encounters a living flame that is simultaneously ruthless in its scorching heat while full of tenderness and compassion for the human predicament. But as the writer begs us to question throughout his essays, exactly who is it who is burned or merely scorched? Who is it who dies? Who is it who does not die, and in fact cannot die? The answer to this question is integrally woven into Lee's essays, echoing the great Song of the Lord, in which Krishna eloquently explains the eternal nature of the soul to Arjuna on the battlefield of the *Mahabharata*.

All of this emanates vividly from the words on these pages. Lee's last essay was written on the evening of November 11, at the home of close friends in Topanga Canyon, where he arrived that day on his last trip—to Santa Monica, California for an Asian tribal arts show. Lee was physically too weak to attend the show; for the next two days he was in virtual seclusion in his bedroom in Topanga, seeing only his core group, who had traveled with him. On November 13 he agreed to be driven back to his ashram in Arizona; arriving that night, Lee retired to his bed, where he remained for the most part of the next two days.

During Lee's life, he had no interest in developing a conventional "spiritual" persona, nor was he interested in ostentatious shows of power of any kind, mystic or mundane. His earthy insistence on remaining "human" was an expression of a natural humility, even though he was a man of great spiritual power and vast inner life. In the last two days of his life, the bhava of *sahaj samadhi*, or open-eyed ecstatic union with the Divine, became brilliantly apparent in Lee in an effortless mood of serenity, communion, and simplicity that permeated his *mahasamadhi*. In the days, weeks, months, and years that followed, Khepa Lee Lozowick continues to make an unforgettable transmission of Grace.

M. Young
February 18, 2013
Triveni Ashram

Everything Is For The Best

February 17, 2008

I'll try to speak as little as possible tonight. I'm sure a lot of you have noticed the various anomalies in my behavior lately. If you haven't—well, thank you! And if you're going to cry, please try to save it till after this, 'cause if you cry, I'll cry, and it'll be a big blubbery mess.

Well, I don't know how to put this diplomatically, but I've been given a death sentence by a doctor who thinks that chemotherapy is the only cure for cancer. He's a very good man, so the poor guy was really upset when I told him that under no circumstances would I undergo chemotherapy or radiation. If you want to know the location of it, just listen to my voice—it should be obvious. Wow, listening to myself makes my skin crawl! So, it's inoperable, and I wouldn't have had surgery anyway. Here's an interesting thing: When I was in California this year, all of the teachers that we met with—all of them—said that I looked brighter and clearer than ever before. Isn't *that* something!

I'm very optimistic, *really* optimistic. I'm on an intensive healing program. I expect to survive this, not so much because *you* all need me to—I think the volume and substance and quality of the Work we've produced together is obvious, I hope it's obvious—but I have some things to do, and I'm planning to do those things, unless not doing them is absolutely necessary. I'm not planning to alter my schedule in any way, but if I keep talking with some difficulty, I may have to, because I don't want to embarrass anybody. I don't mind embarrassing myself, but audiences can be notoriously unreliable, as any of you who have given talks or seminars know, so I might have to adjust my schedule. And maybe not, because most of the talking gigs I have aren't for two months, and I'm optimistic—extremely optimistic.

Some of you have noticed that my diet has changed, and this is the biggest bitch of all: no meat, no milk products, no wine, no chocolate, no sugar. That's a small hell, but once committed to it, it's an easy thing to manage. Like some of you, I can be disciplined when I have to be, and so even though Lalitha has cautioned me not to be too rigid, unfortunately I'm a rigid kind of guy. So I'm on a pretty pure diet, and will stay on that diet and continue the supplementation until everything is better. I suppose I'll know it's better when I'm talking properly, so keep your ears tuned. And remember that it's "not over till the fat lady sings," and she hasn't even started her aria yet, so . . . don't be too concerned. If the healing program *doesn't* work, I'll let you know when to get concerned—it will be evident in my comportment and the grimaces on my face.

With Lalitha's consultation and the consultation of others, I've chosen a healing program that should be extremely effective. So if you know of a miracle cure or a special diet, please save them for *your* need, if you should so need them. I would not appreciate any suggestions on how to speed up the healing process. I'm actively engaged in a very powerful healing process, and it's sort of like supplement poisoning: if you mix too many things, then the effect is the opposite of the effect that you want. So I'm going to stick to what I've chosen and remain optimistic.

I've said many times that I don't want to live past eighty, so I think I have time. In line with Yogi Ramsuratkumar, my intuition rarely fails and is often saying something that you don't realize the meaning of until many years later. So, if I were you, I would not be too worried yet. Then again, if you would like to worry, it can be a fun thing, but don't lose sleep over it—try to worry when you're awake. That would be my recommendation.

So, that's what's been going on, and that's how I'm handling it, and I think that "everything is for the best in this, the best of all possible worlds."[1] Even though that line comes from a satire, in this case we're in the Work and under Yogi Ramsuratkumar's Influence, so we can say that it's true. One of the consequences is that I would prefer to talk as little as possible, although I'm feeling great right now. There are times in which talking is more difficult, although I'm feeling great right now. So, one of the consequences of this is that I prefer to talk as little as possible. If you have questions, submit them in writing, and I will try to answer them in my usual fashion...

Unless there's a dramatic change for the better in my willingness and capability to speak clearly, for the next little while we'll probably watch videos at the After Dinner Talks on Monday and Thursday. Obviously I'm able to talk, it's just uncomfortable at times, and unpleasant to be . . . how can I put this? Well, when I have been speaking as clearly and articulately as anyone has ever spoken for thirty years, and I've been so misunderstood, imagine how misunderstood I would be now, when one word could be another, or another, or another, or just about anything? [Lee chuckles]

So, I'm not feeling like talking a lot lately, although relatively speaking, I'm talking a lot tonight. I do not want to stop communication. I can communicate in writing, although not with the same length and with the same degree of humor and eloquence. However, I think we can get to the point for our important questions. So that's just about it. Jai Guru!

राम राम

---

1 A quote from Voltaire.

Every Act of Dignity

February 25, 2008

Good evening. Well. My difficulties in speaking have nothing to do with cancer. In fact they have to do with mucus. In fact probably every manifestation that you attribute to cancer is most likely no more than the effects of an intense and very rapid detoxification program. Every projection, assumption, expectation, and fantasy you have about what is going on for me is at best neutral, and beyond that a very real interference in the healing process. That is why I am secretive, as a general rule. Who needs to be assaulted by negative thoughts, even when these thoughts are couched in the ostensible context of care, love, affection, even prayer? So please guard your thoughts. To speak such fears, such gross presumptions and most often untruths, is to reinforce the negativity manyfold.

So, please guard your thoughts, and even better, how about thinking differently? Really, it is just a basic decision. Unfortunately it is not a mental decision, as mind can't decide to reeducate and realign itself. Nevertheless, it is no more than a basic decision. It can work here as well as in relationship to other worldviews your mind dominates you with, such as money, anger, music or whatever. Oh, how about pessimism, self-hatred, insecurity, and whatever again?

For the most part, everyone has been quite mature regarding lee's "unexpected adventure." And, I can feel the mind, collective and individual, wanting to definitize the subjective. Don't jump to conclusions until the conclusions are already manifest, concretely and beyond anything requiring jumping to conclusions!

People love to gossip, chatter, blather, and babble, as long as they (even some of us!) can talk about all the senseless data, most of it completely lacking in factual content or substance! So if you will, please do embrace what I have been trying to impart to you for over twenty years relative to this control. You may not be as popular with your average primate as you seem so desperate to be . . . ah well! Every act of dignity has its price in the lower worlds and its reward in the upper world. Where do you want to live when you grow up? Things often seem to be about the practical little things. As the saying goes, "If it ain't one thing, it's another," so don't get fixated. Rather pay attention and catch a few of the flies (but not with your mouth, and don't drool on the table either).

Well this took about a half-hour to pen and will probably take five minutes to read. Hmm. Is that cosmic or what? Two After Dinner Talks this coming week, most likely videos, but, who can foresee the immediate future except in cases when we've overeaten beans and cabbage, or loaned money to an in-law, or have drunk too much coffee or alcohol or argued with an airport security person?

Jai Guru

राम राम

Remember to Practice

March 2, 2008

Good evening. Well, this all puts practice in a different light, doesn't it? What a colossal time consumer it would be if I had to write answers to questions instead of speaking. Maybe I'd have to learn to be direct, to the point, and skip all the long, rambling entertainments. Of course I fully assume that this lack of clarity of speech is quite temporary, and that I'll be talking and singing with a vengeance (more of one than I had before) when the voice is back to normal. Even with my voice as it is, a few people are saying I am still bitter and critical. Tell me, will you practice with greater fervor and intensity if I am only sweet and complimentary? You don't need to tell me to try it and we'll see, because you already know the answer—you know, there in your secret little hideaway.

On the other hand, I am definitely feeling different, very different. And as to how that will manifest (and it won't be deeper antagonism toward anyone or anything, except possibly the evils of technology and the corporate ego), we *will* see.

So what do we mean when we say "practice"? How about Enquiry, Assertion, attention to the basic lifestyle Conditions, especially diet, exercise and meditation—oh, and study and right sexuality (which means no internet porn), the Heart Breath, and practices that you've picked up along the way (circular breath, et cetera), and offering up healthy servings of kindness, generosity and compassion (or at least forbearance if you can't manage compassion) on a regular and reliable basis?

Anything else? Diligent efforts towards projects without overworking or underworking, deep acceptance of the fact that we are different, each of us, and that everyone in the sangha is not going to show up the same, disentangling yourselves from the mechanisms of self-sabotage, self-hatred, and gross assumptions about what anything means without a "reality check." There's more, but that will do for a start. And no whining about not having enough time, because most of the above practices (outside of meditation, study, exercise, et cetera) do not take time at all. They are cognized and engaged in step—literally in the natural process of life as it goes on day to day.

Of course you do need to actually remember to practice: don't we all know how easy it is to be consumed in anything and at the end of the day, "Oops, forgot to practice." The thing is, the more you do any of these things, the more remembrance will arise spontaneously, so you won't have to remind yourself to remember. So . . . time's a wastin'—get to it!

Well, I'm trying to get more than five minutes out of this tonight, but I'm running out of steam. I better not put down the pen, for if I do, that's it for tonight, so, onward for a few more lines.

I plan to recover health. I do not plan to slow down, but I do plan to radically alter what, over the past few years, has become an increasing wanton disregard for a diet that promotes health and well being, physically and subtly and spiritually. I've not been proud of dragging quite a few of you behind me in this whirlwind comet, and if I were you, I'd start to get a bit more serious now.

So prepare to do without meat and alcohol, although every rare once in a while we'll most likely have a small blowout. Can life be fun without all the fancy dietary seductions? Yes, by God, yes! I mean *really* fun—not some dry, boring drudge, where you have to continuously psych yourself up to pretend you're enjoying yourself, but rich, full, satisfying (three words that describe my idea of fun). And can this be sustained over a lifetime, not just for a couple of weeks' retreat? Yes, by God, yes!

Of course if your idea of fun is some kind of screaming, exhibitionist blowout, well . . . I'd suggest a review of priorities. Remember that to be in the guru's world (our aim, in general terms, yes?) is to be in the guru's outer world, to whatever degree you realistically can, as well as to be tuned in to the principles of the guru's Work and Intention. Realistically, most of you *can* be more serious about diet (and the other practices, obviously) if you are willing to concede your own personal commitments to doing things your way. "All life is suffering," so it is our demand to live in a way and practice in a way so that suffering ceases to be what we all think it is. As always, the question remains: Will you? And as always, we will see.

Jai Guru

राप राप

To Speak without Compromise

March 9, 2008

Good evening. And how are we this evening? Relative to this little lila, as the community philosophers and the devotees like to call it, a few things seem to be clarifying. For one (I might not get to "for two" this evening, but we'll see as we go) it feels timely and just for me to start talking straighter. (Or is it more straight? More straightly?)

I have often said what I felt in the moment. Probably more often than not, I have also not said what I really felt. I have been too circumspect, too unwilling to hurt feelings or disappoint tail-wagging enthusiasm. I can feel a lot of that reticence on my part draining away like the beautiful muscle tone of my previous body. (And yes, that is tongue-in-cheek, so for those of you not here to witness these historic events, if your imagination has run wild, it is not dry, parched tongue-in-sunken-cheek, so *cut it out!*)

I can feel the immediacy, in fact the urgency, to speak directly and without personality (mine) compromise. Of course, as always, we will see where this lands. Some of you will most likely applaud this; some will most likely quake a bit, perhaps having felt that you've previously felt the bite of my "honesty."

Well, listen puppies! I am not talking about being more acerbic or intrusive or biting; I am talking about a true and instant response to any circumstance that is asking for input. This does not mean I'm going to prowl the community alleys, guns-a-ready, taking potshots at everyone and anyone. It does not mean that if you ask me for feedback and I tell you I have none, that I am being less honest than I've ever been under such situations. I am already different. What difference you allow my difference to make for you is your business, although I'm always a "silent partner." I suppose, somewhat embarrassingly, that if I am to speak clearly it means positive feedback (dare we say "strokes"—I tremble just thinking of it) as well as a more reflected stab in the "denial body." So, as we say in the industry, "Let's rock and roll!"

On another note—"fa" I believe—we've gotten pretty extraordinary feedback from non-Arizona residents on how wonderful and important it is to receive these written Sunday night Darshans. Go team! And Bala's visits to the European Bordellos is so moving to him he can barely speak of it. So, the Sangha is doing pretty well.

E.J. Gold once told us that until the Teacher gets sick the student body just won't work in a certain way. I think we're all doing what we've always done. It's just that everything is sharper, more pertinent, more real. "Good on ya" as they say way down South. (No, not in Mexico, and speaking of Mexico, I've cancelled both my New York and Mexico trips this year. I do still plan to visit Purna's ashram for his mela in mid-May. I will reiterate, I will *not* slow down, but I do need to get back up to speed first, so . . . I'll be here. Yay!)

As someone said, God being in the details, although our commitment, strength, and devotion are solid for the most part, we still say really dumb and hurtful things to one another—not meaning to of course, but simply not thinking of what comes tumbling or oozing out of our mouths. Thank God it's only occasionally, and we still make lots of foolish mistakes, small ones, yes, and yet ..and yet . . . Lest we forget, the phone still needs to be answered, Elyse still always needs help, meals need to be cooked, Work Weekends continued as well as After Dinner Talks and Sunday morning teaching committee and—you get the point.

No matter how gushing I may become about all of this, please don't get the idea that we should rest on our laurels. Even Lance Armstrong lost...well, sort of. This spate of Sunday evening writing does not mean that my letters will be any different. At least I sure hope not. But this budding writing development feels right—a perfect "fit." I hope it fits you all as well as it appears to fit me. In any case, it is what it is and what it isn't, we might add for a moment of sweet dharma.

And onwards—on words! Let's put the phlegm to rest, so I can get my voice back and let bygones be bygones, if we can. It's a useful ability, that—to let bygones be bygones—and could come in very handy in quite a number of circumstances. As for the future, well, "que sera, sera," which is not fatalistic and does not mean we shouldn't put our ante in the pot, toss our hat in the ring, stand for what is true, vote (in the a-political sense of the word, or . . . ?) or intend. As Arnaud said last summer "Accept what is as it is and act!" When there is a hurricane, we must be the eye of the storm, and when there is darkness, we must be the light, and romantic stuff like that.

We hold something almost too precious to even whisper of it. So please do not feel the need to toot the Community or Teaching horn, to defend yourselves (except energetically of course) by meeting ignorance and abuse with "an eye for an eye." Aggression only begets more ignorance and abuse. Lay low, do your Work, serve one another and others where and when you can and be deeply, even profoundly, alert to the signs of the Path and the Guru's world. We all count on every one of us.

Next week, two After Dinner Talks. Hope to see you there!

Jai Guru,
Jai Guru,
Jai Guru

राम राम

Dignity

March 16, 2008

Good evening! I was pondering, though not heavily, the vast amount of feedback that my little friend cancer has generated around the globe, and I was moved to consider one of the most noble and beautiful of human qualities: dignity. In the torrent of responses to this event, how many people have demonstrated a strong, quiet dignity, and how many have conversely shown themselves to be quite blatantly undignified and clueless. Of course the response of Arnaud and Veronique Desjardins was so ultimately dignified that it is a bit difficult to measure against such a model. But let's consider for a moment what is and is not a function of dignity.

Firstly, of course, dignity is a quality of quietude. As Gour Khepa said in India, disparaging the common man, dignity has no need to "Blah, blah, blah." All the gossip, the speculation, the opinionating, the guessing, ruminating, discussing, the expectations, the assumptions, all, all, all quite glaringly lack in a quality of basic human dignity. Dignity is a quality of such magnificence—it is so attractive, so magnetic—that it is a wonder we don't devote ourselves to its expression. We know it when we are in its presence, and we have the same response to it.

We all have our strengths and weaknesses, our bright radiances and our dull, dark holes. Let us never feel that it is practice enough to rest on the strengths of our mature aspects and ignore—or maybe worse, deny—our weak areas. We must, and I do mean *must,* ferret out every area of lack and bring to it awareness and transformation. Dignity, *please.* Humility, *please.* And the capacity to experience the pure and true joy of heart communion, and the willingness to express this joy in a humble and dignified way.

Some of us have faced death and will never be the same, in a positive way. Others of us have faced death and are still the same, undoubtedly having made great resolutions before our recovery and then, safe and out of dangerous waters, have snapped back into the same primate sloth. This is a vigorous insult to this Path and this Work. We cannot afford such apathy.

As our world at large slides into its own ugly sloth, its complete dumbing-down of decency, intelligence, common sense, even survival instincts except at the most violent levels, we *cannot* afford to be caught in this cultural decline. We must fight tooth and nail to rise to the demands of the triple gem—the Buddha, Dharma and Sangha—and to make a sanctuary of this rare, even precious, little flower we have begun to grow. Please, please, please.

We have been given the gift of friendships with E.J. Gold, Arnaud Desjardins and others. This is a treasure that makes my heart weep with wonder and gratitude. And we have also been given the gift of one another, of sangha—an unspeakably precious circumstance. We can either face one another or turn to the side, even turn our backs. There is no neutral.

Please, please, please dig deeper into the glorious potential you all have and help to build the invincible temple. We all need a haven now and Lord knows, will need one far more acutely as time goes on. And no one will do this, if not you.

Please, please, please, do not be trapped by the sparkling glitter of a world catapulting towards its own destruction. Technology is its own worst enemy. Science is its unwitting criminal accomplice. The internet has adequately proven that nothing is sacred to these people. And you and I should know, and nothing should dissuade us, that without the Sacred, and without dignity relative to the Sacred, there is no true life, no life that can be real, satisfying and fulfilling, neither ultimately nor mundanely. Please, please, please.

I am in a womb. I will never be the same, even though I do not feel that I am confronting death. Cancer is cancer. Cancer is not death. As the founder of the program I am on said, "Hah, cancer, that's nothing." I will never be the same. I am in a period of gestation and the baby is going to be a real beauty (with an ever-sharp tongue!).

I am *not* fighting for my life. I am working, and damned hard, towards perfect health. And I am already planning my strategy, for let me tell you, after six weeks on juice, I am ready to party! So when I'm eating again, I will be like a racehorse in the stall. Of course it will still be no meat, no dairy, no sugar, no wine and no coffee, but right now a little cooked spinach or a yam looks like manna from Heaven. I'm easy to please and can be satisfied for the rest of my life with a few fine vegetables and a little quinoa. Van Gogh had a "lust for life"—I'm up to lust for steamed veggies!

So, remember, what a sweet and soul-satisfying presence is a person with dignity. How much sweeter when you are such a person. Please do not continue to suffer the constant indignity of the "blah, blah, blah." As Swami Prajnanpad said, we are all intrinsically noble and intrinsically dignified, so this is not something we must develop. It is something we must discover and allow through its dynamic attractiveness to override mechanical habits—self-love of the sound of our own voice, the feeling we know better, the urge to intrude, dominate, and aggress upon the other, insecurities that drive us to desperately "blah, blah, blah." Please, please, please. Dignity.

Dignity is its own reward. Dignity is its own payoff. There doesn't need to be an audience. One can be dignified when alone; surely one can and most assuredly should be dignified with one's loved ones, as well as with strangers. Dignity. Please, please, please. Remember "the lilies of the field," the stately oak, the proud lion, and so on and so forth. And remember your sacred artifacts—talking about the embodiment of dignity!

Well, my dears, time draws to a close as this writing takes so much of it—time, that is. So for next week, we have two After

Dinner Videos, and we are one week closer to the All Fools Celebration. Oh boy, oh boy! And for the many of you who have met me in this time with dignity, my very gracious thanks. I touch your feet and offer you a smile, for you relieve me of much irritation and frustration. Alas, I'm not a saint . . . yet. Dignity. Please.

Jai Guru,
Jai Guru,
Jai Guru

राप राप

Get with the Program

March 23, 2008

Good evening ladies and gentlemen. What shall we consider this evening? I was recently cautioned by one of my dearest devotees not to be so critical. The way to motivate people seems to be to trust them, and feeling trusted they will step up to the plate and do what is wanted and needed. That seems true. On the other hand, it could be that part of this training, in no way designed by me but simply as an affect of my often grating personal attributes, is to learn to read deeply into the heart of things. Having been associated closely with women most of my life, I have been not quite inundated but certainly reminded frequently that they don't *feel* appreciated, honored, respected—this, despite a heart that practically melts and weeps with gratitude and love for the profound sacrifices they make, daily and ultimately.

What to do? Am I schizophrenic? No more than most of us, I would suggest. Of course this applies quite equally to all my devotees. I often feel radiant delight and devotion toward someone, then I come to discover that the person is not only completely unaware of my radiance but also believes that I am cold and impervious, and perhaps even actively antagonistic, not even liking them one whit. Well, I am a very interior person, always was, and most likely always will be, although perhaps somewhat less as I get older and more tenderized by the brutalities of such confusion and misinterpretations. For those of you to whom the above does not apply, I thank you, applaud you, and there is no need to write me a letter telling me how clear it is that I love you. I'm not entirely insensitive, even over vast distances; let's assume that I know who you are and how you feel—but be careful, as assumptions can get you in a lot of trouble! In this case, since it's a mutual assumption based on a common agreement, let's assume it is acceptable.

Back to the rest of y'all. So perhaps, once more, we can consider this the training: You have the opportunity to learn to read the subtle signs, to see beyond the ostensible appearances of the gross outer dimensions, to peer deeply into the actual heart of the matter. And once learned as a principle, as a skill applied anywhere, you have the same results: never again to be dissuaded by your delusions, never again to be captured and captivated by the illusions of your superficial and subjective dreams of unworth and unworthiness, of rejection and unnoticeability. I assume—and it's an appropriate assumption in this situation—that to be able to see the *essence,* the truth of any matter always and under any circumstances, would be a talent that you would find not only useful but extremely edifying.

Since this is the way it is, and since I have met you an uncountable number of times where *you* are, in this instance it behooves you—though you aren't cows or okapi—to meet me where *I* am, if you actually believe me when I express the reality of my inner mood. Yes, the voice can be bitingly critical, and yes, there are numerous bumps and grooves that would do well to be sanded down to perfect harmony with the whole. As the tradition says, you are perfect as you are—*and,* it sure as hell wouldn't hurt if the perfection that you are here and now shone with a different glitter in the next perfection of who you are here and now, when that here and now is the next here and now to the previous here and now. In other words, your procrastination, pride, vanity, sloth, greed, aggression, vindictiveness, hurtfulness, anger, self-hatred, insecurity, peevishness, perversity, addiction and so on may be perfect here and now because they *are* here and now, and they don't have to be here and now in the next moment.

So, let's get with the program. I often find my criticality to be unsettling and distasteful to myself. At this time in our sadhana together, I am not and don't seem to be able to merely be content with the neuroses you animate to go unchecked and unobserved, running roughshod over the sweet, delicious, and sacred spaces and moods that the Blessings of Yogi Ramsuratkumar are always offering us as the option to the usual mechanical, mediocre manifestations of the primate without a clue.

Yes, "get with the program" is the operant phrase, for "the program" is the Divine Descent infusing our every action, our every word, thought, our every breath. Is that a program that encourages not only resistance but resentment? If so, who are you and where have you been since you've been here? Hey happy campers, this isn't about s'mores by the campfire—this is about soma in the chakra of initiates, wine in the Tavern amongst the sober drunkards, enslaved by and to the Beloved.

No change is too small to be noticed. So . . . let's get with the program. As I said at Bridge the other night (wish more of you were there), when Yogi Ramsuratkumar shut me off, and He did when I was off, I didn't hang my head in shame; I didn't indulge, even for one second, in remorse for my actions. I immediately got back on track, re-entered His world—the Guru's world—and He immediately turned back on. I had and have only one relationship to Him; I never allowed that singular relationship to be broken even an instant more than necessary.

I suggest you all take up a similar relationship to me. You won't regret it. If I am cranky, sarcastic, cynical, crude, disgracefully irreverent, or personally critical of you, even in a surgical way, don't bow your head like bad children being scolded, don't withdraw inside and go away, don't react with anger, blame, justification or aggressivity. *Get with the program.* My program, which is not other than Yogi Ramsuratkumar's program, which is not other than God's program, which is not other than the Reality of the Universe—the pure, unstained, unitive Truth of all that is, which is begging for your attention, your submission and your Praise.

This is the program that wants the Mercy of Father in Heaven to fill you with beauty, appreciation and compassion. So, what's not to like? And hey, boys and girls, devas and devis, hobos and thieves, I am not just being lyrical and flowery in the above. I am not being romantic, I am being absolutely and positively literal. *Literal.* This is the program that wants your heart to swell with Joy and Love and wants every cell in your body to sing with delight and wonder, with awe and majesty.

Jai Guru, Jaya Baulo Jai, Jai Guru

राप राप

Sahaj Vision

March 30, 2008

Good evening. I receive lots of letters, relatively speaking, telling me how the news of my health considerations has been such a shock that it has propelled the writers into deeper levels of practice considerations. Well, you all know that when I recover and you feel that I am "out of danger" (although in one very real sense it is probably more "dangerous" for me to recover than not), how easy it will be to slide, most likely at the speed of an avalanche sliding down the side of a mountain, right back into the mood of lackadaisicalness (or is lackadaisicality? just kidding, all you English snobs), into the mood of apathy, lack of sufficient motive, or plain unwillingness to step up and keep it up.

If only we all understood that at the most integral level practice is not a luxury; it is a very real necessity. If you will for a moment subscribe to the Buddhist ideal of the Bodhisattva practice, not only do our lives depend on it but perhaps even the lives of all sentient creatures, at least to some degree. You certainly wouldn't shrug your shoulders with an, "Oh well, that's life" if your children—or your dog, if you have completely failed to grasp the teaching here—were in real danger. You'd jump to the need and put yourself on the line.

In fact, according to the serious Buddhist of Mahayana and Vajrayana persuasion, when you fail to meet the practice demand you are allowing your loved ones to slide into situations most likely beyond their ken to manage, and you are doing it with a shoulder shrug and a good dose of ignorance and laziness. If you don't meet the practice demand, you actually suffer less than your loved ones and all sentient beings besides. Can you afford such a consequence? I wouldn't bet on it.

So if my so-called health crisis, which is hardly a crisis, was required to "shock" you, look again and more closely, please. Most shocks wear off, and rather quickly if we are honest. If this "shock" is or was great enough to not wear off, God Bless you and I am grateful, but if it is already wearing off, your ego is winning again. Are you satisfied with that effect? If yes, well let it slide. If no, pay attention, pay attention, pay attention. And while paying attention, pay attention to your paying attention.

I'm not talking about stressing out, paying attention with so much hyped-up tension that your neck muscles bulge and your brain feels like it will drop from exhaustion any second. I'm talking about a serene, relaxed, natural and effortless observation based on the intention to see clearly so as to act in accordance with what we call the Will of God, which could also be called the organic flow of the Universe, unobstructed by the so-called free will of a mind or ego sunk deeply in the illusion of a separate self and a substantial independent existence. Oh yeah. And I mean yeah, not yea. Do you understand, even a little, both the import and the impact of this?

We're here, we're committed, we're all in one big discreet and particular "love-fest," and we might as well get with the program, no? *Yes!* So, what to do? I hope this isn't too sophomoric, but what to do? Start with the basic life Conditions as a foundation, exactly as Hinayana practice is a foundation for Mahayana practice and Mahayana practice is a foundation for Vajrayana practice. And let me remind you that Vajrayana is the diamond vehicle, and you can't just start practicing Vajrayana and be successful without a prior and ongoing foundation in Hinayana and Mahayana—at least not according to the serious Vajrayana masters (and any Vajrayana practitioner who doesn't subscribe to this principle is neither serious nor a master no matter what they call themselves, even if tulku or rinpoche is tacked onto their names).

So it's back to a truly vigorous attempt to take the Conditions—diet, regular meditation, study and regular exercise—as absolutely integral to a life of practice and spiritual health and potential for transformation, consciousness-wise. Upon that *reliable* foundation, we can more significantly consider not only the core practices of Enquiry, the Heart Breath and, most essentially, Assertion, but I can be teased, cajoled and at last convinced to freely instruct more of you in the sexual yoga, the cyclical breath, the picture meditation and the sun and moon practices as well as all the other specific esoteric practices that would inevitably arise were we ready to receive them.

Please, please, please. I'm afraid there is no magic pill. It's slogging through the swamp of all of the neurotic affects—pride, vanity, greed, sloth, anger, self-hatred, lust—that constantly assault and sabotage our attempts to live the basic Conditions as a natural response to the call of the Path. And not only that, it is our failure to bear those neurotic affects that keep us from enjoying and engaging the tantric benefits of having each and every one of those traits serve us as elements of enlightened presence, instead of as habits of self-reference and gross illusion. You don't have to become someone you're not, at least not at the level of activity; you simply must—and it is *must*—make the internal shift from primate presumption, and I would even say at this point, pretension, to Sahaj Vision. This takes no time but does require fertile ground and unrestrained willingness to do whatever it takes to maintain this Natural View. Ah well, yes.

This coming week SHRI is performing on Tuesday and the Celebration begins on Thursday.[1] There will be lots of Bridge

---

1 SHRI is Lee's blues band.

as well, and you are most welcome to come for that. To all who were here to participate in the Work Weekend, thank you for your great service, and for those few who didn't do anything, thanks for contributing to the mass. (I'm serious, I do mean thank you; I am not being sarcastic, although two months ago I would have been being sarcastic.) The few small personal things that didn't get done will unfortunately continue to plague some of us; well, sometimes we miss the trees for the forest. "That's life, that's what all the people say" as Frank Sinatra sang, and if we only would rest in the Sahaj Vision it wouldn't bother us even if it were inappropriate or unfortunate. So . . . kisses and hugs to all, with no suggestion of intrusiveness or partiality and a truly hearty . . .

Jai Guru!

राम राम

Spiritual Slavery

April 6, 2008

Good evening! Well, we have an illustrious crew here this fine evening. We have had so much wonderful feedback on these evening readings that I pray and hope it's not going to turn into another version—spiritual, of course—of the movie *The Fly*: "Feed me, feed me!" (That's the original version, not the re-make.) I too appreciate a good flaming dharma talk, and, lest we are lulled into or back into a safe and comfortable state of comatose denial, ultimately we can only rely on our own practice, our own innate "intrinsic nobility and intrinsic dignity."

The sooner we drop the crutches that we use (because we are afraid that if we put them down we won't be able to stand), the sooner we will realize that the Universe will continue to roll on in its merry way, and we will continue to roll on in perfect synchronization to that Universe, free and easy, open-eyed and non-problematically, even when many others assume our problems for us. Meaning they assume we have problems, even tragic ones, when to us things are simply just, natural, and as they should be, because that is how they are.

Yes, things are how they should be because that is how they *are*, whether they suit our conditional ideas of right/wrong, moral/unethical or politically correct/incorrect or seem irreverent or even nasty and bigoted. As most of you know quite well, at least intellectually, the problem is the overlay we place or superimpose on Reality—due to the deep attachments we have to maintain a status quo, even when that state of affairs is miserable, limiting, unmagical, uncreative, stultifying and in fact, basically illusory—that obscures the way things actually are and the laws by which the Universe works.

Well look, we've committed ourselves to this Work, so why not milk it for all it's worth? I have a cousin who would never smoke dope when he was having sex, though he did pretty much at all other times, because he didn't want any artificiality between him, his experience of reality, and what he felt was the prime expression of human contact. That was, of course, prior to the onset of the virtual revolution: these days people actually do crave the illusion of experience more deeply than the actual reality of life itself, the blood, sweat, tears and the other of the four moons. We, however, are supposed to be what could loosely be called spiritual practitioners. We are supposed to have had a scent of, even to have been stabbed by, the "horror of the situation"—or if you prefer, "the terror of the situation."

As many of you have most likely figured out by now, a lot of people get started on the Path like a racehorse just out of the chute and gradually slow to a peaceful, dull, stagnant stop. Having grown quite attached to so many of you over the weeks, months and years, not only would it be a true shame were you to stall and not immediately restart, but, as we are not just attached in a sentimental way but are literally bonded together, maybe even for eternity, I really don't want to go through all this in the same way again. So please get with the program.

You know the saying: "If it ain't broke, don't fix it." Well the Universe ain't broke. *Every* form of denying the Universe its need, or its urge, to manifest as it is, including to manifest each and every one of us in pure and unobstructed resonance, not just in principle but in actual living fact—yes, *every* form of denying the Universe this reality is an attempt to fix the Universe. Now, put in this way, it sounds absurd beyond belief that we little pissant grains of sand would presume to fix the Universe—the all-perfect, stainless Unity of Truth.

And yet there, and more to the point, *here,* it is. *Every* form, every denial, every neurotic identification, every gesture, when motivated by self-reference over and against Universe-reference, is our attempt to fix what ain't broke. That includes cosmic sex when it is the result of a technology or methodology superimposed on a natural reliance on intuitive movement into the Divine flow of possibility (in other words, ego motivated in order to get something: power, bliss, control, freedom, and so on); that includes service to those less fortunate than us, the healing of others, acts of generosity and social justice. All the "good" things we can do with our lives, when those things are defined by our illusions of separation and fantasy, are attempts to fix what doesn't need fixing.

I, lee, the Guru, the Son of Yogi Ramsuratkumar—transparent, to some degree, hopefully more than not, to the Blessings and Benediction of Father in Heaven—am not separate in any way from our Yogi Ramsuratkumar. I am not here to be an icon, an idol, a figurehead, simply the object, or even Object if you will, of the attention of anyone, no matter how devoted or loving. I am here to Help: to push, pull, wheedle, tease, shove, shock, inspire, jolt, educate, mentor, motivate, or whatever it takes to Help anyone who is deeply and irrevocably serious about continuing through to the end, even in this very lifetime—having once entered the stream of the teaching and taken refuge in the jewels of the Path. And . . . in order to actually be effective in this Help, I need your direct participation.

Listen: We can begin, and often do, with your indirect participation. That is fine for a while, long enough to align the inner vectors, to get the subtle bodies engaged, to create some deeper dimensions of commitment, to educate attention and intention and so on. At a certain point you need to kick it up a few gears and throw your direct participation into the pot. And listen again: If your voice is saying, "Yes, yes, work with me, I can take it, give me what I need to grow, to transform, to *Realize, yes!*" and your body, attitude, and mood is saying, "No, oh no, you're not touching my dream, you're not getting into my bubble, back off or die, motherfucking Guru," I will applaud your sincerity—at least the "I" in you, one part of you, who is completely convinced that you can pull it off. But I ain't stupid, and unfortunately I am neither fireproof nor recoil retardant, so I'm really not interested in walking into your emotional helicopter blades.

So, puppies and pupae, if you want the Help I am here to provide to get off the launching pad, to get out of the frying pan onto your plate, to get past the romantic notion of love and into the heart and soul of the matter, you need to get those "I's" aligned to some minimal degree. There are a whole lot of seats in the Guru's world and a major feast waiting to be put out and eaten.

Impermanence. A great theme and a great "reminding factor." What is a reminding factor? In the Fourth Way teachings, a reminding factor is a catalyzing stimuli (not a stimulant) that reveals to the catalyzee the underlying nature of Reality, which is emptiness. If the catalyzee is sharp—as in perceptive and mature, both as a practitioner and as a human adult—the vision of emptiness, far from being scary, dark, depressing or hopeless, and far from turning the viewer or perceiver into a nihilist or a pantheist, automatically reveals the nature of form, exactly as it is, without seduction or identification. The vision or direct knowledge of form as-it-is returns one to emptiness, the only perfect formula in existence.

So yes, this is a theme to be embraced, investigated, and integrated, for this is the core essence of the Teaching, Spiritual Slavery, the realization without which we cannot progress on the Path. Spiritual Slavery is the definition of Reality as it is, which implies that freedom is not open-ended but in fact is absolutely closed-ended. Freedom is Slavery and Big Brother is not watching; 1984 is long past, a distant memory, if a memory at all (both the actual year and Orwell's masterpiece, if you've even read it, which if you haven't you probably should as it defines our government's game plan quite exactly).

Freedom is Slavery because what is, is and cannot under any circumstances (not even Salvation at the Bleeding Heart of Jesus the Christ, nor bombing yourself along with a bunch of innocent people imagining the reward to be instant entry into Heaven with your own personal bevy of *houris,* and imagine if, as in the movie "Beelzebub," you go to the afterlife in the exact condition you left this one in, wow, it'd be hard, if not impossible, to enjoy those Houri Bliss Bunnies when there's no more left of you than would fit in a thimble, yes, what is, is, and you'd better review the beginning of this sentence) be otherwise than it is, which is Slavery, by definition or in effect.

Spiritual Slavery is the direct realization, the tacit knowledge that emptiness is the essence of the Universe and therefore form is also Real in its context of emptiness. As Werner Erhard said, no matter how enlightened you are, if you walk in front of a truck you'll still be dead meat, a truth echoed by Marco Vassi in his outstanding short story about colonics as a path to Awakening. How's *that*—the truck, that is—for form?

Alright lovers (in the platonic sense), friends, Work teams (you could be all of these), devotees, disciples, Dakinis and Shaktis (no this doesn't apply to everywoman, boo hoo), lords and ladies, Mesdames and Monsieurs, herren und damen, puppies and cubs, apples and snakes, it's truly been a glorious All Fools' Celebration. I'm not exaggerating, at least for me, but despite the magnificence of it all, grow up, get with the program, practice and allow Faith and Surrender to consume you (the emptiness and the form that you are) like it or not, lock, stock and barrel, body, mind and spirit.

This coming week two ADVs, and who knows what magic awaits? It's for damned sure that Father Blesses you always, ongoingly, and under all conditions and circumstances. So, no whining or self-loathing. It doesn't become you.

Jai Guru, Jai Guru
Anande Baulo
Jai Guru

राप राप

I Will Not Slow Down

April 13, 2008

Good evening ladies and all the rest of you who were ladies once and will be again—and I'm not talkin' about lace undies. And what a fine evening it is! Well, we have so many guests here tonight, and I was due to go with several of those guests to Mexico tomorrow to give a seminar. I felt that my voice would not be up to par yet, so I cancelled. And besides that, all my healers strongly recommended that I not stress my system with arduous travel.

That being said, let me make this clear. Before lunch today Purna asked me if I was going on both band tours this summer, with SHRI and the Lee Lozowick Project. Surprise, surprise, I answered, "Yes." He then asked me if I still enjoy the SHRI tour—the implication being, am I just doing it out of some sort of duty or obligation? And I answered, again, "yes," for I still enjoy it immensely. If I didn't I wouldn't do it.

Let me reiterate a short but very pithy statement I made several weeks ago: I will *not* slow down. At the same time, one of the changes—which may seem subtle to some but is not at all subtle—that is cooking and taking shape and form as a result of this little health lila of ours (for what is mine is yours, even if in an altered form) is that I do not plan to continue to pour energy, especially in the forms of time and resources, into nonessential projects and activities.

Yes, "we always make a profit," Purna—and no plagiarism meant, Orage or Mr. Gurdjieff. I am actively optimizing the profit we make and slowing down my attachments to the minimally profitable ventures. So I will not slow down, and I also will not "suffer fools gladly" in terms of those elements of possible engagement that are neither attractive to me or not primary in terms of the vast and limited energy I have with which to serve the Work. And boys and gals, men of the Work and gopis, what is attractive to me *is* profitable, and what is not attractive to me is not (and "no pain, no gain" be damned, and no harm done if it is).

So yes, I will be on both band tours. The Lee Lozowick Project, spurred forward and initially catalyzed by Paul Durham's exceptional efforts on my behalf and Purna's exceptional generosity in many domains, has opened up vistas I could not have foreseen. SHRI is alive and well and still one of my "babies," in spite of small in-band grumbling relative to a few minor details. The Sacred Bazaar, lest it be side-lined or minimized compared to the music projects, looms gigantic on my horizon and shows not the least signs of slowing down. And let us not forget that I, as well, will not slow down unless I am slowed down by the Work—otherwise known affectionately and familiarly amongst us as Yogi Ramsuratkumar and His Blessings for my Mission, and by definition and association the Mission of anyone in this Lineage, teachers and devotees alike.

There are not the least signs of that happening, in spite of my decision to put off the Mexico seminar until a more propitious time. Since Lalitha said that stress is one of the most damaging "foods" I could possibly eat, to slow down when I don't have to would be so stressful for me that I wouldn't recommend it to myself—and don't any of you recommend it to me either, unless you don't mind not being suffered gladly. Yes. And lest you worry, those of you who are prone to such useless emotional gestures, I plan to maintain a fairly religious adherence to my diet until Lalitha tells me I have wiggle room, until I am cancer free, which I still without a doubt expect to be, or until some other reason presents itself. I can't think of such a reason just now, but as we all should well know, the Universe has lots of tricks up Its sleeves (all of them) and likes surprises.

So, you might be asking either me or yourself, or miracle of miracles, someone else in the sangha whose maturity and dharmic wisdom you respect: What *can* I do that would not create stress for my Beloved Guru and would actually help or serve to relieve potential stress? Or even obviate potential stress completely, and maybe even directly aid and abet what is essential and attractive to this same Beloved Guru? Well, let's begin with the basic life Conditions and then let's continue with the core Practices. And, those two foundations—even the core Practices—are still a base upon which the Palace of Realization, the Trysting place for you and the Beloved, can be built and also sustained and glorified. That is your Sanctuary and your warrantee, for *quelle dommage,* unfortunately there are no guarantees.

Yes, these two foundations are a substantial reinforcement, although not a guarantee. In fact, you can manage your mind and bring a mature adult expression to all and any feeling and emotional relationships—not only to others of your own species, organically at least, but to others not of your own species. That definitely includes not only bipeds but also other sentient creatures, ambulatory as well as rooted in the earth, and even goes so far as to include the walls of this room, the pillow you are resting your lively buttocks upon, every space you inhabit now and forever and . . . you get the picture.

And, so, getting the picture, it behooves and benefits you, as redundant as the language may be, to get with the program as well. For, as most of us well know, getting the picture is not only the easy part, but almost tacit, and without getting with the program, the picture is no more than a cheap knockoff, a paint-by-numbers waste of time even if others, in their mostly benign ignorance, think it looks exactly like an original composition by Mozart—or tastes like a Thomas Keller creation, or like a Helen Roy selection of wine.

Yes, please get with the program, as time's a-wastin' and yes, again, even though there is no time, at the same time, it can (time, that is) be wasted. So cubs and kits, the very spawn of the Lord, get with the program, the reason being that if, at the eventual time of my demise, I have devolved to communicating almost exclusively in body noises and movie dialogue, I don't want my last words to be either, "What we have here is a struggle to communicate," or "I'll be back."

Yes. Here's yet another picture I'm sure you get, and another plea to get with the program: being hot into another biography, strong in its descriptions of yet another seriously twisted artistic genius, D.H. Lawrence (though it's a bio of Frieda, his wife), I also would prefer a sangha of grown-up practitioners, well rounded and mature across the board, so to speak, rather than a bunch of spiritual idiot savants, geniuses in dharma and disasters in relationship.

Well, my treasured friends—and I am neither being sarcastic nor exaggerating—another week gone by. Ahh, where do they go? That is not a koan; if we aren't practicing the answer is "nowhere." If we are practicing, ahh, it's a very different answer.

Next week, as far as I know in this moment, two ADVs and lots of teaching lessons in between. Both as usual and as always and not only has it been fun, but, by God, it *is*. Something else I've learned in the past little bit of time.

Jai Guru, Anande Baulo, Jai Guru

राप राप

The Will of God

April 20, 2008

Good evening *mesdames, monsieurs et chiens et chats.* And we hope, truly, that a lovely time will be had by all. A question was asked last night, which question was and still is: "If there is nothing inside of me that can free me, and nothing outside of me that can free me, where do I place my attention?" Excellent indeed! Let's meditate on this a few minutes. Just kidding. The question is: Who am I kidding?[1] Actually it might be equally frustrating to meditate on it for a few minutes. Not kidding. The question is: Who am I not kidding? Listen, *mes amis,* for your life won't depend on the answer but on the success of your practice, at least in this lifetime.

You know, you do, that if it is the "you" whom you have become so passionately and blindly as well as lovingly and affectionately identified with, then of course no matter where "you" place "your" attention, even if it is on guru or God, it will be ultimately ineffective relative to the goal of this Path. (And relative to the *jaol*—old English—of this Path when you aren't piercing the knot of the illusion of separation.) As long as it is this "you" that you cling to and defend so tenaciously, inside and outside, what does it matter?

Yes, of course you can easily create all kinds of phenomena as side effects to the metaphysical placement of attention, but those sparks and lights, sounds and thrills and chills will only add to the mistaken belief that you are getting somewhere—like making

---

1 A playful reference to Lee's teaching on Enquiry, which is the use of the phrase "Who am I kidding?" to penetrate to the emptiness underlying the phenomenal world and emotional states or entrenched mind stream in particular.

progress towards transformation. There is such a reality as the placement of objective attention, but this "you" we are discussing can never place attention correctly, not even by accident. Because this "you" is false, so too is everything this "you" generates, even—oh horrors of horrors!—love, prayer, devotion, faith, whatever.

If we were to attempt to answer this fine question, the kernel of utility is that we must somehow let the Universe place our attention; in other words, when the Universe places our attention we could call this Surrender to the Will of God, for the Universe has Will, momentum, chaotic Intelligence—all quite lawful of course—but no attention. The Universe cannot have attention, although it does have Intention, another word for Will as we are using it. In any case, it is important, probably even necessary, for attention to be placed rightly. We are the Universe's (or God's, if you will) vehicles or agents for this function—as are animals and plants as well, but in a far less sophisticated, less complex, less transformational or alchemical way.

When we are able to allow the Will of God to animate in our field of influence, all dualities (outside/inside, top/bottom, good/bad, yes/no) become irrelevant and the just placement of attention finds itself attentive to whatever, wherever, and whoever (or is it whomever?) that attention can and does serve in that exact "here and now, as it is." Obviously, this can look to the naïve, untrained or ignorant perceiver as dynamically unenlightened behavior. You can be sure that when Neem Karoli Baba, the great Swami Nityananda, or our own Yogi Ramsuratkumar, was slurping down some food and dripping copious amounts on his blanket, shawl, loincloth or beard, that more than a few of those who called themselves devotees were not only disturbed or offended but thrown into confusion and even doubt—if they were ruthlessly self-honest, which was very rarely the case.

Lest we live our lives in denial, and more importantly in a very tentative relationship with our guru, we cannot afford to ignore these common little arrows of poison, for ignored long enough or righteously enough and dogmatically enough, it will be like ignoring the termites that are reliably gnawing through the foundation of our home. You get the picture, or image if you prefer, I am sure. You can be sure that when these eminent gentlemen, great masters all, were demonstrating ostensible anger or jealousy, or envy, greed, pride or vanity, which to varying degrees and frequency they all did, once again, to the subjective view of the student held in place by their "I"—the same "I" as the "you" we are discussing—these seemingly contradictory manifestations will be sources of what could become deep rifts or chasms between guru and chela, something none of us want, wish for others, or can afford.

In the Buddhist world of "form is emptiness, emptiness is form," or in our language, Enlightened Duality, the Universe can place "our" attention on anything, concrete, abstract, sublime or achingly mundane, and can keep "our" attention there for maddening lengths of time—maddening when "our" attention doesn't seem to be where "we" (the same "we" as the "you" we are discussing) assume it should be for success on the Path. At the same time, when "we" feel that "our" attention is on something that is somehow spiritual, "we" are ecstatic. Both views are false, since such views, opinionated and divided against themselves, are rooted in the illusory identification with a discreet individual, also quite illusory.

So, if we aim to live according to the Truth, the only solution, according to the context of this Path that we have so ardently embraced, is to allow the Universe, or the Will of God, to place "our" attention as pure attention, and not only for random and occasional moments (although we all have to start somewhere) but ultimately (a word I probably use too much) moment to moment to such an extreme degree that we aren't dividing and separating, though the proper creation of distinctions is neither dividing nor separating. There, at that point, we aren't even conscious that there is a difference between "our" attention—the "our" of the indentified "I," "me," "you"—and the Will of God. At that point there is *only* the Will of God, not the Will of God and the reflection on or of the Will of God. You know, as the great patriarch of Zen (was it the second or the sixth?) wrote in his poem, "no mirror, no dust . . . "

Well, tonight's discourse—or would we say essay?—wasn't very funny, but if you wish, you still may find a great deal of humor in it.

Next week, as far as I know now, we have two ADVs. Next weekend is a very special Work Weekend; we are planning a new Ashram Beautification Program to renew and revivify the entire "lower forty" (though in fact it's probably only a "lower one-and-a-half"), for real this time. It is a massive task, so we will need a massive amount of help. Please do not gloat if you think, in your superior way, that it's about time—such gloating is unattractive and belittles you. And . . . it is a veritable pleasure knowing you all, even the slackers!

Jai Guru, Jai Guru, Jai Guru

राम राम

The Big Clean Up

April 27, 2008

Well, good evening. So nice to see those of you who are here. It would be equally nice to see those who aren't here, but since they aren't here, we will have to simply think of them fondly, if we wish, since we can see them with our minds but not with our eyes, which is exactly what I meant by the opening greetings. I was not being esoteric. Can I "see" you, as in knowing who you are on all levels and in all times and places? Well, dears, as we used to say in high school, that is for me to know and you to find out—or not, as it is really of no import. Better you see yourselves, collectively and individually. Ah yes.

So, on to the subject of the evening, the big clean up. What a job we've done! You are to be congratulated. Yes, you are to be congratulated, so thank you. Now that we've cleaned up the Ashram and the Case Temple is back to being a temple, a mighty burden has been lifted. I feel so much lighter. There was a subtle psychic mold, and now it is spacious, clear, and ordered. Maybe most importantly, the Case Temple is now defined by its necessary elements; it is free of all of the extraneous, useless, energy-suffocating and draining trivialities that so easily accumulate when we aren't paying attention. It wasn't too late, not too late for Dan—who was and is most gracious—not too late for the Ashram, and it's not too late for me, as Lalitha has paralleled this massive shedding of weight and clutter to my own psychic state.

Okay. Now that we've done the collective work, the Sangha as body is clean, let's keep it that way, hey? The next order of business is the individual side of the coin. I bet most of you got this already, and some are delighted, excited and indicted while others may well be scared, reactive and in recoil, even though those don't rhyme, but neither do the other three in French. Yes, the next order of business is the individual side of the coin. In other words: What are *you* going to do about your clutter? This is the opportunity to shed some weight, lots of weight—recent weight and old, old weight.

The opportunity will not last long. The question is not can you, but will you? The only way to shed your weight is to embrace the experiment fully, understanding that "fully" means totally, completely, without restraint or compromise. Ya dig, hep cats? So, the opportunity will not last long because right now I am resting in the profound clarity of this "clean" space, enjoying the view, but I won't rest long, it's not in my nature; "I" being like a comet and y'all being like its tail, once I start moving I will not be cutting off my tail to spite my burning ball of fire—meaning that I will be on about other business, leaving this business to mind itself, lost opportunity or not. Since I'm leaving for Montana in less than two weeks, my random guess would be that you've got, in a real personal sense, less than two weeks.

So the obvious consideration is: What does it mean to remove your own clutter? Well, clearly we aren't just talking about the external stuff you might be weighed down with, electronically and virtually, like your unnecessary but addictive ego-stroking and ego-satisfying internet projects. We are also talking about all of the psychic/psychological blood suckers—the parasites of mind, cells, and soul—that are leeching you dry and effectively keeping you exactly where you are, unable to move even a millimeter. You know, all the "I couldn't help myself" junk, all the overbearing emotional states, the clinging to childhood dynamics and antiquated survival strategies and so on and so on.

Let's be both honest and realistic (two things that don't always go together very well): Can you do this? The answer, which I bet you guessed I was going to say, is: Yes, you can. Will you? Most of you will not because you will allow yourselves to be effectively stopped dead in your tracks, as the saying goes, by your obsessive mentalizations, the mind parasite that tells you that you can't do this because you don't know *how* to do it, that you can't do this because it isn't your time, karma, because you don't have the skills, the ability and so on . . . ad nauseum.

You all know the party line, which just so happens to be both honest and realistic: There is no "how to"—you just put it down and walk away. Mr. E.J. Gold shared that jewel of a teaching with us because you *can* do it; he wasn't just whistling Dixie, although I'm sure he could if he wanted to. He shared the teaching, which share he called a gift to me, because he knows it is an honest and realistic task, one that you *can* manage. Now to add insult to injury (for some of you), I am not interested, particularly, in a flash in the pan, lookin' good, goin' nowhere, instantaneous manifestation of unclutter, which you then methodically and quickly allow to return to the state of previous clutter.

I am really only suggesting that you take this opportunity if you will maintain and sustain the breakthrough—not to simply commit to it like all the sincere but unfulfilled commitments that litter your past. If you *will* sustain it, then upon that new base, that platform, that radical new context, you can continue to build the Mystical Palace that will house the Beloved. In other words, but saying the very same thing as reinforcement: if you are going to do this—rather, if you have found yourself magically having done this—instead of shooting the baby in the head with your obsessive mental chatter ("Wow, how did this happen, I wonder if it will stay, is it real, what is it, why is it, can I handle it, I don't deserve it," and the common one, "*Help*!"), hold it as your only reality. Begin to live there, learning the territory just like you did when you moved to Prescott, or went to Triveni for retreat, or found yourself being a new parent, or in a new relationship, or in no couple relationship, and so on. As soon as you weaken, thinking of your past clutter with nostalgia, you are dead. As Bob Dylan said: "Nostalgia is death" and he knows what of he speaks.

I would be thrilled, pleased, and overjoyed to welcome you "to town," and what a town it is: no unemployment, plenty of jobs for everyone, and most excellent security (job-wise), with a vast future ahead, no glass ceiling here! If you weren't at brunch you didn't hear Dan thank everyone for saving his life. He wasn't being overdramatic, neither in his gratitude nor his words, and I would like to remind you that he could only say this *after* the events of the last four days.

You are in the same position in the sense that you cannot—not that you won't, you literally can't—see the results of your own overburdening. From a place of burden, weight and clutter, you can't appreciate the spacious unclutter, the lightness of being. You can only know it from its actual presence—that is, after you take the plunge. You can't know what a mango tastes like from a picture of it, or from someone else's ecstatic description; you have to taste it. You can't know how cold the water is until you jump off the bank, and that's the only way to do it—*jump,* not put in one toe to test it out.

Do it or not, but not doing is to remain in ignorance, left to your habits and your insecurities. And doing it, remember there is no formula, no method, no magic wand or magic pill. Simply put down the mass of mess and walk away.

Next week, two ADVs or ADMs but not yet ADTs, and please, if you will . . . next week's Darshan will be the last Darshan that I will be at, personally, for the summer, though I'm always with everyone during the times my body is elsewhere. So I hope to see you there. And thank you so much for cleaning the Guru's extended body this week, as the Ashram is not only my home but my body as well. I feel a great relief!

Jai Guru, Anande Baulo,
Jai Guru Jai

राम राम

We Are Looking for Saints

May 4, 2008

Good evening. Well let's see what we have on the agenda tonight. We will have to see because the plan will unfold as I write, as it always does. It could for you as well, if you allowed some small adjustments to take place on your engine—that is, your mechanicality. Firstly, though, I'd like to reinforce what I spoke about previously, which is that since I've been talking more and been more easily understood (unfortunately only in a linear way), I have noticed that many more people have taken the liberty (an obvious leap of assumption when one thinks "inside the box") of asking me more questions—questions those people wouldn't have dreamed of asking only weeks before. And as I said, just because I am talking more doesn't mean I want to be talking more, except when the choice or option is *mine*. So please, get with the program. And I mean "please," I'm not just being polite. Thank you.

A discussion arose this week about the two polarities of devotion and the ordinary activities of life. It arose relative to a car that pulled into the parking lot of Starbucks as I was daydreaming, peering out the window and lusting after the coffee that everyone who was with me was enjoying, and God Bless them for having coffee when they desired it instead of denying themselves for me, which would have caused me a bit of suffering as well as incurred my displeasure. The car haphazardly and too quickly pulled into a "handicapped only" space, and two women practically leapt out and strode, quite unhandicappedly, into our very Starbucks, which is when I read the saying on the front bumper that stated, "With God all things are possible."

I regaled my associates there and then with my bon mot, which was, "All things are possible except parking properly in an appropriate space," or to put it another way, "Yes, all things are possible, even parking in a handicapped space and a foot over the line at that." And then, ever the lacking-in-compassion-for-idiot-drivers guru, I said: "Hypocrites." All of which led to a discussion of faith, dedication, love, devotion and all of that, and how we can be filled with genuine qualities such as those and yet still be either blind to our contradictory behaviors or really have no clue as to the immaturity of our psychological complexes and their effect on others and on our world. You know, the "praise God" out of one side of our mouths while out of the other side demeaning, in many cases with vicious intent and consequences, our children, partners, and parents.

The point of the discussion revolved around the reality of both sides and what to do—since it was clear to everyone there at our table that I expect consistent and reliable integrity in both domains. The phrase that came to mind was that as a Sangha, we have plenty of mystics and sages; what we're looking for now in these very same mystics and sages, and in everyone else as well, is Saints.

Can you be both spiritually advanced *and* socially advanced as well? Yes, absolutely, yes. Of course we are all polite and appropriately mannered when the corns that we have developed aren't being stepped on, though for some of us it only takes the real or imagined threat of a good hard stomp on one of our corns to elicit the other type of behavior, of which we are so well practiced: the angry, resentful, reactive, aggressive, impolite and unmannered behavior. And that, dear ones, is not Saintly . . . decidedly not.

So yes, our hearts are swollen with truly profound relationships to the Guru, the Sangha, the Dharma and sometimes the "Buddha," and therein lies extraordinary *rasa*, extraordinary *bhava*. People outside of our circle or mandala are tremendously touched by your sanctity, your genuine holiness *and*—yes *and*, for that is not the end of the story—if we wish to be in the "guru's world" we must have or embody a similar "swelling" in the domain of personality and psychology, in all areas and aspects of ordinary life, relationship, creative, professional, monetary, dietary and so on. Can you do it? Yes, absolutely. After all, you've learned to say "please," and "thank you," and "you're welcome," haven't you? It's as simple as that, though it may require a bit more hard work.

Please consider this over the summer while my body, the dense physical one, is in Europe. And for the Europeans, please consider this while my dense physical body is amongst you, even though you all need most to consider this when my dense physical body is not in your dense physical body's proximity and you don't feel a need to be on especially good behavior.

And I will consider this as well while I'm touring with the bands and yelling insults and obscenities at our various audiences. Although I must admit, with some hesitation and embarrassment, that many times I yell loving praise and appreciation to our various audiences as well. Balance is important at times when balance is important.

Thank you, by the way, for your various kindnesses during this healing process that I am in, and though it isn't entirely over yet, there is no need to discontinue these various kindnesses, so please go on. I am very pleased by the various changes that are arising for me, many of which you will discover upon my return from Europe when I can be present for their implementation. While I am away, please try not to let your tendencies toward sloth and comfort allow you to backslide relative to attempting to refill the Ashram refrigerators with all manner of little goodies with personal names taped all over them, or to allow the fantastic Ashram clean-up to be overshadowed by the accumulation of another mess of unnecessary and unneeded mass. Thank you *so* much.

While we're on about recommendations for the summer, please support the Ashram with your attendance to events, meditation, ADTs,[1] Bridge and Work Weekends, as well as remembering to continue the Heart Breath, Enquiry, Assertion, dietary practices . . . You know, the demand and the request is likely to never change, so "get with the program." It's now or later, and there are quite significant benefits to now as opposed to later. To put it another way, there are significant deficits to later.

As far as I know now, there will be two ADT programs as usual during the week I return from Montana.In the meantime, Blessings for great success in the completion of projects for those of you who are in the midst of having large properties for sale; for those of you who are still working out relationship or parenting struggles, Blessings for great success in the resolution of your difficulties.

For those of you for whom life is working quite well, without drama of any sort, high or low, Blessings for great success in the continuation of your ongoing inherence in this Great Process of Divine Evolution, and may the sweet and tragic Realization of Spiritual Slavery in all its various manifestations, transformations, and consequences begin or continue to radiate you, until you are beyond recognition by the usual criteria of recognition. I will await word or evidence of all your many successes with trembling and breathless anticipation

Jai Guru, Anande Baulo,
Jai Guru Jai

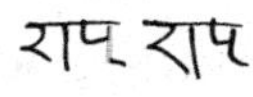

[1] For decades Lee has had two "After Dinner Talks" every week on his ashrams; in these essays he often refers to them using the acronym ADT.

Receiving What the Guru Gives

November 29, 2009

Good evening. I feel that I should write this evening's considerations because I believe I will be better understood, whatever good that may do. (Remember, as Werner Erhard said: "Understanding is the booby prize," and I would add: booby as in last prize and booby as in one who, as well-meaning as they may be, has, as we say, no clue.) The novelty of being "translated" in English, ostensibly my own language (although I've doubted recently whether that is my students' language, given how vast their understanding is and yet how narrow is the band in which this seeming understanding is implemented) has quite worn off, even as it continues to be interesting in French, Spanish, German and Tamil, none of which are my own languages and all of which I've been translated into.

Nonetheless, students we are, and learned we have done, and I suppose that "getting into Heaven" is the point—not whether we slide in, glide in, fly in, or stumble or bumble in. Heaven being what it is, once in, in it is, so I've been told. (Whether we could even get out if we wanted is another issue, sort of like the ultimate socialist civil service job.)

Please do not consider this—the at-least-temporary return to the written darshan address—as a regression relative to the physical health of your spiritual master. It is not, so do me a *huge* favor and stow any projections, assumptions, conclusions, editorializing, fears, concerns and all the attendant stinking mass of putrid shit surrounding those sub-human qualities (or sub-mature human, I should say) and cut me a little slack. Things are progressing nicely despite one hell of a cold that has kicked the crap out of me for a couple of weeks plus. I can feel the sharp claws of some of your mental gyrations like the hounds of the Baskervilles. Thank you.

I hope you have all enjoyed the little satire piece included in the last *Tawagoto.* It was distributed for your enjoyment, not, in your cases, as any great teaching tool, though clearly there is something for the naïve amongst us to learn. And I hope you read and re-read thoroughly Helen's letter. Why, you might have queried (yourself or no one in particular), would someone put up with such treatment by the chef in a fine restaurant? Firstly, because the job they are apprenticing to is something they have always wanted and wouldn't trade for "all the tea in China." It is a dream come to fruition, and there is no price too high to pay for the realization of this dream. And secondly because there are no other "roads to Rome." This is it. There is one way to go and no alternatives and no options. Every *genuine* training ground uses the same methods. No other training produces EXCELLENCE.

To settle for less, or worse, to compromise ideals or integrity—even if that compromise is considered a lateral movement—is unacceptable for the true artist. And make no mistake about it, Helen is apprenticing to a very serious and real art form. Does this sound familiar? Are the parallels obvious? And if not, good God, why not? This sadhana that Helen describes could read like another Milarepa tale, and she's not alone. All over the world, in the most outstanding restaurants and kitchens, under the tutelage of the most outstanding master chefs—artists all—men and women are not only enduring but thriving under such heat, in such milieus.

There is no excuse for settling for less but ignorance, laziness, dull-heartedness, or small-mindedness. I don't believe that many of you are ignorant, dull-hearted or small-minded. Wearing blinders? Yes, perhaps. Tired and frustrated? Yes, perhaps. And called to the limits of what you mistakenly imagine your limits are? Yes, perhaps. That is the pivotal point, the tangent, the launching pad to the next octave.

One of the things that M. Young is realizing, as the first volume of my biography takes shape, is that ever since day one we've had the same opportunity, the same possibility. Times have changed—and how and howdy as well!—but my vision, essentially, has not (though it's certainly dressed far more elaborately) and neither have you. After a fifteen-hour day of being yelled at in ways so deprecating you couldn't have imagined it even days before, when push comes to shove, it may simply boil down to: how badly do you want it? (And incidentally, will it be now or later? Because it *will* be.)

Dear me, forty minutes so far to write this, and I guess the reading of it has taken about five minutes or less. Well, nothing is perfect, is it?

I would like to take a diversion here. It is truly wonderful to host so many guests this season. I enjoy with deep affection the presence of each and every one of you, adults and children alike. If I can speak for those who live here and who work so diligently and so tirelessly every day, it is a joy to have friends from around the world throwing themselves into the mix with such vigor and enthusiasm. Let's do this more often! Yogi Ramsuratkumar knows each and every one of you, and if I can speak for Him, which He certainly has endorsed, supported, and encouraged, He is as thrilled as I when devotees visit the "mother ship," so to say, even as He in no way diminishes His Regard for you wherever you are.

Well, I think this is going well so far, and I am quite certain that had I been speaking rather than writing this, things would have come out quite differently. No less entertaining perhaps but . . . I think this goes well so far. And mind you (or not, as is your privilege), in order to write this, the time has had to come from somewhere. Just now it has come from my rapt involvement with a new Charles Bukowski book, a passion of adoration (with a small "a" but no small thing anyway), so I hope you are appreciating this little essay.

Hell, I'm supposed to be resting, but every time I close my eyes the deluge won't quiet down, so here's a bit more on the above. It is so that each of us must go through our own "corridor of madness" (corridor of bliss) on the Path; at the same time, to have this body, this matrix of sangha around us, is a gift. We have the very, very rare gift of a true family here and wherever sangha is, even if it is one single person living in ostensible isolation. We must face ourselves alone, yes, for no one can do that for us—and, in the context we have established and in the concrete demonstration of that context, we have evolved over the years, brick by brick, tear by tear, pushing against the wind and the storm without retreating. (Oh my, I feel like I should be yelling "Praise the Lord!" here.) We have a support system without which I am sure many of us could not or would not keep plugging away, or would not have kept plugging away. I include myself in this, as I am grateful to (after Yogi Ramsuratkumar, of course) you all for your perseverance, tenacity, and not the least of all, your love.

And, lest we enter the pathologically dangerous territory of "resting on our laurels"—the tulsi ones, not the olive ones—we are far from done and the final aria (arati) is a long way off. I am more touched and moved than ever by what we are doing together, and I am more acutely frustrated than ever as well. Fortunately or not, the higher one climbs, the more one must have skills, attention, perception, and reliable integrity (perhaps eventually we will talk about impeccability). We've climbed fairly high—not as high as some, and quite a bit higher than most. The wider the perspective, the more glaring the gaps, so I am continually more dedicated to leaning on the demand to practice, more insistent on "stepping on the corns" we have so nimbly danced our way in avoidance of, and more committed to an unwillingness to overlook foolishness, sloppiness, and the refusal to grow up or to deal with ourselves with ruthless honestly. I hope that is good news to most of you, and I sincerely wish that you meet the challenges that are particularly evident in these extraordinary, precious, and Work-necessary times.

Another sentence in Helen's letter (to hearken back to one of our earlier stabs at communication) referred to "never apologize." A couple of points I would like to emphasize: When we were in Tiruvannamalai some few years ago, in the once sanctuary of Ganeshan's lovely house, I was sitting next to Yogi Ramsuratkumar. He rested His head on my shoulder in a moment of—what?—tenderness, Transmission, affection. I naturally—as a human, not as a practitioner—rested my head on His, and He instantly slapped my head a good wallop. I got the message, one element of which was: the Guru offers, we take. Simply that. We do not respond as peers, as one human to another. Whatever the Guru gives, it is our job, our *responsibility*, to absorb, stay alert, receive fully and without sentiment.

We don't try to meet the Guru in kind unless the Guru specifically, clearly, and exactly asks that we respond; unless he asks without the need for interpretation or guess work—in other words, through the spoken word, not by inference, body language or implication. Any "normal" human reaction—like "I'm sorry," like the sloppy movement of my head, as if Yogi Ramsurarkumar's gesture towards me was some purely human act of kindness—is a *reaction*, not a response. Let me reiterate: it is the Guru's movement to give, give, give (always some form of Blessing) and our movement should be to receive—passively, calmly and attentively—and never say you're sorry.

Along these lines, I walked into the kitchen early this afternoon and was greeted by a small unpleasant shock that created an irritaton in me. I made a critical comment, and the person implicated responded, "I thought of that before I started." All excuses are just forms of apology. Let me be clear (we can only hope), and let me ask that this clarity may have the chance to show up in some of your subsequent behaviors (we can only hope): I don't give a flea's ass about what you thought about *before* you produced some foolish manifestation, spoke some hurtful or counterproductive word, or spent all of your energy on some internet obsession. What I care about is what you *do* and how what you do intersects with our relationship—more pointedly, with "my" Transmission.

I can feel Yogi Ramsuratkumar listening to this and being drawn deep, deep into one of His Bhavas, weeping silently, with tears moistening His eyes and running down His cheeks. I know that my silly behaviors at times, my irritation, arrogance and impatience, the small errors of the past for which I feel much regret in the moment, are obliterated, blasted out of existence by *this*. *This* is reliable. *This* is rock solid. *This* is who I am and who Yogi Ramsuratkumar trusts implicitly. All excuses, all apologies, have no meaning in the face of *this*. (I hope I am not giving you, any of you, an excuse to stay small and ugly in your behaviors, language, and relationships—when you are ready to speak as I speak, I'll let you know!)

If you *thought* of the right thing to do ahead of time, then I want to see you *do* the right thing. I'd so much prefer that to another apology (yawn), another excuse (yawn), another justification (yawn, yawn, yawn). This cannot be affected with a simple agreement. If you are not Paying Attention and Remembering (self-observation), it is highly unlikely that you will find it possible to quell the apologies and excuses. A bit of retrospective should make that apparently obvious! We all mean well, but no matter how well we mean, when we come across someone in critical medical condition, if we don't have a basis of training, a foundation of knowledge, our ability to help will necessarily be severely limited. It is good to mean well. If we also want to *do* well, the training and knowledge we need to manage our "blind" habits is found in self-observation and in the accrual of results from a consistent, attentive and reliable practice.

I might add a small addendum here, which is for those few of you who never say you're sorry because you'd almost rather be damned than vulnerable: you will have to adjust the above consideration to fit your own particular neurosis. *Oui?* (That's French, not simply the name of a popular girlie magazine.) We have been given all the practices we could conceivably need, and these practices have been articulated in print as well as verbally, by examples of practitioners, and through notable testimony. I guess the appropriate inference here is: "It's now up to you." Oh damn, *that* again.

I guess that at this juncture it is also appropriate to tell you all how much I am looking forward to celebrating my Beloved Master's Jayanthi in little more than a day, so I hope many of you can make it, and beyond hoping that you *can* make it—which is most likely true for most all of you—I additionally hope that most of you *will* make it. And so, unless some forceful addition pushes its way out, Jai Guru!

राम राम

Precision in Practice

December 6, 2009

I apologize for another written piece. As soon as I can rely on putting two or more words together without gushing saliva all over my clothing, I'll return to a more normal converse. I really miss evening tea; it is such a lovely and natural way to end the day but again, unable to sit for more than a few seconds without psychic discomfort, oh well. It is quite interesting how the common things we often take for granted, like a simple conversation with friends or a nice meal together, become so precious when one can't do them. In any event, as the situation is temporary, let us consider more useful things.

I heard a nasty rumor that I wish to confirm or dispel: By a show of hands, how many of those in the room are on, or have, a Facebook site? Thank you.

It has been said, "God is in the details." I hope not, as if so, many of us are overlooking that God. It has not been given us to participate in any major social or political movements, but then again, the mere (although hardly mere) results of a close attention to details in our ongoing daily lives, bringing integrity and right action to them, has most far-reaching consequences. And of course the immediate benefits are quite substantial. I received a letter recently which said that in a hospital in Southern California, nurses who choose of their own free will not to receive the new flu vaccine are forced (or lose their job) to wear facial masks and a large green (how ironic) ID badge to distinguish them so that patients may request another nurse to comfort their hysterical minds. Well, it isn't a yellow or a pink star, but does anyone sense a similarity?

We live in very tense times, as you all know. More and more, it becomes imperative to pay attention to details, none of which should be too small, and to deepen and strengthen the roots which clarify and confirm your choice to lead this lifestyle and tread this Path. Yogi Ramsuratkumar would be (and is) the first one to counsel us to guard our flank and hold tightly to our principles (and hopefully you have embraced the principles that I have tried to instill in you), not only in mind but most importantly in action. The denial some few of us are still in is not only stunning but shocking and saddening. In any event, "Thank God for small favors" and take heart from the vast multitude of those that our lives are replete with. Please do not neglect the beauty and Blessings where they are because there are areas where they are not.

And lest you despair, there are some fantastic movies coming out this holiday season! A small two-hour distraction can be just the thing when needed. And I would say the same thing about chocolate and butter used in cooking. Doing the right thing is one thing; rigidity and righteousness and fundamentalist dogma are another, even when the principles about which one is rigid, righteous, and dogmatic are basically sound.

When I asked one of my students—to whom I have been sending Europeans for years to be instructed in the Heart Breath—to describe her instructions to me, I was a bit horrified to learn that she has been telling people the wrong thing. When S. told me how much trouble she was having doing the Heart Breath practice and I asked her to describe how she was instructed, I was more than horrified, I was aghast. Her description of what she had been told was about as weak as I've ever heard. The instruction was a fair description of the Buddhist practice of tonglen, which, yes, I have considered with you often, but obviously I have not been clear enough in my articulation; although there are similarities, tonglen is *not* the Heart Breath and the Heart Breath is not tonglen.

I feel myself to be an extremely exacting person who expresses a multitude of details when needed. Obviously this doesn't apply to the last couple of years; my mumbling inability to speak clearly and dislike of speaking on that account is one reason. I am exasperated by our willingness to be sloppy and inarticulate about the definitions, boundaries, and essence of our various practices. Many devotees' description of Enquiry is so bizarre, given the extensive instruction available, that it is no wonder whatsoever why it is so ineffectual for so many people. It is disconcerting to say the least when core practices, foundation posts in our entire corpus of practice, are so fuzzily understood. It is even more disconcerting when many of us seem to make no effort towards exactitude and clarity in that regard. Back to attention to details.

To practice wrongly is akin to failing to practice at all, given that each of our core practices is Revelatory and *ours*. To practice something else may certainly produce noticeable results in various ways, but they are not the intended results of the practice and therefore place you, somewhat tentatively and shakily, on some other Path than this one, something I am sure most of you do not intend. The practices are easy to do when done properly, and of course can be confusing and ill-fitting when not. So please attend to the refinement and precision with which I have delivered these practices into your hands and onto your plates (and beware your eager little minds, which have a major investment in obscuring, complicating, and disempowering said practices). As we know, or should, the mind can be a treasure map or minefield, and it is to our advantage to defuse the mines before we step on one and send shrapnel flying every which way.

As you all most likely know, our esteemed President (and I mean that truly, without a shade or hint of sarcasm) has committed a substantial number of new troops to the Afghan situation. On the surface I am sure that many of you had a knee-jerk reaction, wondering what on earth is going on. I must say, with some pleasure, that R., one of the most ardent and politically savvy pacifists, having read a fine articulation of the justification (and even vital need) for such a commitment, had to reassess and rethink her own position. Bravo! The point is that when we jump to conclusions based on established biases, especially when our education relative to the subject is faulty or puerile, sophomoric perhaps, we will most likely "shoot first and ask questions later." Asking questions to a corpse is not likely to be very revealing or edifying. Back, once again, to details.

It pays and pays well to have the facts about any given situation before going off half-cocked, as the saying goes—a reference to guns not genitalia, I believe, or to the rooster domain. How does one collect the facts? Clearly a depth and breadth of study is useful, and perhaps more important is remembering to ask the right questions and knowing what the right questions are. We are often so impulsive, and at times too lazy to be even mildly interested in a proper response to circumstance, that it completely escapes us that we may not have all the necessary data or facts relative to a reaction we are having. Remember that we are called, in maturity, as sane adults and intelligent practitioners, to *respond* in place of reacting.

Arnaud Desjardins might say that all reaction comes from emotions, and as Swami Prajnanpad has said, "All emotion is false." It is, or at least can be, difficult to seek for clarification and facts around an issue when we are so *sure* of our position. Remember, if you will, that positions are just that: positions. As many if not most of you know, our certainty is usually a function of our psychological script, and as many if not most of you know, pathological biases can be amazingly convincing.

Chögyam Trungpa Rinpoche said that wisdom can only be taught in the form of a hint. This becomes more and more obvious to me as all of the direct and unequivocal, unimpeachable teachings I have given, especially in the early days, seems to have become more dharma or obvious truth than pragmatic life action. I suspect that our great strides, our successes pragmatically, have been understood in spite of the rational and logical, not because of it.

So how does that tie in with the need for precision in practice? Wisdom is a ground, a context, of how we view life and reality; the practices are specifics that help us to move with and in life and reality with ease, confidence, and tacit realization of what is true and accurate over and against what is false and subjective—in other words, our ego stories. So, as time continues to unfold in its inexorable way, I think there will be more hints and less eloquent philosophy, and at the same time, lots of exact instruction in *our* practices, so we aren't beating our heads against Buddha's door but rather inhering in the Western Baul Tradition, a tradition which is our unique expression and exposition of the seed of Spiritual Slavery and, hopefully, the embrace of Assertion. Our way is based on Objective Inspiration and deserves to be held in its own perfection, not adjusted to suit our misinterpretations and "creative" impulses.

As a sangha, a community, we have done ourselves a bit proud, but as we considered together last week, we must never rest on our laurels and allow the sled to coast. Beyond that, it is each and every individual's personal task and responsibility to be an exemplar, individually and under all circumstances in every moment, of the same dimension of Divine Influence that is impressive in the body as a whole. We should never hide under the petticoats of the community, imagining we will either be carried on the wave or somehow be relieved of the personal and immediate demand to show up and grow up. In fact there is no place to hide. And what good fortune *that* is!

Well, I think this is a good place to cease and desist. I am a bit embarrassed that tonight's discourse has been so humorless, but I'm sure some of you were laughing inside and hopefully cheering inside now and then as well. Two ADTs this coming week and well, have a wonderful week. Jai Guru.

राम राम

Transforming Every Obstacle

December 13, 2009

Good evening! I hope the discussion on the Heart Breath was useful at the After Dinner Talk last Thursday. Many excellent things were said, and if you put the proper things together in the proper order, you should have quite a bit of clarity about it all. As it has quite wide-reaching implications for our Work in general, and considerable implications for many aspects of our Work in particular as well, one of the elements of the discussion worth reinforcing here is this point: As a technical practice, without any particular goal in mind, simply the activity of doing the Heart Breath has many radiant effects that positively alter our overall practice, our maturity on the Path, and our Being itself. This Radiance does its work over time and shows up in our manifestations, even if the exact trajectories are not so easily or readily traceable.

Much of what we call the Blessing Force of Yogi Ramsuratkumar and the lineage, or loosely call Grace, works in this way. One day we simply show up altered, different. I never recommend questioning such wonderful gifts, but I do recommend simply accepting "what is" with gratitude and wonder (if you are innocent enough to cop to it). As many of you know, to dig around—or more accurately to root around like a pig looking for slop—when such investigations are no more than the perverse wishes to "understand" something, often just creates a big mud hole. So it would do us all well to learn to rest in what is objectively obvious (not what is obvious to an ego full of biases, confusion, misinterpretations and false identifications). We can be present to what is objectively obvious without having to figure anything out about it.

One of the things that never ceases to amaze me, at least when it isn't irritating, maddening, or annoying to me, is how often many of us act in ways that we assume are serving—serving me, or just serving the space or the Work or whatever. So often such actions are in fact no more than our neurotic subjectivity interjecting itself into the given space, occasionally (even more than occasionally) being actually counterproductive rather than helpful. Excuses like, "Well, I thought you didn't like it when . . . " or, "I didn't want to disturb (upset, bother, disrupt, interrupt, etc . . . .) you," are just our own fears, personal trips and self-hatreds being projected onto me or the space.

Clearly, when we are self-observing to a more acute degree, we have a much clearer and cleaner view of the environments and circumstances in which we act out our psychological confusion and even, in some cases, aberration. I randomly find the content of such behaviors to actually be humorous, but I can't say that I am highly developed enough for this attitude in myself to be prevalent yet.

When I was eight years old I was given nitrous oxide for a dental procedure—not unlike the one I had earlier today. I remember counting backwards from one hundred, and the next thing I remember was staggering out to meet my mother. She asked if I was conscious that I was laughing. I said no, then she told me that I had laughed uproariously the whole way out. I expected some nitrous oxide this morning for the procedure, but I didn't need it—only Novocain. I was a bit nervous, but the dentist finished the entire procedure in seconds, literally. A tooth was pulled in less than two seconds. I was impressed and so relieved that I was almost ecstatic all afternoon. Isn't it interesting how often our concerns don't actually materialize to the negative degree that we imagine they probably will? Isn't it a great relief?

One of Chögyam Trungpa Rinpoche's new books is called *The Mishap Lineage.* He says that, in the Kagyu lineage, practice or sadhana is commonly defined by the ordinary life process of meeting mishaps and overcoming them with dignity, bravery and creativity, practicing all the while. I really relate to this in terms of the Western Baul Path as well. Do you agree?

We're flowing nicely, no clouds on the horizon, when suddenly a marital bomb explodes, an unexpected pregnancy arrives, a totally unforeseen financial calamity (or windfall, just another form of "mishap") falls to us, a car crash, a diagnosis of some severe health issue, a family member or close friend dies without warning. All of our lives are certainly defined by such bumps in the road, and countless smaller rough spots. It *is* our practice to meet such unforeseen events directly, without freak-out, annoyance, or breakdown, and move with and beyond them with grace, maturity and nobility.

It might have seemed to some few of you that the Way was about finding some utopian otherworldly "spiritual" Eden and establishing ourselves there, buffered and protected from all and any "mishaps." I think not. We live in a world in which the texture of life includes a vast variety of circumstances, and these circumstances are *not* a test to see what kind of practitioners we are. It is simply life-as-it-is, Just This, meant to be recognized clearly, not avoided but actually respected as a part and parcel of the stream we have entered in order to Realize and Transform.

In one sense, we transform ourselves by transforming every obstacle, large and tiny, into an opportunity to practice kindness, generosity, compassion, forbearance, tenacity, discipline—in essence, skillful means, as the Buddhists say. This is the daily Magic of the Blessing Force of the Lineage—not floating in air, telekinesis, materializing objects and dematerializing ourselves. It's sort of like catching yourself as you stumble and remaining upright and on course. Any "mishap" we encounter—from something as mundane as an unexpected traffic tie-up, to an untimely, unmanageable wave of ecstatic Shakti arising just when we need to be meeting an important business contact—needs to be met with an even-handed equanimity, a good dose of humor, surrender, and an embrace of the *isness,* the reality, of the situation. This is life. This is us.

In our Path and school, we are not defined by an otherworldly haze, in which the actuality of our living, breathing, daily situations are either ignored or looked down on as too mundane and illusory to even bother considering, let alone deal with. Even as vast as the esoteric rays of practice are and may be engaged (if you have the maturity, the foundation, and the ways and means to do so), our Path is also a here-and-now practice. We work with what we are given. We work with what I give you—be that an artistic endeavor, a service task, a relationship situation, or another material issue—and barring or in addition to those, we work with whatever texture, smooth or rough, the Universe lays down at our feet as we move through our lives.

I finished the biography of Dilgo Khyentse Rinpoche, who was a spiritual giant. I have been left with many positive impressions, one of which is that there can be and are, even today, right here in our midst, practitioners of a quality and stature that echo the grandest spiritual heroes down through the ages. And why not one or more of you? As a true dharma genius, the possibilities his life indicates are truly inspiring. It is these small little flashes, sparks that touch us, intersect with us all the time and spur us on, in spite of the massive fog cover that seems to have settled on our struggling planet and culture. Hallelujah!

I want to thank all of you who have been frequenting the Bridge spaces lately. I really enjoy the intimacy of it all. Of course I would prefer that such stark silence (besides the bidding and the ubiquitous "You're in your hand" or "You're on the board" interjections by yours truly) be frequently punctuated by considered questions and active dharma discussions, although I suppose too much of even that could get trying. But, somewhere in the middle, a bit left of middle in fact, would be a very delicious touch to round out the evenings and salve my wounds when I am losing heavily, which of late has been my fate (and that of my partners).

I have begun reading the final journal of Lewis Thompson, who as many of you may recall, is the author of *Black Sun,* a book of poetry published by Hohm Press. It is as much a hagiography as a biography, but within it are many useful points, some few of which I will be reading to you over time, especially an excellent little section on the practice of *sahajiya,* which some of you will recognize as one of the essential and integral elements of our own Path. I think you'll find this to be extremely helpful, if you pay attention, when the time comes. It's nice to have things to look forward to. Speaking of which, *Avatar* will be in the theatres this Friday, and *Sherlock Holmes* and *The Great Emporium of Dr. Parnassus* on Christmas! "Joy to the world . . . ."

I would like to caution you about becoming too myopic. It is true, of course, that we must handle day-to-day business and conduct such business with integrity, with accuracy, with efficiency, properly and correctly. At the same time, we surely do not want to lose sight of the "big picture"—not only why we are here, what we are here to do, and who we are here, but most importantly the Truth of Reality, not through the lens of our psychology but free of all artifice, implication, projection, confusion, and dogma. In spite of the clouds that seem to obscure it (or the moon that may seem to replace it), the Sun is always shining and helping us to conduct our daily affairs with ease, humor, and detachment. So keep this "big picture" in mind; in this manner we needn't get all riled up over small inconsistencies that provoke our failure to Remember.

Ah well, it's been fun and productive, but it is time to get ready to greet you all on this lovely night. . . .

Jai Guru!

राम राम

Seeing the Guru

December 20, 2009

I believe that I understand the desire to, as much as possible, personalize the human relationship to the guru. Whenever I brought gifts to Yogi Ramsuratkumar, I wanted Him to take them immediately, "oooh" and "aaah" over them, caress them and stare into my eyes a secret that only He and I knew. Yes, how true, and that was all about me, not about Him. So, I believe that I understand, to some small degree, why you would like to hand your prasad directly into my hands before receiving yours directly from my hand.

It may be helpful to remember, if you wish, how Yogi Ramsuratkumar left prasad to be distributed when He exited Darshan to return to Sudama House, or to His apartment on the Ashram—when at the end of His earthly or physical life He was staying there, mostly too ill to travel even short distances. And in leaving that prasad, He indicated to me and to everyone there, Indian and Western alike, that I was to give it out. I think it would be useful to many of you to deeply consider why this was in no way a diminishment of His direct Blessing, His love for His devotees, or a lessening of the power of the ritual exchange of prasad.

When someone holds out their prasad and waits, sometimes for what seems a small eternity, for me to take it in my greasy little appendage, in effect that person is demanding that I dance to their tune, jump through their hoop, tap to their piano—or, in effect, become their devotee. When I have to lean so far forward to take or give prasad to any individual that I come close to tumbling head first off of my seat and onto the floor, well, isn't that just a wonderful heart-warming confirmation that in fact I love my devotee so much that I am willing and glad to be completely controlled by their neurotic manipulation?

Yes, I understand that such dynamics are usually thought of as innocent or sincere gestures, and it would be equally useful to allow this moment of embarrassing revelation to indicate the paucity of self-observation that is active in such a person's case, especially if that person just so happens to be you. On the other hand, when I reach out to receive your offering, I hope it is obvious that you can safely place it in my hand(s) without shame, self-consciousness, or untoward self-congratulatory pride. I genuinely hope and pray that none of you feel shamed, attacked, or criticized by this, for our consideration here is not about *you*, but about unconscious or chronically habitual manifestations that are the generative affectations of a life script that you did not choose and are now not willing to deal with ruthlessly (the only form of "dealing with" that will be even minimally effective); a life script that you are now implicated in even though you assumed that script when you were too young, inexperienced and unsophisticated to realize there were alternative ways of seeing your life at the time.

So...onwards. Well, sort of onwards. It's like this: If, even without being conscious of it, you pigeon-hole or diminish the guru to no more than a physical aura or influence, just a kind of "superpal" or "love bomb" or something like that, you misunderstand by "miles and miles and miles and miles" who in fact you are in relationship with and have been since way back and will be until way forward. And in so misunderstanding, your ability and willingness to tap the multi-dimensional, multifaceted, multileveled Source of Transformation, Being, Power and Blessing is unlikely to come to fruition—which *is* the real reason you are here, not the suave, charming, devilish, ravishing, shockingly funny personality you find/found/will find so captivating!

We must exponentially expand our vision of Reality so as to make ourselves available to the Influences of that Reality (and there is only One . . . Reality, that is). Many of you, probably not those who need to hear this so much, have told me that when I am in Europe for the summer, my Presence in Arizona, my closeness to you, the intimacy of this communion, actually feels stronger and greater. *Exactement. Voilá*! When the "human" is not around to distract the lower senses, the Divine Force seems more immediate

Every element of our natural relationship is another window, an opportunity to expand and deepen the recognition and realization of the vast potentials of this unique possibility. Gurdjieff was quite insistent that until a man (woman) realized that he (she) was completely asleep— *completely asleep*, empty of any true knowledge or capacity to Work consciously—they had not yet begun the first step. This "completely asleep" in no way denigrates the vast degree of dream-knowledge we may possess as artists, parents, professionals, collectors of trivialities of information, and computer techs. It means that all our knowledge is relative, unconscious, useless towards awakening from the dream itself.

This, in effect, is what I am pointing to. The guru does not live in the same plane as our dream—although he may be somewhat adept at navigating that territory, certainly in himself, and in you by virtue of that. Referring to a disciple's serious car crash, Soen Nakagawa Roshi said, "One accident is worth a thousand meditations." I think I am beginning to be able to say something similar about the obvious limitations of the body.

I might suggest that until you *see*, in a truly objective way, that you are and have been firmly asleep and coincidentally have a profound wish to awaken from this state of nothingness and meaninglessness, that you cannot *see* the Master for who he actually is, and that in *seeing* the Master truly, such a sight is worth a thousand pieces of prasad delivered forcefully into the Master's hand.

You know, I won't last forever (though I do expect to outlast some few of you!), and I would love to brag on some of y'all, to crow like a rooster about your transformation. I admire and praise many of my students, but I can't get behind too much crowin' . . .

and once on the other side, I'll be much too busy to bother with such things. So give me the opportunity *now.*

To do so, you must see me in a far larger context than the man whose physical acknowledgement you long for and covet. To say I am the same as Yogi Ramsuratkumar is lovely and well and good, but I must ask: Do you see Him any more clearly than you see me, or is He just another human whose attention was desired? No amount of eloquence, spoken or written, can replace the actual and literal *experience* of this "higher" view.

Well, for those of you who want to feel bad about yourselves, this should give you lots of fuel ("let me count the ways..."). I mean this consideration as a spur, a goad, an inspiration to intensify your efforts and your intention to dispel the darknesses of sleep; to remove the veils of illusion from your thoughts and senses and to drive more deeply the wedge of awakening into the sloth of chronic habit and unquestioned assumptions of "knowing" at least something, if not much. Most assertions that we don't know much are just false humility.

The *good news* is that to grasp this, to become aware, to see this Reality is to put the sleeping beast at a very decided disadvantage. This is to be able to truly begin to develop a realistic view, a genuine perspective, which in and of itself will spur you onwards to a more genuine life and eventually to abiding genuineness. What excellence! To have a real chance to be truly different! Not just to morph in the dream but to transcend the entire mold. As Werner Erhard has said, "to create out of nothing." This is actual creation, not just some new variety of the same old stuff. And if you want to be who you can be, in the Work and in the World of God, this is *good news*!

Is there any bad news? I guess you could look at it in this fashion: The more deeply you embrace the "good news," the more profoundly you will realize, in fact and as a fact, how few individuals are actually coming directly to terms with the truth of things "as they are, here and now," how few of your own bonded sangha mates have actually embraced this "good news." You will suffer absolutely commensurately with the shock of these realizations, and they will be a shock. You will consequently realize what you can and cannot do to help or not help. You will realize how great a volume of suffering most people are willing to sustain—along with the whole "catastrophe," as Zorba said, and its commensurate blame, complaint, excuses of helplessness and lack of understanding—rather than vaguely entertain the demand, let alone the actual practice, of radical change from falsehood and lies to truth, from sleep to waking, from illusion and confusion to clarity, which you in turn will suffer to some degree as well.

And beyond the sangha, in the world at large? Need I even speak of such obvious horrors? The bad news, if it is that, is that once aware—not just intellectually insightful but objectively aware—you can't turn it off or turn your back on it all. Of course the advent of the "good news" would be significantly less, if extant at all (at least on this planet), without the shock of the bad news.

So, what to do, what to do? Practice, learn to work consciously, deeply, and clearly *see* the Guru. Do not shy from or turn from, compromise or deny, dishonor or disrespect that seeing. The price is far too high, besides all the other obvious reasons (like nobility, dignity, justice and conscience). I would be touched and enthused if any of you would take these issues to heart and write them in your being, not just in your memories or notebooks. ADTs Monday and Thursday and as the conventional holiday season is just about upon us, "deck the halls with boughs of tulsi, Ram, Ram, Ram, Ram, Ram, Ram, Ram!" And don't forget that the life you are attempting to lead is worthy of daily celebration as each day is, or can be, a true Holy Day. Thank you. Oh, and by the way, after I'm gone, please don't turn all the chants to a cacophonous double-time, train wreck of a disaster. Like, what's the hurry? Oh, and by the way again, Anande Baulo was perfect! So dogmatic dogs—watch it!

Jai Guru!

राम राम

The Higher Practice

December 27, 2009

Good evening friends! This week at Bridge, a guest asked an excellent question, and since to answer it myself I would have had to spew a torrent of saliva upon everything in front of me (I apologize for the graphic description but don't want anyone to worry unnecessarily), I asked everyone present, one at a time, for coherence and clarity, to address the issue. Except for one person (predictably), all participated actively and nicely. A variety of helpful input was given, though mostly it was different ways of saying the same thing.

Most of the contributions were things I have said, probably many times, and/or successful experiences from peoples' personal practice. All of it was true, and not one word pointed to the higher or essential practice. Someone got close but couldn't—or was too insecure or in doubt, meaning wouldn't—articulate their sense of it. All of the suggestions were definitely workable as preliminary approaches, although a few of those present failed to actually touch the core of the issue; they missed the obvious fact that our guest is a fine and sensitive artist, not a wannabe feeling the need to "be creative" as a means of self-expression (in other words ego-stroking), but driven to tap the true source of Beauty through Art.

I will not re-open this consideration here, although I am quite sure that someone in this room would "hit the bull's-eye." At least I certainly hope so! My point is that as well educated in the dharma as we are, it seems that we tend towards the utilization of practice that appears to work quickly and effectively, if not occasionally just temporarily (although "temporarily" in this case could last fifteen or twenty years!), rather than bang our heads against the ultimate practice(s) which is confusing, abstract, ungraspable and therefore just too difficult or impossible to realize for the linear mind, which seeks rational explanations and facile understanding, not to mention the collection of lots of interesting data.

But, lest we fool ourselves, remember that the higher practices are called "higher" for a reason. Once again, as you mature on the Path, it impinges upon you to allow the "lower" practices to take their rightful place in the hierarchy, to understand them in perspective and to be *naturally drawn* to the "higher" or ultimate practice as the just movement of your being craving for a more refined food.

As you make your way on the Way, as you progress in the Work—after some time of course, usually many years (although for a few "natural" mystics this longing seems more constant, even from early on)—if you aren't inexorably pulled to more exalted activities and a more subtle life of practice, you can be pretty sure that one of two things is occurring: either not enough time has passed, or you have failed to practice truly and have finally realized your stagnant state of untransformed sleep.

If you're sittin' on the second egg, you're probably sittin' on an egg that is not likely to hatch, although it's never too late. As most of you know, as you get older (like past sixty), your energy doesn't usually run away with you like it used to. If you have not been practicing profoundly in all domains, including the manifestations of abiding kindness, generosity, and compassion, your longing for a more refined food is likely to clash severely with the demands of family, children, and grandchildren, unless your partner, if you have one, is extremely sensitive to your transformed system and is spacious, embracing and loving enough to support you *completely* in your new mode. It will be an entirely new mode, which for many people is difficult; the clash of vectors can be pretty severe and miserable. You will be left with the choice to suppress your spiritual urges and dance to a tune that feels like you're being carved up by razor blades, or create great suffering to the others who don't understand and in their lack of understanding, cannot support you or accept you as you have become.

Let us not be naïve. This *is* evolution. The Path, as long as you are practicing, even in some cases to minimal degrees, is evolutionary and will not passively "lie down and roll over." It is grow, move, or wilt on the vine. Many of you have now been around long enough to know exactly what I am referring to. I am not talking about the usual life frustrations, disappointments, handicapped or thwarted desires. That is all ego. I'm talking about the literal, actual state of your soul. So perk up, puppies, and pay attention! Or to put it another way, perk up and pay attention, puppies.

I had a hissy fit the other day because someone was assaulting me (and yes, it is an *assault,* not an innocent request for information), having descended to an obsessive neurotic fixation surrounding their personal future. My suggestions to relax, trust the process, stop fixating on the future and be willing to be spontaneous were met with panic and desperate grasping. We all want a nice neat little guarantee that our miserable lives will continue undisturbed as the community changes—as in the move to Paulden and the new ashram. We want to feel that our overwork, our abysmal sense of priorities, our addictions to the internet and other areas of personal comfort (as many hot showers as we want, chemical health care products, unlimited new things—clothes, technology, car, et cetera . . . oh, and I forgot expensive hair stylists and facial treatments), the disgraceful wastefulness of personal habits, the maintenance of our little secret lives (ha, ha), will all be as predictable and stable as we have managed to keep them so far.

I'd like to suggest that, individually, you seriously consider relaxing and cultivating the skills to meet what arises as it arises without this compulsive need to have everything all planned out, hotels arranged, restaurants reserved, all life moves plotted, mapped and resolved. The future is highly unstable, unknown, and both mercurial and in fact not here yet, so why try to have it all figured out? Develop skillful means, lightness of movement, creative ways of dealing with unexpected happenstances. You may well need such abilities, such a capacity. You think you can handle it? You think the future will roll out just as you expect, wish, hope, dream? Uh-huh! You better learn how to dance with reality as it unfolds and stop leaning on the imagined reality of your blind subjectivity.

I have a very concrete idea of how I would like my new home and our new ashram to develop and function. I'm afraid I'm not very interested in talking about it, which was one of the triggers for the object of my hissy fit, propelling her into her nagging barrage and me into my little explosion of frustration (especially her casting of aspersions on my integrity and my reliable trustworthiness). So you'll have to dive in and move with faith and devotion and a willingness to adjust (meaning drop your chronic mechanical relationship to life and transcend your neurotic habitualness) to the situation as it presents itself. I know you can do it. The question is will you? I've already . . . well, never mind.

I am currently reading Shams-i-Tabriz, the Friend who awakened the slumbering Mevlana (Rumi). He likens himself to a mirror-bearer, and the student, who begs to see the mirror, as the reflection. Shams says, "If you see a blemish in the mirror it is not the fault of the mirror, but you are likely to blame the mirror rather than realize, in knowing the nature of mirrors, that the blemish is exactly you as you are." I have paraphrased this in my own words, thank you. Knowing that the seeker has no idea the depth of his "blemishes," the mirror tries to dissuade the devotee from gazing into it; the devotee pleads and promises he will not blame the mirror for what is seen, even though he most likely will. Eventually, as Shams' tale goes, the mirror-holder (the master) gives the mirror over on the sworn condition that no matter what the seekers sees, he or she will not destroy the mirror or shatter it out of anger and outrage.

At Bridge the other night I was thrown into a well of despair at the inability of "seekers" to look dispassionately into the mirror and make use of the objective reflection. We are not horses with blinders on, are we? Then why do we so often act as if we cannot see more than a few millimeters to any side of our achingly narrow life-view? Why, with an almost infinite possibility of options, do we insist on placing ourselves in positively the worst possible position, and then try to smash the mirror when a glimpse is offered us? How we love to bandy around that phrase, "The guru is a mirror." When we notice our reflection, when will we actually remember (and of course some of you already do, with courage and integrity) that what we are noticing is exactly ourselves as we are with not the least exaggeration, distortion, or embellishment? Reality, as it is.

To intellectually hear that the mirror gets blamed for its totally impersonal and objective reflection is as absurd to our rational minds as the notion that the moon is made of cheese, or that the Universe revolves around "me," and yet how often we blame that very mirror when we are standing in front of it, chanting, "Mirror, mirror, on the wall, who's the most perfect devotee of them all?" and the mirror doesn't show us a reflection of our wild imagination but simply reflects reality, often shocking and ugly to our sleeping notions of our own spiritual astuteness and beauty.

As someone commented at Bridge that evening, someone who has a long history and a broad perspective here, "You seem to be fiercer than ever these days." I seem to be driven to be less circumspect and forbearing and more willing to poke around with sharp objects in the dung heap. We're turning up a lot of manure, which could be quite useful in composting gardens, and we're also turning up a lot of biting, snapping, creepy-crawly things. I don't like this little manifestation of mine, even as I see the potential for extraordinary value to you farmers and cultivators of wisdom and spiritual maturity—transformation in fact—if the bull's-eyes being hit are fully utilized to relieve all the rotten abscesses of your personality and psychology and propel you towards awakening and presence.

I've been told by those who believe that their dreams actually mean something that I am in a revolutionary state of transformation, as remnants of "lee" dissolve into Yogi Ramsuratkumar, and that "my" spiny, prickly, difficult expressions are just the outer compliment of that transformation. As I said in Europe this past summer, I have a strong intuition of what this whole process is moving towards, though I must say again that I'm not thrilled with my gestures of impatience, intolerance, and indignation—even if they are aimed at sleep, sloth, and stagnation in those who signed up for the journey to Paradise.

Still, I must and will praise you for your own patience, tolerance, and dignation and indicate my gratitude for your willingness to put up with this difficult transition. For those of you who have no questions, doubts, or confusions, no recoil and reactivity, and are thereby able to truly use the slings and arrows of outrageously excellent fortune that are my gift to you these days, congratulations! I applaud you. And as always, we can *never* afford to rest on our laurels, even be they tulsi, gold, or manna leaves. So don't start congratulating or applauding or slinging arrows at yourselves—leave that to me (the applauding part!).

Thank you all for the wonderful help this Work Weekend. Next weekend looms upon us, and a magnificent weekend I expect it to be. Two ADTs this coming week, and who knows what excellence shall visit us on Monday and Thursday evenings? Who knows but God.

Jai Guru, Jai Baulo Jai

राम राम

To Die Longing

January 3, 2010

Hello, good evening. How often have you heard someone say, "I'm having a bad day" or "I'm having a rough time"? If only we knew what we were talking about. It is, of course, quite accurate to say, "I am having . . . ." Where the problem lies, or stands, as the case may be, is in the habit we have of blaming the "day," the "time," in fact the situation or circumstance for the difficulty.

In truth, as you all know when you're hearing it like this, outside of the immediate events that may trigger the struggle for you, it isn't the movement of life that is making us have a bad day; it is our unwillingness to respond to this movement appropriately, whether appropriately means sanely, maturely, or with objective acceptance of "what is, as it is"—in other words, free of our reactive psychological scripts, our chronic habit patterns of refusal to look at ourselves in the ease of blaming the outside world.

So to reiterate—meaning to iterate again, or once more, to echo or ditto the conversation—life isn't the enemy here. The specific situation isn't the bad guy, the villain, the cause of the rough time we're having. Life is not "doing it to us." We aren't being shafted by the circumstances, though obviously the circumstances may well be quite unpleasant and trying, difficult or problematical. It is our unwillingness to meet the challenge with clarity, creativity, skillful means, and common sense. (If the situation is dangerous or threatening and you are able to avoid it, run! Get the hell out of there, do it!) We can play dumb about this all we like—it doesn't fool anyone but ourselves, and not *really* ourselves either. In still other words, we make the bad day or the rough time ourselves, through our failure to practice. Well,

I assume the point has been made and we needn't continue to hammer a nail already completely in.

In regard to Sufism, Shams-i-Tabriz said: "On this way, to die with the longing to attain one's longing is also a great work." He said it eight hundred or so years ago, but there is no time limit to truth. I know you've all heard this many times before, but it doesn't hurt to reinforce it (meaning to hear it again, not to prop it up with additional bearing beams), especially since various of my devotees are still referring to such things as Enlightenment or Realization.

Shams' pithy statement refers to is the obvious practice of intention, and taking each day as it comes, without relying on some imagined goal or fixed result, as if to realize that end is the aim of our work. To die longing, when that longing is based on Faith, devotion, gratitude, and wisdom, may well be to have attained one's longing. It is the essence of one's being that gets "counted" in Heaven, not necessarily the spiritual goodies that one has collected. So don't despair when your view is faulty, and what you are despairing about may well be quite irrelevant to the path you are on and the practices you should be embracing and integrating.

If someone says to me, "I know you only want what serves my work most effectively," yes, this is true. If someone says to me, "I know you only want what will get me enlightened"—well, what on earth does that mean? To be surrendered to the Will of God may well be, in overt content, quite different for one person than it is for another, given our karmas, our specific work in this lifetime, our level of practice, capacity, ability, possibility (maybe even hillbillity) and so on. Of course in context, what difference could there be? But in the outer world, each of us being unique, there may be vast oceans of variety in how our sadhana manifests from something as ostensibly mundane as anonymously supporting the community with a donation of resources, to teaching in a more public role or function, to creating one objective work of art in a lifetime, to raising children who serve the Work.

So let's try not to be too quick to jump to conclusions, especially when those conclusions are no more than extrapolations of our already false ideas based on our illusory view of life, reality, truth and the Path. Just bear down on practice as you understand it and as you can, and as the poet said, "Bear no thought for the morrow." That does not mean to be stupid and fail to provide for rent, insurance and an occasional ice cream cone for your children (but the gross, self-indulgent over-providing for them through massive material burdens, technological and otherwise, is really quite a blind spot for many well-meaning but equally well-ignorant parents).

It's been a lovely Baul Feast, soft, gentle and benign. There is a time for "demand," for a bit of wildness, and a time to settle into the heart of devotion, to relax and absorb. Of course we can never stop "working," so to speak, but given the intense intimacy of sangha—as in the kitchen and meal prep spaces—we needn't worry too much about being left entirely out in the cold, although we can always hide out anywhere if we want to badly enough, no matter how close the spaces. I often feel the need to push a little harder, to throw a bit more "madness" into the mix, a little more—well, at times a *lot* more—"mirrorness" into the mix to help flush you (the false you, the identified you, the stuck-in-the-dream you, the have-no-clue you and so on, or et cetera, if you prefer) out in the open to the degree that you can't keep missing yourself so easily.

As you all know, denial can be a funny thing. We are committed, at heart and in the marrow of our bones, to clarity and self-honesty; at the same time, that which keeps the denial firmly in place, even gleefully in place for some of us (sort of like a badge of honor), is not only resilient but quite determined in its purpose.

And then of course there's the mind. There are all of those unknowns, our fears: "What will I have to give up? Who will I be? Will I lose my sense of humor, my joie de vivre, my energy, passion, creativity?" (Et cetera, or so on, if you prefer.) There are all the misguided and ill-educated opinions and projections about what surrender and obedience *means* exactly, and there are our foolish, yet very stubborn, notions about "enlightenment" or "awakening" or "freedom."

We have a lot on our plates, a lot to deal with, a great jungle of undergrowth to clear. And we can do it, without a doubt. We have been given the tools, the environment, the company, the circumstance, and most useful of all, the Wise Help of the Blessings of Yogi Ramsuratkumar and the Lineage, and not least of all, the considerable skillful means of our Teacher. So we have all the advantages we need. We just need to put the key in the ignition, turn on the engine, put it in gear (let's not forget that crucial step!) and get movin'. You don't need to be especially inspired in order to follow through; you just need to make it happen—through creature power, if it is necessary to begin there. I don't feel a great urgency, but I am itching for action and I do feel a bit of frustration and impatience in some places, though not all. I see such brilliant potential and talent that is not being utilized nearly to its capacity, although none of that is entirely going to waste.

The suffering in the world at large is not lessening in quantity or in intensity. I think that in our lifetime, the lie, the illusion, the massive darkness, and the illness of the refusal of Truth and Reality as-it-is will only grow more, as will people's general tendency to take it all hook, line and sinker. (For those of you unfamiliar with fishing, "sinker" refers to the lead weights one attaches to the line in order to allow it to sink—imagine that—so that the hook and bait go deep enough in the water to reach the fish!) This suffering is highly likely to increase as people in general continue to be confronted by crisis, by strange behaviors as people go mad from tension and stress, from war, violence, senseless fundamentalism, political and corporate idiocy, greed and criminality, natural earth and sky upheavals, financial challenges, undiagnosable and virulent illness, all-around confusion, doubt, crises of faith and so on and so on . . .

We, *you* in fact, will want to have your "practice shit" together. You will want to be stable and strong and clear in your intention, attention (and not addicted to e-tension), and able to pray profoundly for all that which you can't do anything about hands-on. Never mind being fearless; if you are, God bless your lucky ass! Mostly just be prepared to "do the right thing," fear be damned—and the torpedoes too, if necessary! For if we don't maintain sanity and equanimity and presence, not to mention Objective Work Conscience, who will? I'm not meaning "we" as in you in this school exclusively, but "we" as in this rare fraternity of those who are on the Path, in the Real World, in the Great Work.

This is no time to turn your backs on sadhana and veg out, obsessed with supplements, videos, internet access and "personal space." I wouldn't go so far as to say that we are all called to be "caretakers" of the spiritual purity of the world or anything that grandiose, yet on the other hand there is a certain maintenance that has already fallen to us and those in like positions, and will to greater degrees as time goes by. Believe me, you will not want to get caught short (or napping).

Well, I hope this isn't too "messianic" for you—Lord knows I'm not suggesting that a contingent of the 144 Just Men reside here amongst our august assembly. At the same time, the "state" of your practice, the solidity and reliability of your base or foundation, and the love of Creation, of Life—Creation and Life in the context of Reality, in the sense of seeing "what is, as it is, here and now" and not the view from the balcony of your Mansion of Dreams—are very real considerations.

So, to sum up, or at least begin to sum up: As my health normalizes—and I have no good reason to assume it won't, not investing in pessimism, wild theories, or absurd drama—I don't imagine I will get duller in my thrust of the teaching into your midst. In fact, I expect to be considerably sharper, more directly intolerant of "corns" and bugaboos as well, and more fiercely devoted to your transformation. My ostensible short slide into stodginess (wine, feast, coffee and passivity—and it was passivity, not relaxed and harmonious equanimity; I actually have more of that quality now, despite what may be deceiving appearances) before this little health lila brought me up short and shocked the system into alertness, isn't likely to happen again. I believe we're "on track" now.

Not to say there won't be *lots* of feasting, on many levels and in many dimensions, not the least of these being bodily, but such delights won't be self-indulgent or lazy, sleep-soaked and foolish but will be brilliantly sparkling with open-eyed practice, joy of Divine Communion, surrounded by the beauty of Art, sacred by tradition as well as human, and directly useful, even invaluable to the Work and the Path. We have so much to look forward to, even as some of the challenges may be difficult for sure. Now, as long as "I" can stay "human!" Well after all, if I were to be Anandamayi Ma or Swami Nityananda, I already would have been for a long time, so not to worry too unnecessarily! I think we'll be spared that small challenge.

Ah, that was quite a roll. Thank you all for your sweet devotion, no thanks for the sentimental churchy indulgence, as little of it as there was, and please take all this in the spirit in which it is offered. I touch your feet, by the Blessings of Yogi Ramsuratkumar.

Jai Guru, Jai Guru, Jaya Guru Raya

राम राम

Overflowing with Knowledge

January 10, 2010

Good Evening! I hope you are fine, receptive, enthusiastic, and tingling and sparkling with anticipation on this fine evening. So, to continue considering the need of our times, the deep and often aching confusion of so many people—even some of us—who do not have the slightest idea that they are in such a state. Most who do know have not the slightest idea of what to do about it, although they flail about like swordfish on the hook, imagining that all that struggle will actually accomplish something.

Yes, given all of that, and given the gifts, the opportunities, and the possibilities that we have, by the Blessings of Yogi Ramsuratkumar and the lineage, in our hands literally in every moment, it is extremely irresponsible behavior to fail to act in accordance with those possibilities. Not to mention that it is also extremely questionable as to what on earth and in Heaven (or Hell) we think those possibilities will afford us if we sit with them unused, unexplored, and guarded like some private territory that needs defending.

Are we really in such deep denial? The practices we have been initiated into are sacred affairs. This isn't a casual situation. There is a real *need* both out there and in here. It is our responsibility to understand, appreciate, and actively engage this Work so as not to disrespect, dishonor, and disobey the demand to serve, to transform, to Praise and to fulfill this Mission entrusted to me—and by implication and extension to you as well—by Yogi Ramsuratkumar and His Father in Heaven. In relatively practical terms, this means that we cannot and should not fall into the lackadaisical belief that we can ignore the cries of the Sangha; nor can we continue to be unwilling to confront our own holdouts: our (in some cases) shocking lack of self-observational maturity, our chronically mechanical life-denying habit patterns, and our failure to serve one another, both actively (helping Elyse on phone sales, washing dishes, Work Weekends, phone coverage in the office, et cetera) and passively (again, by refusing to deal with our aggressive opinions, thoughts, gossip and so on).

There is *so* much work to do, and it is not work that can be accomplished optimally in the midst of bickering, petty differences of opinion or activity, withdrawal (both physically and psychically), or all the range of childish and selfish behaviors. To reiterate, it is grossly irresponsible to have the Divine Fiat, which we have, and not do *everything* in our ability—including being ruthlessly self-honest—to show our gratitude inwardly and outwardly for this Benediction.

So please, as the opportunities continue to unfold and be plopped in our laps, or loaded on our spiritually if not bodily sturdy shoulders, please, take this responsibility with the utmost of seriousness. There is plenty of tolerance for much good humor, laughter, enjoyment of good company, celebration and *no* tolerance for wise-ass attitudes, goofing off, or turning one's back on the contract you have engaged and the refuge in which you have ostensibly taken sanctuary. It is not about "shaping up or shipping out." No. It is simply about "shaping up," period. And well, thank you all for indulging this little intrusion into some of your nice, neat little scenarios.

A few evenings ago we watched a video of Gour Khepa.[1] His English is a bit sketchy and he also speaks in highly symbolic terms; someone asked me the other day if I had understood him, not meaning his English but meaning the esoteric (hidden, tantric)

1 Lee met Gour Khepa Baul in Bengal in January 2008.

implication of his communication. I answered yes, but when I was questioned about a specific, I didn't recall it at all. This used to bother me, as if I was losing my memory, but it isn't that at all. It is this: I am full, full to the brim and in fact full to overflowing with knowledge—with intimate, instinctual knowledge of Truth and of Work. There is no room for "data," as interesting and attractive as that data may be. When I read, study, or am in the presence of "information," if I already know something, it doesn't get in because there is no place for it. Sure, an occasional tidbit, a story, some special way of describing something sticks, but generally speaking, when I connect to something—as in "that's correct, I know that also"—there is appreciation and often enthusiasm. This knowledge that I speak of isn't unique by any means, but neither is it common, especially when associated with true context. That which is helpful, useful, or valuable to your or to any individual's Work or Transformation is what moves me and moves through me. That is what fills my mind, occupies my attention, and fulfills my purpose.

At times I've asked Yogi Ramsuratkumar—with great reticence and hesitation, but asked deeply and truly in any event—for His Madness. Included in this domain, of course, is the recognition that the usual points of reference, like a "good memory" for instance, are not relevant. All that is relevant is what serves your progress on the Path and in the Work. To "my" ego such obvious aspects of this knowledge are clearly accepted and very much embraced; at the same time they can be a bit disconcerting, shall we say. For the way we are (I am) used to doing things may well no longer apply. I am using one specific example, but of course, this can, will, and does affect many levels and specifics.

I am more than happy to be so surrendered, even in spite of some resistance at times; after all, this is my Work and "my" gift to Yogi Ramsuratkumar, or rather His Gift to me, and for sure His Gift to you all. Still, I enjoy study and reading, and the data is enlivening, at least momentarily. When I need information for one reason or another, there is always someone who has it, which is very convenient. That leads us to the question: Why worry? When you are committed to the Work, to Sadhana above all, the Work takes care of you, makes sure that you have, even just at your fingertips, those resources that are useful to the efficient, even optimum, completion of the task at hand.

For those of us like myself who tend toward suspicion, it may be a little bit of a struggle to trust this absolute and eternally proven principle, but hopefully experience will convince us of its infallibility. Of course, it is problematical to be a "Renaissance" man or woman when you are so singularly occupied, but on the other hand, the Work is hardly adverse to the so-called finer things of life: deep love, compassion, good art, good food, substantial money and other things resource-wise. Although the vanity items—garish, overdone jewelry or clothing, party bags, one-pack-of-gum-sized little backpacks, high boots, high heels and all those technological feathers-in-your-hat—are not only often counter-productive but may well be directly antagonistic to the Work. So, it doesn't pay to be too attached.

So . . . back to this knowledge we have been speaking about. I am full, full of all sorts of things that I would like to impart to you or anyone who has both the capacity to receive it and the willingness to absorb it. If you are so full of yourself that there is no room for even the Wisdom of the Ages—Truth, in other words—as much as I may love and appreciate you, there is no room to place what I have to offer. There is no space to take it in.

I asked someone to do me a favor and not rush off before completing the moment at hand, and they said to me, "Thanks for letting me do that." I found that delightful, which delight caused me to laugh. It's like this: When you are full of yourself, I don't "let" you do anything. It is *you* who lets me "let" you do anything. The degree to which you obey or submit is the degree to which you—your ego—allows me to direct you. As most of you know from very immediate firsthand experience, when you are in resistance, I might as well talk to a stone, because there is no space in you to plant the seeds I would like to see grow into reliable Work principles and actions. I await the time when you really "let" me direct the play, instead of unconsciously giving me permission to direct you only up to the point at which your psychological script isn't interested in taking direction—mine or anyone else's—as the interchanges at the last couple of Bridge nights should have made very clear to everyone there (except for the one or two human "stones" who were occupying the space in the room and helping to provide "matrix," but not like the movie of the same name).

So this is it: I am full of knowledge and would like to transmit or transfer some of it. The story of Shams-i-Tabriz and Rumi (or Majnun and Layla for that matter) is a classic example of this exchange. I can never be emptied. No matter how much of this wealth I spend, it never diminishes. In fact, it continues to become fuller and fuller. Whenever I come across anything that I don't already know, which is rare but not non-existent, or more exactly, something that makes the explanation or communication of this knowledge more accessible or clearer—then that gets added to the fullness. An example or two should suffice to make that point evident, "Prana follows attention" from Dr. Svoboda being one such little peanut and Swami Prajnanpad's phrase "intrinsic dignity and intrinsic nobility" being another. These are teachings that have stuck, because even though they weren't new to me, they were a spin that really made skyrockets and Roman candles go off when I heard them.

And the point of this consideration? I am, as a "role model," not a unique, exclusive, unattainable Godman, Guru, Awakened, Enlightened, Master, and so on. What I animate and demonstrate, not as Teacher using skillful means, but as one who inheres in the

Work, one who is surrendered to the Will of God, one who is transparent to the Blessings of Yogi Ramsuratkumar and the Lineage, is the mood and context you will animate and demonstrate when you have been de-barrier-ized; when the authority of your own ego (life-script or psychological story) has been submitted to the Authority of Reality, of the Universe. So "don't judge a book by its cover" is a fine cliché here. In other words, if—or as—you find yourselves in strange territory with unfamiliar reference points (for your sense of egoic continuity; for the old habit patterns of chronic mechanicality that rule), rather than rejecting such manifestations as madness, fantasy, hallucination or worse ("possession" or abject failure to be taken into God's World), consider the above issues to be a possible "treasure map," a guidebook, so to speak, for the Alchemy of which you might be at the effect.

Yes, well, I believe that was a conclusion, and I do think it is certainly a hearty (or hardy) stew and should be substantially satisfying and hunger relieving. So go to work on it this week, will ya? Two ADTs this coming week and have a wonderful week besides—if necessary in spite of your pessimism, life-sobering confrontations, nasty people, on the road or on the sidewalk (or in the mall), idiotic e-mail life and all of that. Jai Guru, Jai Guru, Jai Guru!!

राम राम

Faith

January 17, 2010

Hello, good evening, howdy. And a fine evening it is, as it usually is. I think it is a useful not to mention profitable consideration to discuss briefly this habit of jumping to conclusions—making impulsive judgments based on a hyper-emotional state and acting often rashly. It is true, of course, that based on superficial observation, most circumstances appear fairly black-and-white or cut-and-dried, and on that basis the conclusions we jump to equally appear fairly clear and definitive. Nonetheless, most situations are multi-layered, therefore more complex than we give them credit for and more complicated than first outer appearances would indicate. There can be underlying vectors of influence that we would never know about if we didn't stop and sense into the whole complex scene.

As many of our mothers may have told us when we were younger, "Before you act, stop, take a deep breath and count to ten." Things often look different, sometimes very different, after even a few seconds' distance from the immediate stimulus. Of course any emotionally-charged stimulus demands—psychologically, not objectively—a knee-jerk reaction. Well, *mes amis,* you are supposed to be in the Work, as practitioners of various stripes; such a basic circumstance should not continue to blindside you, even if it is relatively intense.

I'm not suggesting that in particularly charged situations you wouldn't feel shook up, fearful, disturbed, even confused and numb at times (as I myself felt, after realizing that the news was true when I first heard about 9/11). But even so, you can practice a kind of forbearance in the midst of such powerful feeling responses. It may be valuable to remember that once you act (or react as the case may be)—which certainly includes unconsidered verbal expressions as well as more physical decisions—you cannot take it back and usually can't "fix" it either, if you decide better of yourself after the fact.

So, the point of consideration: the depth and subtle dimensions of many seemingly straightforward aspects of our lives, as they intersect with the tidal wave of events rolling out of the Universe's sleeve to meet us while we move forward through the world. How do we remember to "look both ways before crossing the street"? By being reminded so many times that it becomes automatic. Apply this same idea to not jumping to conclusions without looking closely at any given situation. Of course, sometimes it takes getting our foot run over or worse in order to remember to check the street before launching into it unaware, but I trust that none of us would wish that analogy to apply to making an impulsive, emotionally driven decision and having to bear or suffer the consequences of inattention or naïveté.

Faith. It's a strange thing, Faith—one reason being that we often don't know whether it is true of us or not until circumstances prove so or not, one way or another. What to do? Prayer is always a reliable process. Not the kind of supplication that asks for Faith, but as Yogi Ramsuratkumar said so often, simply Praise; pure Praise for no reason, or if we want to call it a reason, simply to proclaim the Glory of God. Such prayer is never wasted. It always bears fruit, even if we are unaware of it. Superstition and New Age vibes aside, you can and you may always resort to prayer. You don't need a formula, just start praising the Mercy and Majesty of God and pour it on. If you are not used to being so effusive, it may be a bit embarrassing, but persist; the merits are great and there is no downside. And keep it to yourself. There is no need to trot it around, even within the sangha. Hopefully, the opportunities to test your Faith will be mild and few and far between. After all, there is no need to wish to suffer great trials only to discover whether this elusive Faith is established in us. It is true that certain notable Christian mystics prayed to Christ to suffer what He suffered, as a way to be one with Him, to align with Him, but for most of us such a wish is idiocy. Had you such a wish and were it to be granted, you'd most likely be quite sorry the idea ever crossed your feverish little mind. So . . . glorify the Radiant and Bright Lord above all else, and no matter what anyone thinks (even you), you will be Blessed, all the way to the bank, as they say.

By the way, talking about great sex, it doesn't hurt to praise—full of gratitude and honor, in a human way—your partner either. There is no substitute for deep appreciation of the often extraordinary sacrifices that our partners undergo for us. Whether the sex is good or bad, frequent or not, whether their cooking skills are amazing or lacking in the least infinitesimal excellence, whether they are chatty and social or stoical and reserved, in their own way they make profound sacrifices to serve us, in spite of what may be their outer impatience, annoyance, anger, frustration, irritation, criticism and so on. In our readiness to judge things by the most outer appearances, we rarely recognize what deep and often holy inner lives our partners have. So look more closely, if you haven't yet noticed, and try as best you can to not diminish your partner and their love because of your own frustrations, desires, wishes, hopes and dreams. Praise them to your children, your family, the sangha—yes, praise them, but sensitively, tactfully and humbly. No need to be glaringly effusive in this domain of praise!

Yes, and talking about Faith, I'm currently reading a book by a contemporary (twentieth century) Christian mystic which documents her visionary revelation of the life of Jesus. In one of her visions, it was the time when Jesus disappeared in Jerusalem, and Mary and Joseph didn't know where he had gone. For three days they searched for Him until they at last discovered that He was in the great temple debating with the doctors of Jewish law. Mary was frantic with worry for Him, and when she finally found Him, she rushed to embrace Him and asked why He had left without informing them. His answer, and I quote the document I am referring to, was: "You do not ask 'why' of Him Who Knows. He behaved in a certain way. You do not ask Those with a vocation 'why' they leave everything to follow the Voice of God. I was Wisdom and I Knew. I was 'called' to a mission and I was fulfilling it."

The import of this must be quite obvious to everyone here, and yet I speak about it with some clear hesitation, with the caveat that that was then and this is now. Even so, there were plenty of ego-maniacs and enough hubris (among the Sanhedrin and the temple "chosen") to choke a horse back then, as we say now. In these unholy and vilely materialistic times, when there is a false spiritual teacher—or even an out-and-out quack—around every corner and pathological behavior is almost the norm, if one's faith is simply wishful thinking or psychological transference, the likelihood of being severely hurt or wickedly mistreated by some charlatan is quite high, as you all are well aware.

At the same time, as Mr. Christ was Real in His time, there are those who demonstrate a similar Truth and integrity in these times. Should you be lucky enough to have settled in with one of those rare ones—and obviously I include myself in those august numbers only by the Benediction of Yogi Ramsuratkumar—the above quote must apply sooner or later, if you are to be free (something I am sure all of you would wish for on a good day) of the niggling suspicions and personal holdouts that all act as a veil, thick as a wall (or thin as a sheer silk veil, a "private parts decorator") between your receptivity and the completely unimpeded flow of Grace and Transmission from God to you.

"Why is lee acting so angry/impatient/irritable . . . " or, "Why doesn't lee answer questions anymore like he used to?" or "Why doesn't lee take more interest/more of a role in the Ashram business decisions?" or, "Why did lee get sick if Yogi Ramsuratkumar is protecting him?" or, "Why does lee say 'Do as I say and not as I do'?" And so on and so on. All quite reasonable questions from *your* point of view—from the point of view of the separative ego, of the psychological script, of the life story—but quite unreasonable questions from My point of perspective, from the platform of "Him Who Knows," of "those with a vocation."

I am either the True Heart-Son of Yogi Ramsuratkumar or not, and I am either Transparent (to a greater or lesser degree) to Him or not. If I am, "why" has no place in our ultimate relationship. It destroys trust, communion and optimum Work, not to mention the possibility of Objective Vision, of a similar "Knowing." And if I am not the True Heart-Son of Yogi Ramsuratkumar? That is not a popular option here in our special and somewhat exclusive company, but it is widely considered in the spiritual scene at large and adhered to among the majority of Yogi Ramsuratkunar's followers; in fact it is pretty much universally accepted by all of the "pretender to the throne" (none of whom imagine themselves "pretenders" and equally none of whom understand what that "throne" actually is—annihilation anyone?). Well then! In spite of our building faith, deep devotion, and heartfelt commitment, it is always helpful to remember that Yogi Ramsuratkumar granted us or perhaps ceded—seeded?—me this Mission, and that His overt as well as inner support was demonstrated beyond a doubt many, many times in many, many ways.

Therefore, with regard to the above quote from the mystic Maria Valtorta, I have a "vocation." I am one of "those with a vocation," and this "vocation" was given by the closest manifestation of God I've ever known, Yogi Ramsuratkumar. We would all find it useful to connect the dots, so to speak, to find the harmony between the disparate bits of knowledge that we have come to realize on this Path, in this School, and most importantly, in the Influence of my Work for Father. When the puzzle is completed just so, properly, we will find that this remembrance dispels much if not all of the unexpected little "whys" and more immediately the source of those "whys" (which may seem to be small interruptions or minor annoyances, but often are more devious and sinister than we imagine) that tend to interrupt the smooth flow and progress of our Transformation.

Whew! *That* was a few pages full! Two ADTs this coming week and for those of you who have been working so hard (which is pretty much all of you!), especially at Triveni, thank you again. Perhaps some day my gratitude that knows no bounds will be obvious. Jai Guru, Jai Guru, Jai Guru.

राम राम

What is an Ashram?

January 24, 2010

Hello. Good evening. Howdy do! Well, arid Arizona got its share of water this week, didn't it? Shades (or storms) of things to come as global warming goes along its merry way. And did you pray for the Haitians? I this opportunity didn't slip by you.

So, on to tonight's consideration. A family asked to live on the Ashram for a while (a community family, I hope that inference was obvious), and so I asked them to fill out a "practice questionnaire" on the Ashram diet, meditation, study, exercise, participation in ADTs, Work Weekends, tithing and hours of video/TV watched per week. I asked the ratings to be: nonexistent, poor, mediocre, passable and excellent. Among their ratings there were many "nonexistent," and all the rest were either poor or mediocre.

So, I wrote back and asked, and I quote myself: "Why on Earth (why in God's Name) would you want to live on the Ashram?" This is a sampling of the responses: "Because we want to be different. Because we want to engage you/practice on a deeper level. Because *not* practicing has created nothing but discontent, confusion and misery. Because you are the core—we want/need to honor and delight in that." And finally: "We hoped to be thrust into the river of practice . . . sink or swim . . . and take that reconnection with us . . . "

I don't relate all this to mock or deride these devotees, for they are some of the sweetest, most genuine, and finest people I know, and I do call them devotees for in their hearts they are. Obviously this mindset is catastrophic and shows signs of such misunderstanding that I felt, with their permission of course, a pounding wish to consider it with you all tonight.

First of all, I am *where you are.* (We had a most lovely German devotee leave the school because she lived geographically isolated from Sangha and didn't feel "connected" enough.) It is absurd to assume that my physical presence or proximity is needed or more useful for generating a desire and willingness and practical circumstance to practice. If you can't find me where you are, you will *under no conditions* be able to truly find me in my physical company, even if you are with me twenty-four hours a day. And furthermore, if one was truly committed to the reasons stated for wanting to live on the Ashram, one would demonstrate that commitment by coming to *all* After Dinner Talks, Ashram Work Weekends, Bridge nights and chanting *saptas* instead of one ADT a *month,* zero Work Weekends a year and . . . you get the picture.

If I had the *slightest* indication of a true willingness to sacrifice *now,* not expecting to be pushed, prodded, and led by a ring through the nose *after* moving here, I might (and only might) be a bit more inclined to toss the dice and hope for a winning roll. As the famous line from the movie *Jerry Maguire* proclaimed, "Show me the money!" 'cause baby, I ain't signing no contract until I have some reasonable encouragement.

Secondly, and equally as relevant and important, and I hope and pray this is something I will be able to hold when we move to the new Ashram in Paulden: What is a real Ashram? Well, surely an Ashram is not a substitute for a mother, a boss, or a "half-way house." It is a true, orthodox, and traditional Sanctuary, a Holy Place which houses, honors, and cares for on every level the most sacred elements of the School and the Teaching: the Guru and core group, empowered spaces and artifacts, the essential archival teachings and so on.

An Ashram is not a place to use as a trial balloon, hoping that by living there a bit of its intensity of integrity will rub off. On certain very specific occasions, it may be used as a training ground or facility, but this is not its purpose and it certainly is no "safe house" to shelter us while we get our lives together. It is not a homeless shelter, though it might provide that function as well from time to time and under very specific conditions. And it is not a sanatorium, though that too may be an occasional situation.

The Ashram is the home of the Revelatory Source of Divine Influence, including the Sanctum Sanctorum, whether this be the Darshan Hall, evening tea space or whatever. An Ashram should be profoundly respected, honored, and treated as such by all those who presume to worship in this Way or be adherents to this Dharma or profess to love the Guru. To despoil the Ashram purity (as Arnaud has tried to educate his students relative to Hauteville, with some, and only some, small success, which is why he has said in the recent past that it isn't an Ashram) with constant use of cell phones, internet, abysmal standards of practice, glaring lack of attention, hurtful gossip, ugly attitudes (as we discussed heatedly at the Bridge table this past week) such as resentment, anger and aggression, not to mention territorial coups and counter-coups, is to turn the Ashram into just another worldly arena in which to play out one's neurotic attachments and psychological script.

And by the way, the person who generated the Bridge table discussion about resentment, anger, and aggression resoundingly denied demonstrating the least evidence of such traits, even when everyone else there testified—as a chorus, almost ten people including her ostensible Guru—to not only observing but being regular victims of her anger, resentment, and aggression. So, neither is an Ashram a museum or a laboratory for testing stones, but on rare occasion an exception may be made. And remember, even stones are sentient—the human ones more that the inanimate ones. As the poet said, "To err is human, to forgive Divine."

On another note—*La* ♪♪—it becomes clearer as time goes by that there is no such thing as an oversight, error, or failure to serve, too small to pay attention to and to feel remorse about. Even the tiniest of habits, when blindly mechanical, leads to larger and larger consequences. There is an obvious hierarchy of "sins" on Earth, in our three-dimensional, five-sense psychological world.

Blatant and intentional deception, for instance, is a greater crime than so-called innocent "exaggeration." But in Heaven, so to speak, there is no such hierarchy. To miss the mark is to miss the mark, and the distance is not judged or considered, only the fact of having missed the mark. I think we would all agree, perhaps with various considerations, that life surely and certainly is not limited to our infinitesimally short blink-of-an-eye time here in this body, as this finite character on this planet. Life was before, and life goes on in a great and fluid continuum. Yes? And so it would seem to me to make sense to "lay up stores for the future" so to speak—call it the accumulation of merit or the generation of good Karma, if you will or wish—and to pay close care to even the smallest or slightest detail in our daily existence, for nothing, as mentioned earlier, is too minor to overlook or neglect when it comes to the effect of that sloppiness in the Holy World of God.

As we all know, myself included, it is an almost constant dynamic to be inattentive when faced (or confronted) with the endless glam and glitter of the snares of ego—the fascinating seductions very intentionally designed to distract us from our Purpose, from our practice, from our Faith in what on another level we know beyond a shadow of a doubt to be true and real. These are the dramas that grip us where it hurts: pride, vanity, lust, desire, competition, bigotry, anger, gossip, resentment—all affects of our self-centered refusal to surrender, or to allow ourselves to be surrendered, thereby placing the other, not to mention God, before ourselves.

Now *that* is hubris, but we don't see it that way, for the most part. We see ourselves being helpless in the face of unconscious domination by our life script, our psychological story. But we have been given a way out, a doorway—no, a runway—to freedom from this imperious and devilish overseer. We have found the Path, entered the stream, joined the Work force, and are guided, protected, and supported, not to mention loved, by Yogi Ramsuratkumar and His Father in Heaven. How much better help could you get?

We have been given a Way, practices, devotion (dare I say even Adoration?), Benediction and Blessings more profuse and copious than we can count.

All that is needed—and yes, it is a big "all"—is to give ourselves to this Grace unreservedly and uncompromisingly. Can we? Yes. Do we? You can answer that one. Will we? In some cases, absolutely. In most cases we will continue to do our fancy dance routines, suffering and crying and apologizing all the way to the next transition. And let me suggest that looking back from over there upon what could have been done or engaged in this life and wasn't will not look as attractive as your egos now make sloth, comfort and the illusion of "there's plenty of time" appear.

So . . . attention to detail. Nothing, *nothing*, is too insignificant to sidestep or deny. Every detail here, no matter how tiny, is glaring and important in Heaven. Yes, we all get busy and lost in our own groove, we all have "things" to do, *and* we should never be too consumed to stop for a small moment, or even a large moment, and provide what is "wanted and needed" in the way of genuine service, to act when needed—or just to listen when needed. Believe it or not, we can put our annoyance, our irritation, our time concerns and our victim positions aside and serve the other with kindness and generosity, both of resource and of spirit. Better to please God than our egos!

And so my friends, another week has gone by, and by next Sunday still another week will have passed, but since we have eternity, let's not be too concerned about the mere onslaught of time. Live rightly now, and life will do right by us then, whenever "then" is. I will not be here organically for the next three Sundays, as my body will be travelling, but if you recall the very things considered just a few short moments ago, rest assured and Faithfully confident in that which is important, that which is True, that which is heart and never leaves you, never leaves here. And wherever you are is here. Jai Guru!

राम राम

A Small Rant

January 31, 2010

Good evening all! As most of you probably know by now, the Landmark Forum is the new buzz around here. Tuesday, this past week, was the Introduction in Phoenix, and a fair number of people from here attended. Through an intermediary, I invited a few people to take the Forum. Some others were suggested, and I said okay. Others I felt didn't need it—though would probably love the stimulation and therefore imagine that it was useful. Still others were suggested for taking it, and I rejected them as candidates because I felt they were far too closed to possibly make use of it, or because the time is not right. As with all tools, if you don't use them, then you don't get the advantage of the tool. As I told one of the people who took the Landmark Forum this past weekend, "If you don't play, you can't win." A few of us are simply too defended to make the effort worthwhile. Some of the people who attended Tuesday are massively defended, but the odds favor them. Go figure.

We were playing Bridge on that same Tuesday and my team was winning, winning, winning, but I wasn't enjoying the win because one of the opposite team had fairly consistent excellent cards and was, for the most part, blowing every advantage—and had they not, we would not have been winning so consistently. So I emphasized the need to pay attention and she said, "Whenever I try to pay attention, I never do it to my satisfaction." After a bit of banter, I said, "I don't do *anything* to my satisfaction," upon which comment I added the non-rhetorical question: "What does that tell you?"

The answer was not forthcoming, though enough stabs were taken at answering to whittle a large branch into a small twig.

So I've decided to share what that tells us tonight. It tells us that our personal sense of satisfaction, the bar we set for ourselves, is totally subjective and is often completely unrealistic, meaning that at some level we don't really want to do or accomplish that thing. I've learned to just do and accomplish anyway, regardless of whether the action, completed or not, meets "my" satisfaction. Nobody gives a fig except me. But people do give a fig about the opportunity to be a part of "the action."

So . . . a small rant: I was sitting at dinner Thursday night feeling quite cold, with the heater behind me turned off. I was told that it was on before dinner, until someone came and asked whether it should be left on or not, saying, "There was a complaint." I didn't complain tonight or ever about it being too warm with the heater on—although, yes, I have grimaced and moaned and rolled my eyes. But in this context the only thing that is a complaint is when I *say*, when *I* say, "The heater is too hot." This whole thing of "there was a complaint" is a total justification for being irresponsible at some level (usually unconscious, or subconscious, although I'm not quite sure of the difference) and allowing someone else, *anyone* else but me, to abdicate our personal common sense and authority. Well, abdicate is not the right word—I believe commandeer would be more accurate.

I often feel as if—again, at the unconscious or subconscious levels—my devotees believe that I am helpless and haven't the slightest ability to ask for what I do want or mention what I do not want. As if I couldn't say either "yes" or "no" and required other people, who are more than willing to speak on my behalf without my direction, to handle things for me. This is doubly painful because I believe myself, or my preferences at least, to be quite transparent. I have demonstrated my likes and dislikes, my preferences, my ways of functioning, and my ways of doing things for so many years that it is really hard to understand why so many people seem to have no clue, including people who have spent and do spend a considerable amount of time around me under quite a variety of situations and circumstances.

So this "there was a complaint" is a really irritating burr under the saddle, a really annoying pea under the mattress, a really warm heat (talking about heaters!) under my collar. So whaddya think? Is there any possibility that we could learn something here and perhaps minimize the lack of verification with me relative to things that directly concern my person? Well, it's worth a try, worth the commitment to and subsequent practice of "Paying Attention and Remembering."

Oh, and talking about "remembering," on a purely mundane level, since I mentioned my extreme dislike of the use of paper clips on things given to me—and this is not a Divine Fiat, it is only my personal thing—I have not seen *any* diminishment of paper clips used on things put in my mailbox or handed to me. I know for a fact that the majority of people perpetrating said abuses upon my unstable frame of mind were at the Darshan in which my preferences were stated. Similarly, those who continue to demand that I talk—almost but not entirely about matters quite irrelevant to my Help but certainly relevant to the use of wise counsel of Sangha—have quite completely failed to respect my preferences in this area as well, with a few notable exceptions (and thank you).

Believe me, when I am talking again without extreme discomfort—I mean physically, for any psychic or emotional discomfort is meaningless to me—and with no barrier to communication, I expect to be talking up a blue streak, so . . . patience! And besides patience, get a grip on the lack of necessity for most (but again, not all) of what you ask me, if you would so please. Ah yes. This is all I've managed to write for tonight, so profuse Blessings on you all and Jai Guru!

राप राप

To Grow into Devotees

February 21, 2010

I was sitting at the opening night gala event of the Pacific Arts of Asia Show in San Francisco and watching women stagger, stumble, or barely walk by in six-inch-high spike heels. I'm talking about eighty percent of the women who walked by—the remaining twenty percent comfortably strolling in flats or short heels. Occasionally one of the women managed to appear able to walk on these spike heels with a modicum of grace. The others were noticeably strained by the severe physical tension of maintaining balance without falling over, tripping, or spraining an ankle. And I'm thinking, again: What have we become when vanity is more important than health, ease, and self-respect? I'm sorry to say, enough of that goes on here, in milder and more subtle forms of course. Or should I say *still* goes on here. Well, back to paying attention, if in fact we ever did pay attention—and if not, well then forward to it!

So, here is a very useful consideration on the point of using the Guru as an excuse to completely put aside common sense, good sense. I hope the person who is the excellent example for this point will not take this as a shaming, humiliating, redundant (after my yelling at her in the office), and unnecessary blow. I was over it seconds after I made the point, though she may well still be carrying it these three days later. When faced with the obvious error that generated my fierce little outburst, the person in question said, and I quote, "If I were late for any other reason, I would have done it differently," meaning that she was late for an appointment she had with me. She entirely, obviously failed to understand me—even knowing that I knew her schedule and how uneven these things can be—and assumed I would have been angry if she were two minutes late, for that is the ostensible amount of time that would have been saved had she not "erred" in her common sense and good judgment. (Yawn . . . failure to understand me is so common amongst devotees, short- and long-term, it's a wonder I'm not used to it enough to stop being annoyed, given the fact that even *minimal* observation of the way I work and have always worked could, should, produce the desired insights of "understanding.")

Okay. The point: "If it were for any other reason than disobeying, disappointing, dishonoring the guru, et cetera, et cetera, I would have . . . ." fill in the blanks. First of all, if one doesn't understand the Guru, any idea of disobedience, disappointment, dishonor, et cetera, et cetera, is our own totally subjective projection, no more than a function of our life script (neurosis). Secondly, as examples: "If anyone else had wanted to sleep with/rape my thirteen-year-old daughter/son (besides the guru/reverend/minister, et cetera) I *never* would have agreed!" Or, "If anyone else had asked me to bomb/poison gas, et cetera, the whatever, besides the guru/reverend/minister, et cetera, I *never* would have done it!"

"If anyone else had asked me to kill/abuse/beat/humiliate"—as in the events at Guantanamo Bay Prison—"him or her, other than the commanding officer, the President (guru), et cetera, I *never* would have . . . " and so on and on. Oh, I forgot one: "If anyone else had asked me to smuggle drugs besides the reverend, the guru, et cetera, I never would have . . . ."

Becoming a little child in the presence of the dominating parent is a dynamic that creates what Gurdjieff called "followers" and is not something we want to encourage or support. Of course there is the ubiquitous dynamic of transference, which we need to understand and to allow a process for in terms of time, clarity, developing self-observation and ruthless self-honesty. We can't just take a new student and crush them into a senior student mold, but then again we also want to maintain an educational influx for everyone, without police state tactics. We want to grow into devotees who honor and obey the Guru out of love and gratitude, out of maturity and conscious understanding, out of an adult freedom of choice, rather than from fear, projection, or obsequiousness—in short, psychological complications relative to our mechanicality, our "story," our compelling and compulsive neurotic needs.

A real "no" is certainly healthier than a false "yes." Obviously, "No, I am not going to do the dishes because I just don't feel like it right now," is not very healthy. (At least I hope it is obvious. And could that *ever* be real?) A bit of sacrifice to what is "wanted and needed" (as Werner Erhard said) in the moment and in the daily routine of an Ashram and the Path we have committed our lives to is always appropriate. But then, this too is simply common sense, good sense—a recognition of service to the "other," whether that other is an individual or an organization like the Hohm Community.

I would personally appreciate not being related to like a vengeful dictator who will lop off your head psychically or otherwise if you "displease me," when you are categorically unwilling to see me—*see me*—without the blindness of your psychological veils and personal bias. I'm not suggesting casualness or laziness, but a clarity that understands the relationship between guru and devotee, and who I am in that and who you are in that. Well . . . thank you ahead of time—or in time, if you are one of those who already has a handle on this.

I'm sorry the considerations of this fine evening are so mundane. I would much rather be set on fire by a sublime Dharma-jewel but, alas and alack, that doesn't seem to have been tonight's fare. For those of you who purchased the book, *Poem of the Man-God,* I would like to suggest that there are gems aplenty studded within its pages. Of course the book isn't about Mr. Christ as much as it is about us, our sadhana, our "call" so to speak, and perhaps our "calling" as well—not that we should rush into becoming teachers, so to say, but that our service, our offering, is always relevant. If you are turned off by things Christian, remember Jesus wasn't a Christian, profit from the pure Dharma, and never mind the trappings.

I also hope that you found the stories from California useful. We tell stories not purely as entertainment but hopefully so that you may use their value for your own refining and maturing practice. They aren't as much about the people they happened to as they are about people in general—that is us, if we relate and can apply the lessons.

I received another letter from Europe asking me how to handle a situation, the exact situation this person has been asking me about for several years, which I have addressed multiple times, always in the same way. I replied that I was finished answering such questions, which I have answered over and over, as I expect my input to be applied. If it isn't, well then, at least I expect it to be remembered and applied when the horror (terror) of the situation finally dawns on the person, which often is enough of a shock to actually create some movement out of the sloth and swamp that we seem to be so comfortable remaining in, despite of what we claim to be great suffering. How strange, how strange.

On another note, we had a lovely "group therapy session" in the office this afternoon, and I was quite impressed with how well the women—those giving, not receiving the help—handled the situation. That is all we can hope for: maturity in being, in delivery. We have absolutely nothing to say about and no control over how the person receiving the help will make use of it, but we do have a say in how we comport ourselves. It was an excellent comportment, I must say, giving me confidence in my ongoing recommendation to so many people to seek help from within the

Sangha body instead of feeling that only I can make the difference, which reinforces my confidence in the certainty that those who complain about the Sangha failing to serve them are basically simply unwilling to take the help offered and unwilling to listen to honest feedback.

If you are one of those who has been at the brunt of my impatience, annoyance, and irritation this week, I apologize, not for the direct utility of my feedback but for the vehicle through which it has been delivered. I will probably apologize many more times before we're on to something less strident, so thank you for bearing with me. Steve opened the announcements on this Work Weekend this morning by thanking everyone who had joined us. There were two—that's *two*—people present out of the fifty-plus who live in town. Yes. Heartbreak comes in many forms.

Well, two ADTs this week, and if you don't manage to attend those either (remember they are called "after *dinner* talks," not "evening talks"), have a most productive and a most wonderful week, truly. And on that note, *Jai Guru.*

A Far Deeper Work

February 28, 2010

Hello. Welcome. Though I moan and bitch (no sexism implied, I sincerely hope), I am well aware that I am really extremely lucky with this little health lila of mine. My "suffering" is annoying irritating and frustrating, and at the same time, as I said just a moment ago, I am well aware that it is quite minor relative to what it could be and relative, I imagine, to what some few of you have endured. So I am very grateful for such a small thing to endure.

Some of you may have heard the phrase "a tempest in a teapot." This describes what is a pastime for many of us, and a favorite pastime for a few of us: the dramatization, exaggeration, and magnification of some minor disturbance into a life-shocking catastrophe that we can worry, yell, pout, and stomp around about. "Oh, the *injustice*!" or, "What have I done to deserve *this*?" Well, my friends, my allies in the Work, it behooves us to get a grip—in other words, to develop the Work skill to maintain a genuine perspective on Reality as it actually is, rather than making it into something to feed our life script and fuel our self-importance and illusions. It doesn't pay to waste invaluable work energy on pettiness. Save it for when you need it, and as you all should know, inevitably you *will* need it.

It is only our own identification with the willing victim "I" that creates such furor over insignificance. Why be a victim of the victim? With a modicum of awareness, you won't be so easily trapped in such grossly obvious situations. If you simply try, try, and keep on trying, and if your efforts are sincere and not motivated to make points with the authority, be it the Guru or God, you will inevitably build Work success and find those attempts rewarded, and quite richly I will add. So if you must react or recoil, at least keep the scale commensurate to the actual provocation, and please *do* try to pause for a moment and think before you blurt out or do something truly vile, for which you will be very sorry for a very long time.

So, friends, here's the thing about questions to me. As you all know, I receive many sincere and honest appeals for information, direction, decisions to be made—all in all, answers to various of life's sometimes confusing opportunities. And here's the dilemma (mine, not necessarily yours): if you have context, for the most part questions are not needed, except to possibly clarify details or get an overview, a long-term vision that opens the immediate need to act, to move to a broader field of perception and possibility. If you don't have context (as in wishing for a parent figure to absolve you of responsibility by making the decisions for you), then any answer I might offer will probably be wrongly and strategically used, with shortsight and even direct antagonism to the issue at hand.

It is frustrating to me, because the questioner fully believes in their own sincerity, even when self-honesty has rarely graced their consciousness, and my unwillingness to answer the question directly is often seen as a lack of interest, caring, attention or even love. Context, context, context.

As an example: Parents often idealize their children to such a romantic or sentimental degree (yes, Virginia, even here in our sacred enclaves), that they totally blind themselves to their own glaring selfishness and soul-deadening lack of genuineness in relationship to those very children. What to do when these parents ask me heart-rending, and by their own perception, heartfelt questions about how to handle various details relative to their children? Unfortunately, if we are unwilling (and it is almost always unwilling, not unable) to see ourselves clearly, we will be unable to implement input or feedback that demands as a foundation for success this very real self-seeing: an objective assessment or knowledge of who we are now as we are, not as we imagine ourselves to be or hope to be some day.

As some of you have undoubtedly noticed, more and more these days I am not answering your questions with data or factual information, methods, the nuts and bolts of what to do, but rather with pointers about working with one's own lack of context. You know, the old "physician heal thyself" paradigm. As we converse, Rami is finishing the Landmark Forum Advanced Course and one of her comments is: "This is really different than the basic course. They don't hold your hand in this one. It's entirely up to you to do the work." Bravo! This is similar, in some ways, to what y'all are being asked to do—to take the initiative to put yourself on the line. When you do, I am two hundred percent here, there, everywhere for you, to help, guide, inform, educate, push, pull (even shove or yank, if needed) and get the Work in progress, in process, and flying instead of crawling.

Most of our irrelevant questions or idiotic chatter could easily be eliminated and illuminated by simply stopping for a small moment to consider or ponder before speaking. It is the chronically mechanical impulse of our life script, our psychological story, that produces *all* of these useless leakages of energy that keep our Work efforts mediocre and dull. It is true that the vast majority of visitors who discover us are highly impressed by our spiritual force and integrity. Not enough, not enough. As I commented in a distinction on literature Thursday night, I want people to be *compelled,* not simply moved by admiration.

No, it is not time to rest yet, if it ever is! A far deeper work and a far more profound effect is requested—in fact, required—if one is truly serious about pursuing this Path to the sweet end, for a half-assed pursuit will most likely only introduce us to the bitter end. Of course the Influence, the Blessings are not bound by time or space, and at the same time there is the Sanctuary of the

Ashram and the Refuge of Sangha. ("When two or more are gathered. . . . ") A question might arise, which is: When we have spent time here, be it a couple of hours or weeks, and received a mainline injection of the Force of Benediction, how do we hold this power, this light? How do we hold it in order that it can continue to feed and fuel us at all times, whether we are in Remembrance or in forgetfulness? Obviously the essential answer is consistent practice, reliably paying our dues with active engagement, even if our fickle and insecure minds tell us (and you know they will) that we are just going through empty motions, and why bother if it isn't "real" or "true" or heartfelt and so on.

This alone is a good enough reason to not allow the mind and your psychological script to dominate your behaviors. While there is no substitute for consistent practice, at the same time it is most helpful to be willing to be reminded; to be willing to allow our artifacts, *murtis*, or *vigrahas*—and our memories of past "glories," we could say—to bring us into resonance, into sync. If in fact we are a bit off the track, this willingness to be reminded is not only appropriate but may at times be crucial to a continuity of budding faith and prayers to be Surrendered to the Will of God. In fact, it is our responsibility to maintain an ongoing relationship to these ways of strengthening the container, to embrace and keep the Heart of Sanctuary active in our hearts, cells, beings.

It is always a joy for me to have guests, whether they are from America, Europe, or even right here in Prescott. Often we see a few people exclusively on Sunday evenings, such as this delicious Sunday evening, and it seems almost (not quite, but close) as if we are hosting guests, as the Radiant Aura of Yogi Ramsuratkumar's most immediate Presence seems to be particularly tangible here in Sanctuary. It is always a touch sad when people confess that when they return "home," usually after some time, they feel that they have "lost" that razor's edge of brilliance, of Transcendent Oneness, as if it has faded away due to distance or due to a return to the busy engagement with the ordinary and countless distractions of one's family, professional, or creative life. This perception is not necessarily accurate, for mostly these perceptions are false, even though they may seem so alive and so pressing.

Have faith in the words and in the doctrine (not dogma) of the Guru. In fact what often happens is that the dynamism of this scintillating and sublime Effect has become more subtle, more refined, rather than the gross affectation that captures an attention that we cannot miss. Yes, this is true. Someone said, "You can't lose what you never had," and we might ask, or query or even suppose, in the sense of the present discussion: "Can you lose what you have, when what you have has permeated every part, dimension, and level of you?"

Ah well, enough for now.

This coming Saturday Ravi Ravindra is speaking in Mesa; I will be going and would be thrilled to have a community trip organized—something we have not done in simply ages! Perhaps someone can post a sign-up sheet, and if you remember from those long ages ago, when we last did something like this, I dislike sign-ups who cross out their names just before the trip. So please do not sign up if you are not *committed* to attending, for in spite of what the office biddies and Sangha Nazis propose, you can *always* add your name to the list the morning of departure—there is *always* room to fit a few more enthusiastic sangha into such a venture.

Bravo brave souls, for your deep, abiding, and loving involvement in this sprawling yet perfectly focused attempt to actually create some semblance of the True Work, Objective Community, and Divine Life on the face of our rapidly deteriorating planet and in the midst of a common value system amongst most of humanity that is a criminal shame and an insult to intelligence, sensitivity, and God.

May you all be mightily Blessed, deliriously happy, successful in choosing what is, and at peace within yourselves. *Jai, Jai, Jai Guru!*

राम राम

Faith and Surrender

March 7, 2010

Good evening, as it most usually is on Sunday and hopefully on most other evenings as well. And talking about optimism, I think a major dose is called for, in the specific sense that as my healing program continues to drag on, with my great faith in its success and at the same time my frustration with the length of time it is taking to demonstrate its efficacy, it becomes imperative for you to see things in a "big picture" kind of way—which, when carried through, directly helps and serves me.

It is like this: The Universe doesn't make mistakes. Its timing is exactly what it needs to be based on the Universe's (Reality's or Truth's) own imperative. Try as we might, we aren't often privy to that. We like to think that we know what is best for ourselves and others, especially our loved ones, and in our rigid or orthodox views, we quite commonly deny the fact that the Universe is always an Objective Creation machine. I am very optimistic about my own staying around for a while, and I could easily be wrong. So, not to try to prepare y'all for bad news (to the ego), but this situation demands that you not look at my staying or going in a narrow way—as if either case actually *meant* anything beyond that the Universe decides what Its program is often lifetimes before our current little candlelights of consciousness exist, and the dictates of this marvelous Universe will out.

So, as always, we are called to profound Faith *and* Surrender (meaning to not fight, struggle, or argue with however Existence rolls down the pike). We are called to the knowledge or presumption (do you have the gumption for such a presumption?) that whatever occurs is the perfect unfolding of destiny as it is meant to be, in the integrity of the Path and Yogi Ramsuratkumar's Blessing Force, Guidance and Protection.

Why am I considering this with you now? During the week a conversation was had with Lalitha (and nobody here better call her and scold her!), and although I was not the ear on the phone getting the download, what I gathered reading between the lines—and of course Lalitha would swear that I misunderstood her implications—was that she isn't as optimistic as the optimism I am suggesting you all cultivate. Certain of those close to me were a bit shaken, so to speak. As I go along my merry yet cranky and irritable way, I need your understanding as the container in which I am held as your Guru and Teacher or whatever. I need you, I *want* you, to trust the Universe.

To walk around here and notice looks of worry, sorrow (as if you've already decided on the end result, timing and all), sentimental concern and the whole lot of it, is a real downer, let me tell you. I'm not asking you to just plaster on a happy-face mask, but to truly confront your own pessimism, your small worldview, your own failure to see clearly, and your own tendencies to imagine that you and not the Universe control life and its pleasant or unpleasant manifestations. I hope it is obvious that I'm not suggesting a deadening passivity; I am suggesting a passive observation of what arises and then an appropriate action, mild or dynamic, founded in wisdom, Faith in the Universe, and a "big picture" panoramic view of the rightness of the Universe's activity.

Many if not most of you have asked for my input in various aspects of your lives—personal, creative and professional—ostensibly with the willingness to follow the feedback or direction that I offer, even if it conflicts with your wishes. That implies that you trust my judgment (and I assert that you do, even those of you who have resoundingly rejected my advice and gone on to the poor choices you hoped my advice would confirm, which you have inevitably come to realize).

Well my devotees, the Universe has upped the ante. I'm begging you—and begging does not come easy for me, even though I've been more driven to it over the years—to trust me in the case of my health and its obvious effect on whether this body remains here for some time or goes.

M. Young, my biographer, just asked me if, relative to Yogi Ramsuratkumar, I ever felt that I had "bitten off more than I could chew." I answered "How could I? Of course not!" This ties in with our consideration of this evening. How could "I" have "bitten off" anything when "I" made no decision? There were no choices (only the quite transparent appearance of such) except those already made by the Universe. There was a seamless flow from one form (lee with no guru, directly "hit" by God, et cetera) to another (lee as devotee and disciple of Yogi Ramsuratkumar, his eternal Master, Father and Heart).This is the kind of shift of context I am outlining tonight, a vision of the fullness and justice of the Universe's incarnations, in a personal sense, replacing our small belief in our own universe, the universe of opinion, dogma, psychology and misperception, confusion and doubt. How could "I" live if it wasn't "fated," and at the same time how could "I" die if it wasn't "fated"?

So . . . back to Faith and Surrender, the two qualities that Yogi Ramsuratkumar said were the essence of it all. He also said that until Faith and Surrender were true of any individual (us!), we must practice, study, perform yogas of various sorts (not that any of these would necessarily fall away after Faith and Surrender were true of us) and commit to rigorous discipline and discrimination in regards to "right effort, right behavior, right speech, right contemplation" and so on. I may not be bringing the kind of cheery joy to my situation that Yvan Amar brought to his, yet at the same time, I am held in the Grace of Yogi Ramsuratkumar, and He will handle the major details, leaving me to handle the minor ones, in which handling I am bumbling and stumbling around as they do get handled.

An example of a lack of Faith and Surrender: We were at a program this week, and we were all given name tags to slap on our shirts, blouses, dresses, suit jackets or pocketbooks, and it struck me how wrong it was that my biographer and otherwise had "Angelon" on hers. How much more obvious could it be that when we were in India in the nineties, 1998 I believe, and Yogi Ramsuratkumar made this fabulous lila with her, demanding directly and unequivocally that when He asked her, "What is your name?" she should answer, "Mary." Twelve years ago (!!!) she ceased to be Angelon and was offered the rare, priceless Benediction, the opportunity, to be M. Young . . . Mary.

I think that there is absolutely no question about the magnificence of her work tasks, her writing, when she *is* M. Young, and I think it is obvious to her when she suffers the great crises of "Angelon" that many of those conflicts, much of that suffering, would have dissolved into thin air if she had been willing to have Faith in Yogi Ramsuratkumar's Genius, if she had embraced and Surrendered herself to who He told her—with no fuzzy edges—that she is.

Such responsibilities are not easy to bear. Well, sometimes they are, but not usually. To shift identity in a real and abiding way and to live on the basis of that shift (which I suppose is what "abiding" means) requires a tremendous leap, if not into the Unknown, at least out of the known—as far as we actually "know" what is really going on in that persona that we are and have been identified with for a lifetime. So, it usually isn't easy, and especially with a name like Mary, given our Christian references—more accurately our churchy references. This is one of the reasons we do sadhana: to prepare for such "leaps of faith," so to speak. As some of you know firsthand (or second- or thirdhand from your observation of family members, especially brothers and sisters), most everything in us wants desperately to minimize the demand, to make it something that it isn't, or to forget completely through trivialization or "trance." And yet, here it is, when it is and how it is.

I'm sure many of you have similar stories you could relate, in relationship to my instruction to you—stories that would delight me if any of you would be willing to tell them at the ADT tomorrow evening. Thank you ahead of time.

So, my health, as it will develop for better or worse, isn't personal to one or two of us. It touches us all. Well, good work, lee. Hallelujah! What a powerful tool, a powerful and ever-present reminding factor. Go Yogi Ramsuatkumar! Please, let's make use of it, for I surely wouldn't want this most annoying and bothersome little ugliness, which is certainly Reminding me, to have all been for naught. (I know it won't, absolutely *can't* be, for naught, and still we want to optimize its effectiveness, don't we?)

Gosh and golly gee, I'm sorry tonight's discussion has been so lacking in a good dose of humor—it has seemed so heavy, at least while I was writing it. It actually is quite light, so be enthusiastic, if you will. It is easier to be humorous when I'm rambling and every off-the-cuff stream of consciousness little tidbit can be turned into a grinning or laughing matter. Let's all vote for that back again! Two ADTs or ADVs this coming week, and perhaps when you are visiting with the those folks who are not here tonight, please fill them in on our conversation with as much optimism as you can bring to it. Yes.

Jai Guru, Jai Guru, Jai Guru

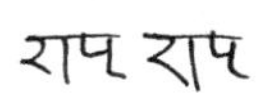

Who Will Make the Gesture?

March 14, 2010

Several weeks ago at an ADT, Nara decried the common, all too common, lack of practice amongst the Sangha at large and Ashram residents in particular. Someone didn't talk to him for two weeks and finally told him that they were angry at him for what he said because it made them feel guilty for not going to meditation. Oy vey! Such things continue to show me that I am still soooo naïve. Such a reminder from Nara should be hailed, celebrated, applauded. Such reminders, including more personal direct feedback, should be embraced and welcomed because it gives us one more immediate opportunity to clearly acknowledge our avoidances, our denials, our mediocrity, our middle-class, lazy-ass, practice-crass, Mama Cass (jes cause ya got one fabulous voice don't mean you ain't still sound asleep and jes markin' time), passive-aggressive sass, lookin' good, goin' nowhere blind spots!

When will we be truly enthusiastic and grateful for this amazing and exceedingly rare Blessing of Guru, Dharma, Sangha, and Path? When will we throw ourselves into the opportunity to cultivate the attitude that *anything* which helps us remove blocks, obstacles, or veils that stand between us and Faith and Surrender—Yogi Ramsuratkumar in fact—needs (not *should* but *needs)* to be received and used with delight, pleasure and profound thanks? When will we be truly happy when one of our own (or not) shows us where we are hiding, lurking in the swamps and shadows of unobserved and unowned neuroses, cramps, "sins," false views, deluded opinions, bigotries and the whole catalog of darknesses and vilenesses?

We are not here to simply spin our wheels in the mud. We are not here to become churchified machines to replace our alternative machines. And we are certainly not here to demonstrate petty, fickle, petulant, self-obsessed childish reactivity to genuine frustrations on the part of those who wish to see us whole, adult, mature practitioners, even if that frustration bursts forth in somewhat accusatory tones.

There was recently an article in *Rolling Stone* magazine about a new cult led by another megalomaniacal, sadistic, self-centered, criminal Korean man who thinks he is some holy personage. And where did he place their world nexus of operations? Sedona. Yep. Sedona, our own Arizona Garden of Eden. The list of abuses is mind-boggling, but what is even more mind-boggling is how many gullible followers he was able to attract and keep attracted in spite of horrendous physical conditions, unconscionable psychological conditions, nothing less than financial banditry, thievery, and a dharma stupid enough to be a stand-up comedy routine if the leader wasn't serious. I listened to the article as it was read to me and just kept shaking my head, having no comprehension of what makes people so willing to be grossly taken advantage of, even to the point of a tragic breakdown of health, financial stability, family relations that were previously loving and healthy and so on.

In a very small way, our refusal to grow up and even to beg for input that could help us and serve us—and to actually allow that input (with our active participation, obviously) to make a real and *lasting* difference in us—smacks of similar "cultic" behavior. That includes our unconscious reactivity in the face of such help, from absurd comments like the one mentioned earlier, to angry and attacking outbursts, to the one most common in relationship to me: to smile, thank me, and promptly ignore whatever utility my words or gestures could have effected. Such people, given free reign to exercise power or authority over others, are likely to use that freedom to abuse and suppress, to unrealistically accuse and repress others who are trying to see Truth and Reality gain the upper hand. (Although such likeliness isn't guaranteed, for we do have our Master's and our Master's Master's Guidance and protection and the momentum and force of years, even eons, of practice.)

As the adage goes: "Better safe than sorry." This kind of weakness needs to be addressed and rooted out. Everyone is enthusiastic about the seminar program we've been doing in Phoenix, which is all well and good—and, as you know, if you aren't *self-observing* in an objective way, all that rah, rah, rah jazz will be just as useless as Nara's plea to practice was to the person who was finding themselves in recoil and full of guilt.

Guilt!? I cannot count the times I have considered the absolute uselessness of guilt with y'all, and how feelings of guilt are illusions perpetuated by an unwillingness to leave the child behind in favor of the now obviously grown-up person. Y'all have closets full, drawers full, storage lockers, attics, basements *full* of gifts that have been given over the years, gifts that you unwrapped in front of the gift-giver (the three refuges) so as to be polite or politically correct, and then threw them, still in the boxes, into their resting places to gather dust and maybe someday be listed on your resumé or in your inventory of possessions. Many of us have become or are becoming classic spiritual materialists (as Chögyam Trungpa Rinpoche pointed out); if your personal Path is to be optimized successfully, you must dig these weeds out and throw them away.

I have both faith and confidence in you (most of you, not as a personal selectivity but as a Universal potentiality) that you *can* do this Work effectively and rightly. You can do it *now*, not someday in the future. You can do it *now*, not will do it whenever. I trust you. I better trust you, for I have placed my life in your hands, in the sense that even though I belong fully and without reserve to Yogi Ramsuratkumar, this School is about *us*, not about me. I am submitted to you, to y'all, in the Work Chamber that is about Transmission, communication, about *your* transformation.

My transformation is not at issue or an issue. My transformation is solely Yogi Ramsuratkumar's business and is a done deal. And, I don't live in a vacuum and *you*, y'all, are the content of the world I do live in. So it is *us* or nothing. Who will make the gesture? Who will make the gesture, beyond that dumb, Japanese-doll, head bobbing, "Yes, lee, thank you," trance-speak? And who will understand that to make any gesture in this context means to demonstrate the results in your life and the lives of others in a *noticeable* way?

If you think or imagine that you are or have made a difference, but this is merely some kind of internal intuition or belief, unsubstantiated by having been noticed by others in the environment who know you well enough to be able to tell when a difference has been and is being made, you are still lost in your own dream, buffered in your own bubble, and still failing to self-observe to any degree that can possibly be effective or valuable. I'm not talking about a subjective difference; I'm talking about a *manifest* difference.

Abraham (of Bible note) was sitting in front of his house in ecstatic communion with God when he happened to notice several travelers passing by on the road. He jumped up immediately and ran to them to offer them a drink, a meal, some rest. In Orthodox Judaism hospitality is a high law, and *acts* are prized over internal considering. Abraham broke off his inner conversation with God Himself in order to *act*.

Okay, okay! The seeds of being different are planted in you, and they need to be watered, fertilized, cared for in their gestation. Instantaneous, full-grown, fruit-bearing plants are unrealistic, isn't that the way the process *always* works? Okay, okay. At the same time, to plant seeds and then fail to provide water, fertilizer, and shelter, and to deny the new delicate shoots the appropriate amount and degree of sunlight needed for healthy ongoing development, is a bit cutting-off-your-nose-to-spite-your-face foolish (even if clearly self-serving and ego-guarding), don't you think?

So it's *you.* Y'all. I'm not looking down the road for the real devotees to show up. You're here. It is *you,* y'all. We are the "A-Team," and it is high time we got to it, or actively sped up our continuing of getting to it. *Doch. Voilà.*

Two ADTs or ADVs this week. And even if you are not in meditation in the morning, which costs me a lot on my expense account, it is still a truly joyous affair to see you here tonight and at the After Dinner Talks (which includes dinner, by the way, in the same way that mediation includes Arati). So, "Come on in, the water's fine!"

Jai Guru, Jaya Baulo Jai

राम राम

What Is It That I Trust in You?

March 21, 2010

I was having a bit of a—oh, good evening, by the way, and welcome!—yes, a bit of a bitchfest with one of my household, with me being bitch number one, of course, as is the current state of affairs and has been for far too long to suit my tastes and the tastes of some of you, I am sure. After I had ostensibly been demeaningly and disrespectfully critical of the other person (calling their motives into question), one of the salvos fired at me was something to the effect of, "Thanks for supporting me," or, "Thanks for trusting my work," said, of course, as if I didn't, wasn't, or hadn't supported them.

Knowing full well that everyone else in my household has seen my absolutely reliable support for this person on many occasions, I took this occasion, when the object of my so-called annoyance and two others were in the kitchen with me, to ask the other two (and I quote), "Have you ever seen my support for this person?" They both immediately and with gusto answered, "Yes." So I took the opportunity to suggest that they, one at a time, tell her about those circumstances.

The first person said that it was obvious that she had my support based on the jobs or responsibilities I had given to her to do for me, to which answer I "snapped" (*again*, yawn) and said, "No, no, no, *that's* not it." (Another quote by the way.) Then I turned to the second person and asked her to make the communication (she had been in the kitchen the whole time listening to the conversation), in answer to which she promptly said *exactly* the same thing as the first woman. Oh my God, oh my God, how two mature, intelligent "dharma mavens" could so widely miss the mark and assume that gross outer-world tasks were indicative of acknowledgement and support for someone's Work efforts was and clearly still is mind-boggling and unbelievable to me! Without pussy-footing around the catnip, I was floored, aghast, frustrated, and more than a little bit depressed.

So listen puppies, yes it is true that the Ashram and this whole system could not function if many people didn't manage all of the necessary external projects, from dishes, phones, garden care and property upkeep, to Hohm Press, financial management, cooking and all the rest of it. These are all things that roll down the pike as life rolls up the pike and have to be handled in the process. And for your hard work, your sacrifices of time and energy, your dedication, I am profoundly grateful and shower Yogi Ramsuratkumar's Blessings on y'all by the truckload.

At the same time, when one talks about "My" support, it always has to do with your Work, your "spiritual" practices, your transformational or alchemical engagement, your aim (in the mystical realms), your Attention and Remembering, and so on. Anyone who has studied this Way for any length of time could only make such a gross and unconscionable error if the response comes thoughtlessly and unbelievably (at this stage of the game) directly through ego's eyes. And the person I had been harping on, who had stopped for a moment to listen to what *should* have been said, was basically blown out of the potential chamber by ridiculous miscommunications.

This is for *all* of you. You are not—and your Work is not—your external activities, except in *very rare* cases in which all any given individual can do is give resources (in money or materials) or some personal skill, such as carpentry or chefery. But this is hardly the case of y'all—you are *not* the exceptions to this particular rule. So once again I ask, when—*when*—will you stop "seeing the Work through the eyes of the world?"

When I say that I have faith in you, as I said exactly one week ago, I am hardly talking about trusting that you will show up for your task on time (if at all) or finish your job in the time I wanted it done. It should be obvious by now that some of you always have such integrity, and some of you are sloppy and unreliable in these domains. And yet, still, I have faith in you. Did you ever actually stop to think about what that *means*? Or do you just take it in through the ears and into the brain and never give it a moment's consideration?

What *exactly* do I have faith in? I'd really, *really* like you to answer this for yourselves, because if you do not, you are very likely to expend a tremendous amount of time, energy, and resources completely barking up the wrong tree (when the cat is in another *universe*) and even losing your Work over it. Obviously, when you are terrified to "be wrong" in some superficial or even highly subjective situation, this is actually what you are doing: no more than protecting an ego that has little if nothing to do with our Work together and My Advent here in this time and place. A colossal waste with no value whatsoever.

So what is it, *exactly*, that I have faith in? What is it that I trust in you? What is it that I am continuously (up to a point) giving you the benefit of the doubt relative to? This ain't Zen, or I would yell, drooling and spitting like the Trevi Fountain, "*Answer Now! Now!*" So, answer it within yourself, but do answer it, so you don't be fools in critical moments like my two special and lovely devotees in the kitchen the other day. What is it in you, *exactly*, that I have faith in?

On another subject . . . well, is there really another subject? Ah, but enough of philosophy. I would like to thank you for being so spacious—those of you who are—around my irritable, nasty, aggressive outbursts these many months. I am sure that some few of you harbor great fears, or at least worries, that I am fast descending into an abusive, selfish, uncaring, loutish pig of a man. Many would assume that—especially those with no depth of education about this process (mine and yours, not just mine as an isolated situation, separate from my Post as Guru and Agent of Yogi Ramsuratkumar's Transmission).

I am hoping that over time this all will be seen in a perspective that firmly establishes it in the overall flow, the "big picture" if you will, of the ongoing communication of the Work. Historical precedents aside, of which there are many, it is our own personal task to make as much use as we can of whatever comes through our Guide—whether it be sweet and blissful or ugly and harsh. It is our own progress on the Path that is at stake. Of course all this is dependent on the Reality that I actually am the Mission Holder of Yogi Ramsuratkumar, the transparent and hopefully faithful and surrendered vehicle of my Master—the genuine article, not some fool who believes himself to be that which he is not (as is epidemic in the spiritual field these days).

So your willingness to embrace or merely bear with this phase that is being animated here through lee is not only vital but may even be pivotal in your own practice. And again, having some small sense of the difficulty of these manifestations, especially for those who are the direct objects of my "poison darts" or "poison pen"—not to mention those of you who may feel like you are back in your childhood with your family once again (curse the thought!)—I want to bow before you in gratitude, as I assume, I hope accurately, that it is your faith (there's that special word again) that keeps you "truckin" and not fear or co-dependency or stubbornness.

I need you as much as you need me (or at least close!). May Blessings pour upon your devotion and more, for most of you know full well that to remove yourself from the active chamber, whether that be by physically exiting the space or by closing down or off inside, is to cease to work and to cease to be available, in fact, to actively block or deny the flow of Benediction and the potential or possibility of using the input, whatever it is, even if it seems to be humiliating or simply useless.

I'm hardly suggesting that every single one of the Guru's farts needs to be inhaled lest you miss a grand treasure, but on the other hand, gestures as loud and unmistakable as these "I" am making so frequently in this pivotal time are situations you may not want to avoid, at least not if you wish to maximize your "profit." And, while we're at it (we are "at it," aren't we?), just to be cognizant of what is going on in any given space and able to repeat it with some fair degree of accuracy to others does not mean that you are getting or have gotten it. If it suits your psychological script, you can keep *all* of this neatly confined to your mind, to your mental gyrations, without making any value of it or being touched by it at all. This is a complex, tricky, highly sophisticated labyrinth that we are called to traverse here; tears (especially later when you're alone in your room) or a look of shock or horror on your face during the "storm" aren't necessarily indicative that you have allowed yourself to actually participate, rather than allowing the mind to co-opt the whole potato with a little emotional buzz to convince you that you "got it."

So, once again, thank you for not only your patience but in many cases your kindness during what, for me, is a time of trial and travail, even as I can make a fair to excellent argument for its viable utility (fair to excellent depending on the listener, not depending on me).

Well, there is so much more, but I think this is enough to chew on for the nonce. Two ADTs or ADVs this week and a very important Work Weekend this coming Saturday and Sunday, so if you can at all and in any way free up your time, please attend (and keep in mind that the Work Weekends include the meals). And even though we are far from the holiday of Thanksgiving, "Don't let the turkeys get you down!"

Jai Guru,
Jai Guru,
Jai Guru

राम राम

Sanctuary

March 28, 2010

Welcome and good evening as well as glad tidings. We have been considering Sanctuary for a short while at the After Dinner Talk spaces and an excellent subject matter it is indeed. It is true that the world is "going to hell in a handbasket," and that human suffering is at epidemic levels. Of course there are those who suffer in ways similar to the incredible agonies of the Middle Ages, but at the same time today's suffering is more in the soul-dead category: the abject separation and active rejection of our essential humanity and humaneness both. As a race, we have and are turning our backs on our true and deep natures in favor of flash-in-the-pan gimmickry, quick satisfactions, and massive attempts to guarantee ourselves comfort and the illusion of health, well-being, and success.

Sanctuary is even more important now than it was when we began this spiritual school this time around. To deny its holiness and its refuge is not only unwise and foolish but bad "business"—meaning quite unprofitable. Most of us do not deny our Sanctuary in gross ways; it is all the small abuses, so glibly excused to ourselves, that build up a quite significant charge of negative energy. It takes an inordinate amount of effort to counterbalance that accumulated charge—especially in relationship to how little energy was required for each small insult (to your own intelligence and dignity) or oversight to slip through the dharma facade and weaken the foundation of our commitment, our integrity, and even our devotion. So please take our discussion of this subject matter seriously, give it careful and deep consideration, and integrate it into your behavior and not just into the wonderfully encyclopedic data banks of your dharma intellects.

Sanctuary, we could loosely say, is the physical or subtle space in which our connection to the Guru, the Path, and to God is held somewhat consciously. Sanctuary is the mood or the context in which content is solidly rooted in our Work together, in which the active qualities of Radiant Love, Mercy, Generosity (both of spirit and of resources), and Nobility are dominant, alive and permeating the physical or subtle space.

There are times, yes, when such a space just seems to descend or open up in spite of ourselves. Such spaces usually seem wondrous, magical, deliciously sweet, profound, and graceful, and we should not be sitting around twiddling our fingers or toes waiting for them to arise. Reality is not the great or foreboding mystery that it often seems to us, unbeknownst to all those who are not ruthlessly self-honest. It has been given to us to *actively* involve ourselves in doing as many of the things that are possible to do which encourage the evocation or creation of Sanctuary (although in actual terms we never "create" Sanctuary, it is always right here waiting for us to enter), and once there, to invoke the ongoing Blessings that are so clearly evident when we are awake in that space and to maintain the Presence or the sparkling brilliance that touches us so deeply.

These are not times to be lazy. Like the usual psychological script, which is triggered by various stimuli and reacts completely automatically—often so seamlessly that we don't have any idea how mechanical our lives are—the training must be embodied so fully that it activates almost automatically when needed. We need to replace those psychological automatisms with Work automatisms, so that when we have the option to "sin," which we pretty much always have because it *is* the stuff of our life story or psychological script, we act in a manner that is in accordance with Truth, with conscious life, with the laws of the Work. We could say that we automatically chose—or it is chosen for us—to be in perfect alignment with the Will of God.

This is only one reason out of many that Sanctuary is so crucial. Sanctuary is a training ground or chamber in which our entire unconscious—our unquestioned and unobserved faulty worldview—is adjusted and transformed. It is the training ground in which the lead of our being states is turned into the pure gold of a life lived in and for the Divine.

So please let us not get (or stay) sloppy and inattentive. This past week someone did a very impressive and major piece of work, and for a week or so afterward showed up particularly, excellently clear in way that was uncharacteristic of their normal state. I complimented this significant demonstration of possibility, and literally the day after my high praise, this individual had snapped back, like a stretched rubber band, into their out-of-touch, chronically habitual dream-world trance, buffered from Reality and my Help.

We cannot afford such "luxuries." Once we step strongly forward, we must maintain this momentum, stay sharp and alert, and capitalize on the breakthrough or it will mean *nothing*. Once in Sanctuary, we need to *use* that space to anchor ourselves, to "tie ourselves to the mast" so to speak—or Circe and the Sirens will capture us, effectively neutralizing our ostensible advantage.

Sanctuary. There is no substitute for these spaces, these opportunities. Sure, great advances and great changes will be evident over a lifetime of even mediocre practice. But do we have a lifetime, not just now, but *ever*? I do not, and I would suggest that you do not either, regardless of your chronological or biological age. As Elvis (Presley, not Costello) sang so passionately lo, those many years (lifetimes?) ago: ♫ "It's now or never, my love won't wait . . ." ♫

So, while on the subject of Sanctuary (not Elvis Presley, and yes, he has reincarnated, and he ain't one of *our* little darlings), and while we can almost taste, almost touch it, let's not allow it to fall by the wayside and stagnate, drying up and killing all the tadpoles.

As I was lying in bed falling asleep I had a fantastic flash about a further consideration of Sanctuary, but unfortunately I didn't anchor it—I didn't key or highlight it in consciousness—and so for the life of me, try as I might (even ceasing to try, which usually is quite effective), it hasn't come back. Ah, but not to worry, because another one has taken its place!

It is said that to advance in the Work, one must replace one's self first (or *be* replaced, heh, heh, he chuckled conspiratorially). Another way of saying this is that when our heads are above the clouds it is not because we can fly (or levitate), but because we are standing on someone else's shoulders. To belittle, demean, be ungrateful to or criticize, to judge unfairly and condemn on the basis of our judgment those individuals whose shoulders we are standing on is foolish, self-defeating, and ultimately may even cause the entire structure to collapse—for *we would not be where we are* were it not for them. To be unconscious is one thing (no excuse, but still, what is, is, as it is, isn't it?), but to fail to capitalize on the knowledge, experience, and efforts that have been made by others for so long is nothing but sheer egoism and power lust.

Yes it is true that the vision above the clouds, the vast perspective, the endless horizon, the magnificent heights, is heady and exhilarating indeed. Yet to lose our heads over it is certainly counterproductive. We need to be able *and willing* to "hold our seat" whether the horse is bucking, galloping, or just peacefully ambling through the glorious spring fields of flowers and ambrosial perfume. We need to "Pay Attention and Remember" not only in times of stress, crisis, and demand but in times of ecstatic revelation and even bliss as well. For Sanctuary is no Sanctuary if we lose sight of it the instant we are presented with a bauble of desire, some responsibility, some authority, praise from the guru (or even better, from someone famous or who we feel far inferior to), or even the dawning of wisdom: classic "spiritual materialism."[1]

---

1 "Spiritual Materialism" is a dharma term coined by Chögyam Trungpa Rinpoche.

We need to remember that Sanctuary is the aim, not control, being "right," or domination over others, even if such domination wears the smiling face of "good reasons"—you know, the sheep's clothing, so to speak. As more of you begin to assume posts of responsibility for the teaching, whether overtly or more subtly, by serving me more directly or personally, as is clearly the case these days—and I see no reason that things should not continue in that direction, even when I regain a more functional vocal health—ideally, we need to have profound gratitude for both those who came before us, who paved the way and mapped the territory, and those who will come in greater and greater numbers (with all of the attendant headaches, irritations and frustrations for us, and with their own confusions, doubts, anger, fear, denial, ignorance, hot-headed righteousness, self-hatred, lack of clarity and so on).

We need to have profound gratitude for those whose shoulders provide the foundation upon which we stand and which would collapse, even at times instantaneously, were those shoulders suddenly removed—and that would be shocking, surprising, and unpleasant, to put it mildly. If you are a shoulder upon which someone else stands, it greatly behooves you to stay steady and solid and try not to topple those relying on you to maintain them—even if that is insidious, unconscious, and consistent with your psychological script, since so many of you have self-sabotage issues.

So, my dears, the importance of these ideas cannot nor should not be disregarded or under-appreciated, for the health and sanity of your actual transformation (and your accumulation of "good" karma) may depend upon your serious engagement and embrace of them. As they say, "forewarned is forearmed," and it certainly can be when one is willing to dig in and respect the Laws of the Work, the Realities of the Universe, more than the mechanical and empty respect we have for our own life choices—choices made not in consciousness, wisdom, or knowledge but out of terror, survival, projection, illusion and misunderstanding.

राम राम

Being Straightened

April 4, 2010

Hello. Good evening. *Bonsoir* and welcome, welcome with open arms, with delight, and all the good stuff.

Straightened. Most of us don't like to be straightened all that much. We have talked quite a bit, both in quality and in quantity, about this subject of feedback. Earlier this week a bit of feedback was immodestly offered to someone about the brunch meal on Friday—feedback that was taken stoically (on the outside) when it came from me, but with a bit more evident steam coming out of all upper orifices when offered at a slightly later time by someone other than me. (Is it possible that anyone is "other" than Me?) Afterward, I was ruminating that perhaps "straightening" might be a more useful and more accurate word for this exchange, this process. For after all, by virtue of our identification with our psychology and personality—our false selves, illusions, and delusions—yes, we are bent, crooked, stooped, twisted, "arthritic" in our attempts to function in a real way.

So really, what I aim to do is bring clarity to one's crookedness, to shine a light, or a battery of carbon-arc lights, on the self-denial that maintains anyone's dark twistedness. This applies equally whether the arthritic condition is verbal (in hurtful and proud use of language) or more physical (in gross errors due to a lack of paying attention, or in poor work, as well as Work, habits), or psychological (in sabotage mechanisms, passive-aggressive behavior, unwillingness to give anyone the benefit of the doubt, and an almost endless list of other idiosyncratic gestures of a failure to be in relationship and to seek refuge in Sangha—or the general public, for that matter).

But most of us surely don't like to be straightened, as evidenced by our snarling reactions, defense mechanisms, blame of others, accusations, arguments, stony silence (while we simmer inside, nodding our heads as if we actually had taken it in) and also by our out-and-out failure to implement the information, which is due to either stubborn unwillingness or pretense at confusion and not understanding said information. Somehow it may be extremely useful to your Work efforts, to your transformation, to actively cultivate the wish to be straightened, or at least to take advantage as much as is possible in this straightening help offered, both by myself and by others, when, in regard to others, the help is timely, appropriate and accurate.

Asking me for such input isn't necessarily the best way of approaching such cultivation—in fact it is most often exactly the wrong approach. Better to be aware of when help is flowing your way, as if you could miss it if you were even minimally alert. It is also useful to hang yourself out there—to be who you are, as you are, here and now, even if in this stage of your spiritual maturation you are a ruthlessly self-lying (as contrasted with ruthlessly self-honest), totally mechanical, blundering, fear-ridden, self-hating, pessimistic (but deeply sincere at heart) poseur. Hang yourself out there, and when I am moved to "straighten," I certainly will not hold back, as can be attested to by several of you in reference to this past week's "action."

I came into the Bridge space about fifteen minutes after three people had gathered at my table to play; the table was set up and ready to go, and not one of the three players sitting there waiting for me had dealt the cards. Holy bejesus! I mean, how much trouble could anyone possibly get into by taking the insignificant risk (as to be absurd in its insignificance) of dealing the cards, even if terrified (but not frozen) that such an act of insurrection or rebellion would evoke my displeasure? I mean *really*! This level of paralysis is almost epidemic in the community, and I wish it would take a turn for the better, toward growing up and acting our age. Sometimes it seems that some of the teenagers are more mature than many of the adults (or maybe they just don't care, but I doubt that that's it). So, be willing to make a mistake, and then ingest and digest any direct straightening advice that is the result of your mistake—this is a most important and profitable skill.

On a related topic, at the Bridge space the other evening I was asked an ostensibly innocent question—and of course from ego's perspective, it was innocent, ego-innocent—and, after a simple "no," my response was blunt, unpleasant, harsh and sharp, although could have been, could still be, incredibly valuable and useful to the one who asked the question. So I hope (but doubt) that it didn't go over their head completely. You know, if one gets caught with one's hand in the cookie jar, (or even more embarrassing, in bed with our mother-in-law or stepdaughter, in the act, so to speak), it is pretty hard to pretend that we don't know what point is being made. And yet, when we are caught in the act of asking certain totally self-referencing, Work-irrelevant and Dharma-useless questions, we get this (usually) blank look on our faces as if we have not the slightest idea in the world what is being pointed out.

This brings me to the topic of the vast volume of letters, appeals, and verbal queries that I receive, a great majority of which are about meaningless, insignificant aspects of our lives—but surely not so to ego, to which such little match-head flares are seen as raging forest fires! It is no wonder how little energy we have for sadhana, practice, and grown-up actions, including financial responsibility. (Not only for our self-indulgences but for our obligations, for our Sacred Art. I realize that I have teased, tempted, and cajoled you into much of that obligation—for which I have my most excellent divine reasons—but this is no reason to be sloppy, irresponsible and excuse-making. You may feel that your excuses justify your behavior, but they merely make you appear weak and in denial—not everyone, but most.)

We have been considering, actively discussing, and engaging the Work for almost the entire life of this community, and you should know by now that *energy* is needed to progress and that "prana follows attention," to quote Robert Svoboda. Obviously, when your attention is on minor things, your prana flows to minor things and is therefore *unavailable* for more major things. Needless to say, although you all know, how much *energy* you put into—use up, in fact—on these "tempests in teapots," leaving not enough for the real storms of life. It's no wonder that so many people are tense, stressed-out, and living in fear and/or survival, which is for the most part (but not exclusively) unnecessary and due to bad decisions. These are mostly the result of a failure to follow my advice or input, to take seriously the straightening that is offered, and a lack of energy needed to keep things in perspective—to see or recognize Reality as it is, in fact.

I don't really expect most of those to whom this applies to do anything about it. Why would you? You've had countless opportunities to do something about it over the years and haven't yet, but nonetheless (or nevertheless, if you would like) I offer it as a possibility that *anyone* amongst you has the skills and the being to actually *do* something to alter your neurotic self-serving, chronically mechanical, life-deadening and Path-denying behaviors. After all, what are we here for?

This ain't no weekend workshop about how to change your ego-life to a better ego-life; this ain't no therapeutic modality that purports to give you sanity and clarity. This is a traditional Transformational Workplace, a genuine alchemical laboratory, if you will—and that's transformation in the vertical, not the horizontal. This is not a consciousness-raising, coffee-klatch-cum-bridge-club, garden club, Jay-Cee, Shriner-convention social scene. Where is your "magnetic center," your "center of gravity"—to use Mr. Gurdjieff's language? If it is fixated and focused on irrelevant and insignificant drama with regard to the real demand or Real Work that you are presented with *all the time* (and on a silver platter, I will add), then what are you doing wasting your time and juice? You all know better that that. You do.

Your grossly exaggerated concerns (relative to what they are concerned with) are not only burdensome but counterproductive. How about putting all of that "buzz" into *attention* on the teaching, practice, *tapas* (not just going through the motions because you "should"), and developing maturity in action and speech, in thought and emotion. If you're going to use up whatever available prana you manage to reap, why not use it up on sadhana instead of on petty egoic concerns? That would have many benefits to you personally and to the Sangha at large, as well as to me. So, instead of my scurrying about chanting, "I'm late, I'm late, for a very important date!" I can get on about more important business—sacrifices that Yogi Ramsuratkumar would then be free to Surrender me to. So, when I finally do get to the Mad Hatter's tea party, I can be relaxed and radiant. Yes?

One last thought for tonight. It is ongoingly amazing what a fabulous body of talent, skill, and potential we have here (and in Europe, Canada, Mexico, et cetera) in the Sangha. At the same time, it is frustratingly maddening how much of that talent, skill, and potential is handicapped, in some cases severely, by the blinders we wear—by our in-the-box, dogmatic, self-sabotaging, narrow, and unnecessarily limited views of ourselves and the possibilities outside of ourselves. To a large degree, we *will not* step out of our orthodox, stilted, miniscule worldview into the vast plane and multi-dimensional world of *drala*, of Objective Magic.[1] And we *will not* "jump the octave," because we are unwilling to be straightened—in spite of mental wishes to, often accompanied by

---

1 Drala is a word from Tibetan Buddhist teachings meaning the natural magic and essential wonder that informs the Universe and all worlds.

many tears and much heart-beating and in some cases not a little bit of guilt (as if we didn't deserve the largess of the Universe poured liberally into our lives).[2]

It is nothing more than our own psychological scripts that keep us under the thumb of diminished function, struggling to get our heads above water but struggling uselessly; we *are* our own failure, our own refusal, which is far deeper and more powerfully defining than our lite wishes to be different. (The attendant emotional dramas don't necessarily make our wishes more than "lite.") *You are working against yourself.*

Of course in a few rare cases we could say that there are karmas at play, but hey, doesn't the power of the Guru—not to mention the overriding Benediction of the Divine, of Father in Heaven—transcend Karma? It damn well *can*—but it depends on you. So this straightening that I offer so liberally and so unsentimentally these days is *for you*, to serve *you*, to be a source of Help so that you have aid in breaking out of the stultifying "glass ceiling" limitation that keeps you just sitting on the shelf gathering dust (and paeans of denial, doubt, and insecurity) rather than fully expressing and *enjoying* the vast creativity and profit-earning realities that, in essence, are true of you! (Profit-earning for the Work, of course, but hardly free from worldly profit, something many of you seem to be quite lacking in these days, and some of you for years and years . . .)

I don't seem to be slowing down in this straightening function but, things being what they are, it could cease in a heartbeat, in the blink of an eye. So, while it is so prevalent—both through myself and through many individuals in the Sangha, whom I have asked specifically to carry on these efforts—it would greatly avail you, all of you, to take full advantage and throw yourselves at the

---

2 "Jump the octave" is a term used in the Fourth Way teachings of G.I. Gurdjieff, meaning to make a spiritual leap to the next level of evolutionary potential.

mercy of the straightening and beg for more, in fact. But listen, you can't just make the gesture, if the gesture is not truly surrendered, backed up by your utter helplessness and hopelessness. As most of you should know by now, empty gestures only produce empty (or *no*) results. So, the plastic false smile you plaster on your face while nodding your head in agreement, mouthing "yes" or "okay" or "got it" when I provide you with a moment of straightening, just will not—*will not*—effect the desired ends. You have to really bow, on bended knee or in full-out pranam, to the illusion shattering that is inevitable when you are moved beyond your personal world and into the mad, mad, wide world of God, Guru and Path. You can't fake or out-wit this one—not that you ever did or could, which was just one more of your arrogant delusions.

If you truly want to be straightened at last (and what a relief *that* would be, though so different at first as to feel wrong, out of place, and ill-fitting), stand up "straight" and take the place in the Work that you took incarnation to realize. Get with the program—Mine, not your habitual one, which you are already with more than enough! If you truly want to be straightened—not just tonight, when you are carried by a wave of enthusiasm or inspiration, but ongoingly—you will need to Pay Attention, Remember and submit. If you don't integrate and digest and *act*, the input is no more than hollow words, a kite blowing flightily in the wind, looking good but still firmly attached to the string of your denial, refusal, lack of honest self-observation and chronic illusion.

Remember, *I'm on your side!!* I have Faith in you. (I better, eh, since we're what we've got!) And I cannot turn away from the needs and demands of the Path. So . . . the ball is in your court, to use an apt sports analogy. Thank you for your patience. This is a rich, rich time in our community history, let's reap the rewards!

Jai Guru, Jai Guru,
Jai Guru

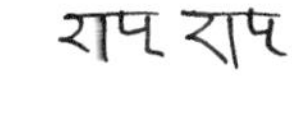

The Spirit of the Law

April 11, 2010

As the first volume of my biography is underway and Mari plows ahead, skillfully of course, in interviewing those students who were present during the 1975-1980 inception of this community, it becomes increasingly interesting how the stories, memories, and accounts of happenings vary—in some cases quite dramatically. Were one a stickler for the "facts," for an exactitude of accuracy relative to events, such a one might well despair of ever coming to the "truth"—that is, to the "letter of the law." Even amongst accounts that were written then and there, at the very time of the experience, given a few weeks for reflection and penmanship of course, there are disparities. And this is only a few years ago!

It sheds a glaring light on "historical" data, eh? If one were to somehow measure the "spiritual maturity" of those telling contradictory tales, one would find the results to be fairly even across the board. That could, or may, lead us to the conclusion that our memories and our interpretive faculties do not necessarily have anything to do with our maturation as devotees. Now *that* is fortunate, is it not?

Recently a black man, somewhere in the western USA—an excellent student, a hard-working and responsible employee who was born in America but had no "papers"—was recently caught with one joint (marijuana ciggie) in his pocket; he was sentenced to ten years in jail. Should we still be exceedingly naïve and consider ourselves an intelligent culture? Yes, there is the "law," and it is important, even vitally so; at the same time, there is the "spirit of the law," which embodies a mood of spaciousness, heartfulness, an ability to see beyond or rather through the outer appearance of things—a view of "what is, as it is, here and now" on all levels, which is Reality. To adhere to the rigid and unyielding not to mention unfeeling, unempathetic, unrealistic, and uncompassionate "letter of the law" when circumstances prove to be unique or circumstantially "special" in some way (à la the tale *Les Miserables*) and in turn to ignore the "spirit of the law" is to live in a world of sorrow, injustice, righteousness, frustration, anger, blame of others, vengeance, pride, arrogance and ungodliness. We wouldn't want to live *there*, would we?

In this case, a reasonable question (although I would add that reasonableness is not *always* an effective response to the calls of the Work) might be: How to distinguish between "letter" and "spirit," especially when either one could be applicable under various situational manifestations? I might suggest that a mood of generosity, of kindness, of *good will* never hurts and usually helps.

Someone was on the phone two weeks ago fielding a call from an obviously distraught person, and the man on our end said, "I refuse to be yelled at!" and slammed the receiver down without hesitation or a second thought (or a moment's consideration or remorse). Now, I don't imagine any of us likes to be yelled at, especially in accusatory terms, even when it is the Spiritual Master who is doing the yelling—not even those who are adoring, worshipping, dogmatic zealots and Hohm Church fundamentalists. I am not a friggin' idol, and although your love is precious and divine to me, when it fails to take into account your egoic failures to practice rightly, it is of little avail in the big picture—it is neither entirely wasted or useless, nor is it entirely productive and profitable either.

In any event, I don't imagine that any of us enjoy or delight in being yelled at. But suppose the caller was dying, or imagined themselves to be, or had been in agonizing pain for years? What if they had seen their personal, professional, and creative life disintegrate around them, and they had three fairly young children to care for and had been abandoned by friends and family alike, and they discovered a Hohm Press book that they believed might relieve their suffering or be the cure, if not the answer, to their prayers? Do you not suppose that such a person would be anxious, keyed-up, maybe even hysterical, and would be upset if the conversation with someone on the phone didn't go as they had hoped or imagined? Well, you get the scenario—a very plausible one, I will add. Do you suppose that being hung up on instead of treated with patience and understanding might be devastating? The "letter of the law" is: If you attack me verbally I will cut off communication, even shockingly abruptly. But the "spirit of the Law"? A very different possibility, both for the giver and the receiver.

Lee has said to some of his students, "In all these years you have not moved an inch," or words to that effect. If that is taken according to the "letter of the law" it would be depressing and crushing, maybe even *devastating*. To appreciate a statement like that from the "spirit of the law" would be to comprehend that Lee is talking to *one* of the "I's" and has to because there is no unity, no single "I," no unified "I." Lee is talking to ego, to the psychological script, the life story, the refusal to surrender and to accept "what is, as it is, here and now." To take such a statement, which may be made in a public or semi-public space, and repeat it with the phrase "Lee said" before it, is not only to sow seeds of confusion and doubt but to absolutely misrepresent and *insult* the integrity of the Teaching, the skillful means of Lee (which under other more sympathetic circumstances we laud and applaud as if we know what we are talking about and can be trustworthy around that knowledge), and the "spirit of the law."

We surely wouldn't want to be the object of another's crude and gross misinterpretations, but then we seem to have little problem when we are the one demonstrating exactly such misinterpretations. Sooner or later this needs to stop if you wish to truly be an exemplar of the Three Refuges. Well when, if not now? As I've said to more than a few of you, you need to *RELAX*. You need to be able to apply your better sense to things instead of being imprisoned by your paralytic fears and insecurities. When many of you were children you probably heard, as a way to defuse anger and impulsive reactivity, "Stop, take a deep breath, and count to ten before you say or do anything." Once again, mother was right. Can you do something akin to that now? Instead of counting to ten, repeat Yogi Ramsuratkumar's Name a few times, or remember your Teacher, your Path, your practice.

If I could spend all the time *serving* you instead of apologizing to those in the Sangha who want to apply the harsh and punitive "letter of the law" to those whom you unfairly accuse of injustices due to your narrow and biased viewpoints, the results would be most efficacious, don't you know! So be willing (as it is more willingness than ableness) to apply the "spirit of the law," because it has many wide-ranging benefits.

Please realize that I am talking about an Objective Absolute—the *"Spirit of the Law."* I am not suggesting that in your relaxation you begin to apply the shotgun blast of your worldly subjective personal army of "I's" as if such pathetic attempts were any more than your own wish to be in control and maintain the mechanical and chronic status quo of your ego-script. Please, please, spare us all. The "Law" is not at all subjective. It is defined and exact. Yes, each specific and unique circumstance in every moment demands a specific and unique response or application of the "Law," but this in no way redefines or negates the unyielding, pure, perfectly Objective Nature of the "Law."

In fact this leads us directly to the key point: *You* as you are, cannot—*cannot*—hope, dream, or *do* relative to this issue. In fact there is no individual, no separate one who can effectively apply this principle. Only God can. Only Reality can. Only Truth can. Only Life can. Only the ultimately intelligent Universe, the Divine, Holy Presence can.

Aw shucks! And here I could feel some of you just on the edge of an inspirational event, almost a conversion, feeling, "Yes, *I* can do this!" No, you cannot. *You* as you are cannot! You must be taken, Ravished, Ruined, consumed, abandoned to Surrender, for only in a state of Surrender, of tacit Faith, can this *Law* be both realized and lived. The dictates of the *Law* apply to God. Man, as he is, is like a fish out of water, flopping around, twisting and turning in paroxysms of survival, occasionally hitting the mark, more often missing the mark, but still untransformed—still lead, not yet gold.

What to do, what to do? Prayer is always an option, and not a bad one, I would add! And let us not forget practice. For example the "spirit of the law" is to eat *on the recommended diet* unless specific circumstances demand or suggest a more liberal approach, such as the need to be a good guest, to make your parents happy by eating what they offer you (without saying that they are just under the illusion of separation and *you*, ah yes, *you* are a real *sadhaka* doing *tapas* maybe even for *their* sins as well as your own!), or to share a bite of your child's food. The "spirit of the law" is to meditate daily unless you are either too ill to get out of bed, carrying a communicative illness which you would do well not to bring in the hall (but you certainly can meditate in your own space), and so on. So let us take this consideration deeply to heart and see what results transpire, eh?

Oh hells bells. There I was, eyes closed, just about to drop into a fitful nap when the momentum of this bright consideration just wouldn't trail off. So a few more thoughts on the matter. Surrender isn't a "thing," a discrete object (or subject), and yet it just needs a space in which to abide. That seems paradoxical, but really is not. As simple as that. Several things define this space or "chamber," if you will, such as Faith, reliability, integrity of action, word and thought (but not necessarily impeccability—after all we are human) and, perhaps most importantly, *emptiness*. If *you* are present, there is no room for Surrender, which requires *a lot* of *room.* You cannot and will not be Ravished if your ego is poised (poisoned) and ready to co-opt the Beloved's Attention and Gifts.

These ideas do not demand an aggressive approach, such as more study, more meditation, more, more, more, more japa, more intensity. Neither is a totally passive (by ego's definition of that word) approach necessarily effective. One needs to empty out, to empty the vehicle of *you,* of your personal, psychological preferences, demands, and so-called needs, most of which are not needs but desires. You need to serve others radically and dynamically whether you agree with them or not, and serve quietly and unobtrusively (if possible) without saving chits or IOUs that you plan to redeem later.

Do you think some people spend an inordinate amount of time catering to blood family? Serve them without complaint, animosity, envy or criticism. You think some people are massively self-indulgent? Every time I read Brother Juniper's Tariqat about what goes on "behind the scenes" so to speak in the Ashram kitchen, I weep—the selfishness, the refusal to take responsibility to do the dishes or to stop using the Ashram as if it was your personal apartment, and in so many other ways, like the grossly irresponsible relationship to the Ashram vehicles. Yes, every time I read his *accurate* accounts, I weep bitter tears, for *you* my dears, for you. I appreciate that these things do *not apply* to everyone, but nevertheless they apply to those to whom they do apply, and it's a stain on all of us. You think some people are so self-referenced that you'd like to choke them? *Serve* them, freely and willingly without aggression or hoping they get their come-uppance. How to become empty? *SERVE.* Surrender doesn't like "roommates"—it likes an empty space, clean, free of garbage and clutter. *Empty.*

Can you do this? *Yes,* a thousand times *yes*! Will you? I am counting on it. I have Faith in you, so "throw me a bone, will ya" and get on it as soon as possible, so I can celebrate your Ruin with you. I'd love that, and I'd fully appreciate it as well.

Listen: Give the Beloved an inch and He'll (She'll?) take the mile. Don't make it a business deal, full of *mutual* reward and expectation. Give the Beloved an inch completely free of contractual obligation and the Beloved will pick up speed—cautiously at first, we being the sneaky, sophisticated ego-beings that we are—but finding you Faithful in your resolve and in your Adoration and free as well of wants and supplication, the Beloved will fill the emptiness with Itself and all that implies.

Ah, that's better, now that that little addendum has been added, so good evening, good tidings and Jai Guru, Jaya Guru Raya.

राप राप

The Refusal

April 18, 2010

I've been being a bit blunt lately, so if this is too-too, forgive me. There I was at the Bridge table and someone says to my partner, "I can see your cards," because my partner's cards were angled in a particular way. And I said, "They have been holding their cards that way for fifteen years, so I'd just look." And I added, "Anyone who has been told that three times should never hold their cards like that again. They deserve to lose."

And there *we* are. It's not that habits are so difficult to self-observe and coincidentally alter. No, no, no, no. It is that we REFUSE, we categorically refuse to shift our internal relationship to our psychological script, to our life story. We are rarely conscious, though not always, of this absolute REFUSAL, and that is the addendum. We REFUSE to become conscious of our REFUSAL, in spite of our profound commitment to the Path, our Teacher and Sangha, and the breadth and depth of help that is available at our fingertips.

So, as I am fond of saying, "What to do, what to do?" I might add, and will in fact, that such REFUSAL is a burden to the teacher, and after a certain amount of time, such burdens become heartbreaks. Do we care? Superficially, of course, but it seems not enough to actually *do* anything about it, even though we have a workshop full of tools at our beck and call and at our disposal as well. Pay Attention, Remember, Self-Observe, really take the help offered seriously enough to be willing to admit that not only are we wrong, *dead* wrong, but that we cannot do this without help. Take the help seriously enough to understand that as smart as we are—as talented, creative, wealthy, successful, healthy as we may be—we are not always right and others always wrong; understand that all of our so-called gifts are no more than ego's manifestation and will pass away with our bodies (or minds—dementia anyone?).

Do you want Heaven or to remain in hell? Sooner or later you need to decide—soon enough to be able to do something about it, but not so soon that you are completely incapable of any real transformation. You need to really decide, not just make a decision with the "I" that has found the spiritual river and dipped its toe in. You need to decide so firmly that you are willing to see yourself as you are: asleep, a liar, totally self-referenced, abusive and inconsiderate to your friends, family and teacher, especially when your desires contradict the direction of life and the needs of the immediate space. As they say in the Landmark Education programs, you are running "a racket," and unless you see it for what it is and stop its dynamic dominance over you, you will never be who you can be.

What inspires us, what provokes us, what actually *moves* us to do something about this state of invulnerability that we allow to persist? We have to allow the Truth to penetrate the almost impermeable skin of our fortress of ego. We have to hear and see objectively. And we must have true empathy—called compassion?—for all those whom we criticize, feel superior to, dislike, have personality clash with and so on. "Love thy neighbor as thyself"—something almost impossible to do if we are inauthentic with others and with ourselves.

There is no gradual path to Surrender, Faith, Obedience. Of course we can and *should* "fake it till we make it," and we can "practice like our hair is on fire," and we can make strides towards maturity, but in fact we are or we aren't. As the "one rotten apple spoils the bushel" adage goes, one area of REFUSAL effectively avoids Grace.

The Beloved cannot be bothered to do therapy on its host—or to clean the space because you have failed to do so. If you want to be ravished, your Essence must be truly pure and *reliably* trustworthy, not merely situationally so. Look puppies, you can flit around the edges of this business—as some of you are still doing in spite of huge sacrifices you have made to live this refined life—for lifetimes, but such tentativeness isn't really profitable. No one is getting any younger, are we? And there is no time (literally as well as metaphorically) like the present. When will you do it, and if not you, who?

You need to pierce this REFUSAL, this petulant teen-age REFUSAL, this resistance to the wave of the Work. Will you be inundated? Yes, of course, but after all, that was your entrance fee, your Cosmic Agreement. You can plead ignorance or confusion all you like, but all that is just wasting time and causing great frustration to your teacher. You have already "taken refuge," so how about honoring that vow, that contract, that commitment? How about honoring it with real sugar on it (not all those rainforest plant saps they use for sweeteners these healthy days).

Here's another small point: The REFUSAL cannot be hidden. It is certainly not invisible to just about anyone except maybe you, and it cannot be suppressed, as that within you which suppresses things isn't nearly as powerful as that within you which is the REFUSAL. This REFUSAL cannot be overridden by an act of will or by an ongoing effort of will; it is stronger than your puny will. It is a force of nature, ego nature. The only way to begin to deal with it is to admit that it *is*, to allow yourself to see it clearly, to accept that it is true of you and begin to notice it *whenever* it rears its defiant head. And later, even to notice it in its quiescent state, which is *all the time* when it isn't being overtly expressive.

In other words, you are not the innocent victim of circumstances or of your teacher's personal animosities (of which the teacher probably has many). You are a false self who assumes you are true; you are identified with a vehicle that perpetually lies and cheats, is devious and even sinful, one could say. The being in you which is conscious (or can be) never questions, as the false self has convinced you of its integrity, its trueness, its reality. But it is all one big, albeit very complex and sophisticated, illusion.

So first, as a primary step, you must begin to question not your dharmic certainties but the tacit certainties of your "rightness." The vision of how wrong that assumed "rightness" is will most likely be quite a shock. At first you won't want to believe it because it will seem so foreign, such an ill-fit to *everything* that you have blindly accepted as real. So be prepared to persist, to be tenacious, and to consider a profound faith in the Truth of the Way. (Even if the Teacher is a bit "eccentric," don't ya know!)

You will need to be able to hold (and hold on tight) to the "big picture"—the perspective of how much time, long periods of time, it takes both to mature and to begin to realize the universal pattern to this all, as well as the internal mechanisms that need to be aligned for it all to make sense. Patience, forbearance, spaciousness. Please. Yes, *please.* I have taken to pleading, begging, *imploring* of late, as I'd like the seriousness of this situation—of your REFUSAL, how counter productive it is to you, and how painful it is to me, beyond painful—to sink in somehow.

For I am here for you, for your transformation, and as long as there is REFUSAL, well of course there will still be progress on a horizontal level, a deepening of practice both in terms of understanding and action, but I'm here for the *vertical* movement—you know, up Jacob's Ladder. After all, any decent healer or therapist, coach, or seminar trainer can facilitate horizontal maturation, as you all know full well from all your seemingly endless love affairs with healers, therapists, coaches, and seminar trainers, all of which may have moved you *along* nicely, but have they moved you *up*? If you are truly self-honest, you must answer "no." And if I cannot do my job, for whatever reason, I am not fulfilling my obligation to my Master, to Yogi Ramsuratkumar, and barring that, I really have no reason to continue to be here (as much as I love my children and granddaughter and those others).

So . . . Refusenicks, check it out, check it out, and let's get down to business (and it ain't business if there ain't profit, as Mr. Gurdjieff said) and down to Work. The Laws of the Work do not bend just because someone has a good heart and a bit of sincerity. We need to "fall in line" or drop and give the Sarge about 250. And that ain't no fun, especially in the mire of one's loose "ego-bowels." I realize, of course, that many if not most of you really don't want to let go of your "precioussss." You love it, you worship it, you enjoy it, even if that enjoyment comes in the form of misery to yourself and to your loved ones.

Ah well, *mes amis,* sooner or later, you'll have to make the choice of perpetual stagnation or Divine movement—the choice to stay in the School as baggage or as one who serves the process, the Work, or to be spun out to rot in purgatory, one form of which is "ignorance is bliss." Many if not most of you have already seen too much, so your options are "get with the program" or continue to suffer—that of course is your privilege, although the suffering you cause to others is not your privilege but is sacrilege. Many if not most of you are far too self-centered, far too deep in your REFUSAL to care enough to make a difference, but it doesn't hurt to consider the ideas, at least.

To return to the Bridge table, where we began this illustrious sermon: It is shocking to see how many smart people absolutely REFUSE to make the truly *insignificant* effort to familiarize themselves with the guidelines of the game, which the Bridge fundamentalists call *rules,* so they can play intelligently as a matter of course rather than doing the proper thing purely randomly, or by accident even. And it is further mind-boggling to recognize how many of these geniuses REFUSE to apply the even more insignificant attention to the game to remember whether they are in their hand or on the board at the play of each round.

These are *blatant* slaps in the face to your partner (and yes, you can apply these principles to your relationships in general, as it *does* apply whether you like it or want it to or not), and a gross insult, a dishonoring, and even a violent act of aggression towards the game, the space, all the players and guests in the chamber and in our case, to the revelatory insight from which this gift came to us. And the saddest part is that many if not most of you *just don't care.* Sure, I know, you have a mental block against card games, or competitive play or whatever, or you just play because you think you're "supposed to." Un-huh. It is a REFUSAL to budge one millimeter from your "script," from your "story."

If you were snakin' after some desired love affair, you'd have the attention of a riveter on the sixtieth floor of an open construction sight. Sure, because that is for *you,* for a you who is a complete lie, a total illusion, a you who exists in fact only in its own mind. I have some bad news for y'all chickens, ducks, and turkeys. This ain't about that "you." It is about service to the other, whoever that other is; it is about surrender to the flow of the Universe. It is not about putting "your" flow on a pedestal and admiring and even idolizing it.

And you can't surrender by your own muscular attempts. You can only be Surrendered. Call it Grace, Blessing, Benediction, whatever. How to negotiate that deal? Apply whatever recommendations I have made in the body of this discourse. Deal head-on with the REFUSAL. Realize that it *is* and work *with* it. For sure if you are working against it, it *will* win.

Well, worms and devotees, I could go on and on, and on and on, but I think I've said enough. Many if not most of you must feel a bit inundated (though I wouldn't say intimidated, as your REFUSAL is too self-referencing to be intimidated). All right, let's rock & roll!

Jai Guru, Jai Guru,
Jai Guru

राम राम

On the Gospel of Judas

May 2, 2010

Jesus, that's Mr. Christ for whom B.C. was established, was often criticized—even by his disciples, but heavily criticized by many others—for the company he would keep and for those to whom he so freely and generously offered his miracles and his Regard, not to mention his forgiveness. Those such as the whores, the publicans, the poor, orphaned, leprous, and mad amongst the Jewish population but also among the Gentiles (the non-Jews) who he commonly preached to: the Samaritans, the Greeks, the Romans, all of the so-called heathen peoples who worshipped idols and practical polytheism.

He always said, and repeated this many times, that he came to teach the sinners, the non-believers, not those who were already leading lives of true practice and abiding by the Laws of Moses. He was also much criticized for shunning the oft-offered hospitality of the wealthy Pharisees, scribes, and other religious leaders of the time, who were all very wealthy from their usury, taking bribes, extortion and so on. He would not capitulate for comfort or ease, and especially not for social or political advantages, when these were offered with hypocrisy and veiled contempt. Bravo Mr. C!

Bill Clinton has said that the biggest mistake of his presidency was not the Monica Lewinsky "affair" but his failure to involve the U.S. in the Rwanda genocide tragedy—he having turned his back on the whole potato, most likely hoping it would blow over or just go away. The violence still goes on today and the details are too horrid to repeat.

As one person aptly testified, some of us will keep a foot in both worlds, this one and the other. For many of you, who are much involved in the "other" world—working in business or as healers or school teachers—it is imperative that you not bring untoward prejudices to the "sinners" whose company you keep. After all, who needs the Teaching more than the lost and suffering hordes of the naïve, confused, and even ignorant?

And how does the Teaching get communicated? Not by preaching but by *being*. A compassionate, forgiving, and forbearing comportment, actively expressed through one's manifestations in relationship, go a lot farther to touch the heart of the needy than your words, which are often the wrong words for the person or circumstance. If we are to function freely, clearly, and effectively, we cannot ignore the vast landscape of denial, psychological aberration, misery and pain, doubt, depression and epidemic narcissism. Of course there is a long tradition of those whose lives are defined by a more contemplative or renunciate practice—the Christian monastic orders and convent orders, the Cistercians, Benedictines, and all the rest, and many of the Tibetan Buddhist orders of temple "live-ins."

In our tradition, there must inevitably be such practitioners, but they will always be, at least quantitatively, in the minority. For most of us, it is the very world we shun (and with extremely good reason) that most needs what we have to offer. It is here within our own tradition, within our own energetic body, that the toxic cells, organs, glands, and systemic orders of flow, metaphorically speaking, must be purified and cleansed if the Blessing Force and Drive of Benediction of Yogi Ramsuratkumar and the Lineage is to be optimally effective.

The Gospel of Judas is a recently published historical document, with scholarly commentary by the translators of course, that was unearthed with the treasure trove of sacred Coptic scripture that came to light in Egypt in 1970. In this gem of a fragment, Jesus is bemoaning to Judas the fact of how many of his disciples, even the closest, are unreliable when tempted by the glitter of the world at that time—wealth, religious authority, devotion from adoring sycophants—all in Jesus' name of course. In our time and place, obviously fame, wealth, influence, power and so on are temptations, but it is the subtle ones, like Facebook and the ease of unnecessary email communications, that are at least as seductive and as big a trap—to varying degrees, some truly quite high on the scale—to invalidate our so-called disciplic transmission.

In the ultimate sense of things, in Reality—Transcendental Reality in fact (not in the reality of "thingness")—there is no "other" world; there is only one continuous existence, and it is not separate, any part of it, from any other part of it, in any way. Still, this knowledge, which many of you profess to have and some of those many actually do have, can be the very buffer that our psychological script uses to ignore the world that has such an immediate need for the dharma. Based on that same knowledge, while we put ourselves high above that world (at least in our own minds) in a nice, neat, holier-than-thou fortress, defended by indisputable rhetoric, we are weak and untrustworthy at base by also indisputable personal falsity and lack of authenticity.

We need to figure out, in practical functional terms, how to accept the whole "catastrophe" without being implicated in the "catastrophic." We need to understand what it means, and *how* to "render unto Caesar" as an act of Lawful Justice, not as a collapse into fear, weakness or personal advantage (and without oozing critical expressions such as cynicism, barbed, mocking humor, or sneering contempt). For like it or not "Caesar" *is* and isn't about to disappear in the face of a little "green consciousness." The overriding domination of the political corporate monster is more entrenched than it has ever been in the history of the world; it is more sinister, more devious, and there is no end to its lust or vile evils in sight.

It does not pay to be naïve on any level, including in the knowledge of the wide use of technology as tools by the "dark side of the Force" and their insidious galloping (they left creeping behind decades ago) domination or attempts at domination over every living and non-living being on this planet (with aims and even active plans to extend that to other planets in this and other solar systems). So open your eyes, puppies, for the fate of this here school, this here gen-u-ine Lineage of the True Work will be in your hands soon enough! And as it is said, "charity begins at home," and the most home home is our own personal entity, our body-mind complex. It starts by refusing to be "bought," to be "tempted," to be infiltrated, though many of you already are. And it is twice as hard to fully extricate yourselves from these demonic entities once they've become established in you than to refuse to accept this establishment before it gets in and grows roots—or tentacles, which is a more apt description.

What can I say that I haven't said many times? A friend and mentor of Purna's has said, "If they aren't practicing by now, they're not going to." I don't want to fully embrace that, and yet, and yet . . . I'd love for you to show me that he is wrong. As I've said many times recently, can you? Of course. Will you? That's the real question. Will you?

Listen once again pups and kits, babes in virtual reality land: You only have one Soul, and if you sell that one out, there just ain't no options for what it is you've come here to do. When that one Soul is gone, in the grasp of "the devil"—not the devil who helps and serves us but the other devil—what to do but weep? For there is *no* viable alternative to the value of that Soul; there is no other aspect of you that can both be fed and do the Work. That Soul, your *only* Soul, seduced, fascinated, captivated and thereby captured, effectively stymies and obstructs the Work—and the Blessings—that I can pour upon you like gentle spring rains or monsoon torrents, as is your disposition and more importantly your capacity to use them.

When defined by distraction from the True Work and attention on the false, that Soul, that *only* Soul, is out of touch, out of range, and out of most of its possibilities to advance on the Path, to be Alchemized, to find the inherence in God and Truth that is its birthright and potential, here and now. Why are so many of you so willing to opt for blindness and misery? And not even for thirty pieces of silver, but for a tentative, strategic, and unreliable smile from your "lover," or for your child to do what *you* want them to do because you're unwilling to release them into their own life, or for success in a world that would just as soon crush you into flour and bake you into a loaf of bread for its insatiable lust, greed and inhumanity. Or for recognition or acknowledgement from someone who isn't worth the turds you flush down the toilet (hopefully on a regular basis, and well-proportioned and well-constituted—the turds, not the object of your desperate seeking for "agreement"). Why? This is a question you should ask yourselves and an answer you *need* to realize to move forward, to consider the Transcendental.

Why indeed. In the *Gospel of Judas*, one of the Gnostic sects is implicated in the testimony of Jesus. According to this gospel, this true secret teaching was imparted to Judas and no one else, not even to any of the other disciples. It is this: *This* world was not created by God, by the Almighty, the Creator of All, the Source, the One, but was created by an emanation of God the Almighty—an angel gone bad, incidentally with the name of "the Fool." Jesus was here on Earth to transmit the actual dharma that to free your Soul, you had to submit to *God the Almighty, the One,* not to the creator of this realm. How's that for shocking and dangerous news?

Is it true? What does it matter? Is it useful? It could be if you gave it the benefit of the doubt (like any data that can be valuable nutrition for our sadhana and realization), and let it work on and in you, and if you took it seriously enough to be willing to extract the barbed hooks that have lodged themselves in the gullet of your illusions and your psychological script . . .

राम राम

Vanity, Pride, Lust

May 9, 2010

Good evening. How are y'all? Well, I hope. Glad to be here, I hope.

Ah yes. Vanity. Deal with it now, my friends. There's not too much more humbling an experience than an illness that takes your idea of vanity and puts it through the meat grinder or the shredder, as some of you know full well. Vanity. What is it anyway but a grossly subjective view of a self which you have not been ruthlessly self-honest about, a self that many traditions claim is not more than a fantasy, a phantasm, pure illusion, projection, imagination?

Vanity is personal to our tastes, most of which are obviously defined by environmental factors in our childhood: parental, societal, political, peer group and so on. You all have seen the person with no "style" by anyone's view, who features themselves a real peacock. Vanity. Deal with it now, my friends.

I am hardly suggesting that we become completely lax in personal hygiene and sloppy and uncaring in appearance Simply that we see vanity for what it actually *is*, "as it is, here and now." That we see the essence of vanity (or lack of essence as the case may be), that we detach from and get a perspective, and then a grip, on our investment in having to look a certain way, think a certain way, dress, appear, groom, speak, move, act in certain ways and so on. Now. Before life itself forces us to deal with it.

It's always better to decide for self-observation and objectivity ourselves than to be pushed by mild or harsh circumstances to confront our delusions, our dreams, our opinions and assumptions of grandeur. And unlike myself, who is handling my own situation with somewhat less than dignity, learn to be noble and elegant in your comportment, even on a bad hair day or with soiled pants. Back to that old Brazil nut, "Do as I say and not as I do."[1] Ah well. It's fine to be a bit of a fop, a dandy—as Baudelaire prided himself on being, at least in his early life—as long as it is a clear decision that you hold with humor and a very light grip. But to choke the life out of yourself because you've dripped a bit of bean juice on your clothing doesn't serve you or anyone else. So, vanity. Relax!

Pride. Deal with it now! What is pride anyway but the ego believing itself to be right, accurate, superior to others—not to other egos, because the ego doesn't acknowledge that it is "just" an ego and not the entire truth, life, and light of the being itself. Pride is our way of remaining separate, uninvolved, superficial, and imagining that we are feeling great and fulfilled when in fact we are deeply suffering and something in us knows it, which makes pride a bit hollow, don't ya think? You know, the old struttin' around acting like we're on top of it all when in fact we are just spinning our wheels, lookin' bad (to others, not our egos) and goin' nowhere.

Pride. What to do? Cultivate a sense of equanimity, rather than differentiation, develop a sense of humor relative to your own pomposity and posturing, and those two would be a fabulous start. Have you heard people admit when they are overweight, over-worked, over-stimulated (caffeine or . . . .)? Sure y'all have. And how many of those people take an immediate and *reliable* decision to do something about their admission, *now*? Yes, very few *is* the correct answer, and no one is a strong possibility as well.

1 "Do as I say not as I do" is a teaching phrase coined by Lee in the late 1970s referring to the guru principle as an objective function that operates by dharmic law rather than societal norms, and as such, should not be emulated as a role model.

You all know—or you certainly should by now, as this is hardly the first time we're considering it—that every time you commit to something (even when you're just "shootin the breeze" knowingly or not) and fail to follow through, you reinforce the habit to not do whatever it is. When you admit to something within yourself that, in your admission, implies that *you* would be better if things were otherwise, it is a commitment to actually *do* something about it. Every lack of follow through is another "nail in the coffin," so to speak.

Without an organic gesture or action that is not merely mental or emotional, our desires, wishes, and intentions are all well and good but don't go very far except to generate the very mistaken belief that we are covering ground, when in fact we're planted firmly, rooted (or tied down) and not moving in the least. So if you are going to talk about your need to be different in any domain, along with that testimony there must the agreement with yourself to make a move, to start the process of "recovery," without which the whole shebang will be ineffective and impotent, as flashy as it may appear behind your charismatic "stand."

No need to huff and puff when you're up against a steel wall, one version of which is the momentum you have built up in *not* doing anything about anything, by continuing to reinforce empty dreams of magical change with no personal effort toward the realization of these dreams. If you aren't willing to "stand up and be counted," don't throw your hat in the ring. Such manifestations make for victoryless victories indeed. We all know those who love to mouth platitudes, and who are in no way examples (let alone exemplars) of the fruits of such statements. Try your best not to be one of those.

Back to pride for a moment. As I can well represent the humbling effect of certain breakdowns on vanity, what of it I had, so too can I evidence a similar relationship to whatever pride (more than vanity, much more) has tainted my efforts at integrity and purity.

"My," rather "the," unconscionable snappishness and vile impatience demonstrated so commonly and seemingly easefully have reinforced my plea to you and my prayer to you: Pride! Deal with it *now* before *it* deals with you . . . an unpleasant dynamic for sure.

Lust? It may well be overrated as well. "Sex is only a great thing if you're not getting any." Charles Bukowski. Of course that can be argued. I suppose a lot of it is what kind of sex (poor or unsatisfying vs. great and elevating). Still . . . Obviously lust applies to a far broader category than merely the sexual domain. And what is at the base of lust? The wish or need to fill a hole in ourselves, which selves are completely false and inauthentic to begin with. Hmmm. Does that give pause for thought? It should, though if the pause is a mere few seconds and the thought is flighty and superficial, well . . . I think you can make the connection and grasp the inference.

We are always lusting after something: sex, fame, power, money, comfort (though we usually don't lust after comfort but creep into its clutches with eyes lowered and spines less than erect), material things or more ethereal things, like attention and acknowledgement. We are always lusting after something, and if we stop to examine the roots, the essence of this lust, we cannot help but see that it all comes from that within us—call it ego or chief feature, or the "devil made me do it" syndrome—that in fact *cannot* be satisfied beyond a very temporary euphoria or self-satisfaction. The emphasis here being not on satisfaction but on "self"—obviously the illusory self of the dream, the mechanical demonstration of the psychological script, which has no consciousness of the truth or reality of the matter and therefore no real appreciation or gratitude for the so-called fulfillment of that lust.

Of course it's nice to feel passionate and alive, which we often do during the "chase," during the active process of pursuit of our lusty goal. But hey, why not feel such things because the Divine has infused and is infusing us with Its Radiant Brilliance, with the Light and Glory of Its Magnificence and Its Regality? Why not feel passionate and alive out of a certainty of the intrinsic nobility and intrinsic dignity of our Being, rather than out of the unexamined tumult of the drive for control, domination, possession, and personal territorial aggressiveness, whether that manifests as accumulation of "things" like King Midas' gold or feelings of vengeance, jealousy, envy, competitiveness?

All of these are, of course, very self-satisfying and equally self-aggrandizing, but only to the false self and only in the dream, in our bubble of imagination, fantasy, and hallucination. So . . . check it out, check it out. Remember that even though most of y'all trust me as your Guru and as the wise elder of this here spiritual school—and I know you do, at least to a certain degree and some of you beyond that degree, which *will* (you can count on it) be proven over time—it is best not to swallow what I am saying without personally verifying the truth of these accusations in your *direct* experience, not merely through corroboration from other "dharma mavens"—like M. Gurdjieff, Chögyam Trungpa Rinpoche, and Arnaud Desjardins.

To not *personally verify* through direct, *immediate* (meaning "here and now" and not "quickly") experience is to make an assumption that you've "got it" and based on that assumption can practice it. (You know the old, "I can quit anytime I want to," as related to cigarettes, alcohol, or whatever, turned on its head and metamorphosed into "I can practice anytime I want to" bluster—or is it gambit?) In that case, you have most likely deceived yourself once again and relegated the gems of the Teaching to mentalizations and philosophy.

So . . . one ADT this coming week, which is tomorrow—Monday, for those of you for whom "tomorrow" is too meaningless a generalization. I will sincerely miss you while I am stirring up a few hornets' nests (hopefully) at Purna's Mela in Montana this week, so please do the best you can to be here for dinner and the talk tomorrow—oops, I mean, this very Monday.

I hope to send a reading for next Sunday, a week from tonight, from the sizzling-hot essays I've written that will be read and discussed in Montana, so you *will* be missed, but not forgotten. "Out of sight, out of mind" is a *wonderful* thing, because if we are properly and objectively situated, "out of mind" means firmly ensconced in the "Heart of God." Memory being what it is, would you rather be remembered by ego or by the Absolute? By ego-memory as flakey, hit-or-miss, strategic, and unreliable as it is, or by the memory of the Absolute as a nonseparative, unitive, permanent, ever-present Regard? Hmmm?

God may "forget" your name, your face, your precious hopes, dreams and pretensions, but God will not, *cannot*, forget *you*. Now *that* is good news, if only we could fully appreciate it for the Truth of it and the Nature of it. Ooops. Here I was trying to end and that little jewel popped in! Ah well, God never sleeps, just like Rust. So I will be leaving early Tuesday and would like to wish you—even to *offer* you—a most excellent, wonderful and fulfilling week, free of the evils of vanity, pride and lust and full of the Beneficence, Mercy and Glory of God.

Jai Guru, Jai Guru, Jai Guru

राम राम

"Not What Should Be, but What Is"[1]

May 13, 2010

On this evening Lee was visiting Sat Loka Ashram in Montana; he wrote the following address to be read aloud in Arizona during the darshan program while he was away.

So, I wished to send a package of art to France, and I asked Dasya to check for a price and shipping details. In the process, each time he calls and speaks to a different person, all the "authorities" give him a different answer about the requirements. Does this seem strange, given that the shipping company is very competent, and one would think that the rules for a specific shipment would be exact, clear, and consistent? Well, yes and no. This should be obvious in our multiple dealings with overseas travel, visas, luggage requirements, and other details of "regulations," which are wildly mercurial, all relevant to whoever happens to get on the phone at any given time, and not necessarily in relation to their position or rank within corporate hierarchy.

There are two primary issues: to consider protocol, which includes legal criteria in various circumstances—real estate dealings, financial dealings, et cetera—as well as our particular social and spiritual guideines, and taking into consideration the Laws of the Work. The second issue is the familiar old chestnut, or pecan if you prefer, "the Spirit of the Law" in each circumstance, our ability to read what is "wanted and needed," as Werner Erhard said, and to trust our "read" well enough to act justly and with commitment rather than to capitulate to the easy way out, therefore defaulting to habit, fear, or insecurity.

---

1 "Not what should be, but what is" is a teaching phrase from Swami Prajnanpad, the master of Arnaud Desjardins.

I know that some, maybe many of us, wish desperately to trust "the powers that be"—our government (though it really isn't "ours," even in this Great Democracy), our educational system, our medical system, our financial institutions, insurance companies, and on and on. Ah yes, but alas—and quite possibly alack as well, though I have no idea in the world what "alack" means—none of them as systems, as entities, are reliable in any conceivable way. Some of the individuals within those systems are wonderful, decent, truly good and sensitive, just, and "by the spirit" people. Such people are always working against the devious and oftentimes evil momentum of the juggernaut known as "corporation, legal entity, organization" or whatever.

And why should a spiritual community be any different? Are we not made up of individuals? Individuals at all levels of personal maturity with all degrees of neurosis, even to the point that every spiritual community has a few benign borderlines and even one or two—sometimes well-hidden, sometimes not—psychotic personalities: in other words, individuals at every conceivable karmic dimension, including those whom we could loosely call "spiritually developed."

Even though we have the definition of "community" and the clear intention to work together toward the Great Work, up to a point (which we are clearly attempting to meet and exceed), the individual intrudes his or her priorities—the demands of the psychological script—into and onto the body of practitioners. This is simply "par for the course," in spite of the occasional "holes in one," and in spite of occasional forays into the sand traps or pools of water that inevitably make up a part of the "course."

This entire paradigm is one that we need to recognize and factor into our daily function so we don't spend all of our time reacting to perceived inconsistencies that are just natural elements of the whole. At many times, we have five to seven people actively busy in our ashram office. Any of those people could answer a random phone call: one will take down the message exactly, be polite, pleasant, and competent, while another will be annoyed, impatient, never ask who is calling, get a return phone number, or write it down incorrectly. This, even though both people have been trained the same, have equal intelligence and an equal sincerity relative to their commitment to the Path, equal devotion, and so on.

Each of us needs to be able to work and practice within the given aspects of the field in which we are living. Instead of wishing that reality would conform to our ethical, projected ideals, we need to see reality as it is and work with it, rather than be polarized against it because it annoys or tweaks our sense of "what *should* be." We need to stop being harder on our spiritual community than we are on any ordinary circumstance because we assume that—being involved in the "higher" pursuits of the spirit—we should necessarily be "better" or more competent, less problematical, than any "ordinary" primate and sleeping-world situation, group, or organization.

People are people, and our task is to transcend illusion, not to transcend our humanity. In transcending illusion, yes, much of what defines the average person—blind, mechanical behaviours, hidden motives, all of the psychological weaknesses and aggression that are counter to a life of dignity, nobility, compassion, and in short, a life consciously lived—will be eliminated. True true. At the same time, we need to recognize that this is a process that is often effected over a fairly long period of time, and we need to stop expecting things to be other than they actually *are*—especially when our expectations are tinged with intolerance, unrealistic demands, righteousness, or dogmatic zealousness.

So, patience, forbearance, great spaciousness, and a healthy sense of humor—or a healthy "dose" of humor when our lack of humor is more illness than isness. Well, as is often the case, I don't know how to end these things. So, feeling that the main issues have been adequately covered and not needing to keep making the same points over and over, at least not in this one essay—though obviously repetition has its great value, repetition in the appropriate time, place, and context of course—we will sign off, over, and out (for those of you listening to this on CB), and bid you, as usual, our wish that you take these ideas, make them your own, and allow them to define or redefine your immediate and practical interactions with your world and the larger world of which your world is an integral working part. And, if you do that, my job will have been done and I will be pleased, whether I ever receive direct feedback relative to these issues or not. So I thank you in advance, as a commitment and gesture of my faith in you.

And thank you for your enthusiasm over the small orange booklet.[2] It is the first in a series, of how many I have no idea, but the second one will be in production shortly, and I have ideas for the third and fourth. Then we'll see . . .

And please continue to energize your enthusiasm for ADTs, Bridge nights, and Work Weekends, as well as for Guru Purnima. Your active participation will feed me as I traverse the European continent, holy hollerin' and writin' up a storm!

Please do not judge my current physical state as you perceive and imagine it to be, with judgment, projection, or assumptions. I don't even share with my family what is actually going on and do not need or appreciate a lot of wild fantasies about my health. Hold it without judgment, as much as you can, and live or die (me or you), there can only be profit in cultivating such a mind state. Thank you again, and when I start talking again, you can be sure that news will flow from Europe at the speed of light. I am not being stubborn or naïve, but I am still quite optimistic, if a bit worn out by holding strong in the face of gale winds, even as mercurial as I assure you they are. So, "parting is such sweet sorrow . . . " Have a gloriously profitable summer in all domains.

Jai Guru, Jai Guru, Jai Guru

लाल लाल

2 Lee is referring to the original small booklet titled *Words of Fire and Faith* in which five of his written addresses were published at his request.

Yes

May 14, 2010

Hello. Welcome. I would like to make a request of you all. I have spent much time, energy and effort maintaining an optimistic overview of this little health lila. I realize that the failure of my voice to function relatively normally and the failure of my saliva glands to stop working triple overtime and the fact that I have aged ten years in the past year may appear to you, may seem to indicate, that I well may be on my way out, that things are goin' downhill, gettin' worse and that I'm bettin' on a losin' hand, and so on.

Spare me, please. I don't need, and certainly do not appreciate, to put it mildly, a bunch of negative, short-sighted, uninformed, ignorant, maudlin, sentimental, and culturally-biased projections, comments and/or concerns, silent or not. I have enough to carry and bear enough burdens already to actively wish to discourage any unconscious and mechanical reactions to your subjective and myopic observations. Once again, spare me.

I, or my appointed spokeswoman, will be reading this request for context prior to the essay of each session when we come together over the days, so no one misses the point (except those who miss *every* point, which includes a fair number of ya'll, but ah, that's another story for another time). Onwards...

Yes. It's a versatile word, used to affirm, assert, or to hide behind, and it's the subject of this small epistle. In its objective meaning, it defines reality as it is: a submission to truth that is reliable in its consistency, trustworthiness, vision and wisdom.

Yes. I accept life in its full spectrum and in its total beingness, as surrender to the Will of God, as the nature of "intrinsic dignity and intrinsic nobility," to quote Swami Prajnanpad, the guru of Arnaud Desjardins, a genuine representative of "yes," as was his guru and his before him, and his before him (which is a not-too-subtle indication of the value, maybe even *need*, of lineage). Ah, but as sweet as that is, that is not the topic of this little sermon.

I recently pointed out to my bridge partner how a play he made was basically senseless. He noticed it and said "Yes," with some enthusiasm, I might add. This is the same partner whose cards were visible to the person on his right, on the opposing team, and who had been holding his cards that way, and still is (!!) after over fifteen years of reminders, including my recent public teaching about such things.

Do you think, can you even imagine, that his "yes" meant anything? Of course it did to him. He fully believed that he got what I was pointing out, and in that moment he well might have. But in the *very next moment*, and certainly by the next morning, that "yes" meant nothing; he will continue to play according to the logic, faulty though it is, that caused him to manifest the offending play. (It was only offensive to me, as no one else in the game noticed anything, bubbled and encased in their own self-centered logic, such as it is, as they indubitably are.) And guess what, predictable automatons, just a couple of days later, he did exactly the same thing! Literally. The next time we played bridge, he did exactly the same thing in exactly the same circumstance.

For most of us, our "yes" is just a way to get the hound off the scent, to keep the piercing eye of the Work at bay, or/and (for they all may and probably do apply) an ostensible wall to hide behind, even as we believe that we are sincere and authentic in our agreement or affirmation. But when our "yes" is so immediate, thoughtless and glib, how can we take it seriously?

I have been poking one stalwart devotee for years, and more vigorously of late, relative to her lack of self-honesty, self-observation, and ability to follow through; just about *every time* I launch a dart, or missile as the case may be, she nods or speaks a "yes." I've been asking her not to say "yes," as her "yes" is so far from a real or objective commitment to do what she is affirming that she understands—all to no avail, because she continues to "yes" me with predictable regularity while she continues to REFUSE, to resoundingly (resounding to everyone but her) fail to *implement*.

We say "yes" within the belief that we are definitely "on the same page," but we aren't. We are avoiding the real issue, which is our REFUSAL to look at ourselves unreservedly with the microscope of the Work; to feel into the indicated help offered and to begin to practice with intelligence relative to the laws of the Work and the graceful offerings of the Universe.

So our "yes" is not the "yes" of recognition, the "yes" of wisdom, the "yes" of a sophisticated embrace of the teaching, but is the "yes" of avoidance—a weak, albeit unconscious (which need not be so if we are self-honest, ruthlessly self-honest, and profoundly practicing self-observation of our internal and external states and what is, as it is, in the wider sense of our environment, circumstance and field of activity) and chronically mechanical (which need not be, if we are willing to *study* the ideas of the Work, eat them and digest them) attempt to remain as we are, undisturbed, unruffled and blind, mired, comfortably of course, in our psychological script and life story, convinced of our personal authority, our rightness, and our superiority in spite of massive amounts of data to the contrary.

I'm talking about our belief in our rightness and our superiority in spite of massive amounts of data to the contrary. Data we have avoided like the bird flu—Ah ha! Bird flu...pitiful! "Oh my God, the millennium is coming! Water! Rice! Toilet paper! Oh my God! 2012 is coming! The end of the world is coming! I remember what the Mayans said!" *Pitiful!*—or shrugged off as the poor and helpless frustrations of a Universe and a circle of friends and family who just don't understand us. What fools we are! How lost and how defeated we will be when our suffering becomes unavoidable in the awareness that hopefully will come before death of the body or mind. Madness, anyone?

Here is the domain of our work, not there. Here. Yes, here is the domain of our work, not there, and how shocked we will be when we recognize the illusion of our identification, our seamless identification with the false self and our delusions of clarity and spirituality. As usual, it is "if not now, when?" and "if not you, who?"

It is so simple. Such a tiny, teeny, but not weenie, exercise to see our "yes" for what it actually is, to acknowledge the paucity—or poverty if you will—of our working being. To come to terms with our *lie*, our *deceit*, our *refusal*.

As usual, I would suggest: Can you do it? Without question, or of course, if you prefer. But the real question is: Will you? (It's a question that most of you, even those of you who are here, have answered "no" to, after your inauthentic and unholy, not to mention hypocritical "yes," time after time and time again for *years*!) The real question is: Will you?

Well, I think we've at least scratched the surface of the subject, eh? Thank you for paying attention, at least with the "I" that is paying attention, and no thanks to the "I's" that will disregard this consideration as soon as it feels safe to do so.

राम राम

Legacy

May 23, 2010

Good evening, hi, hello. For those of you who were at brunch this morning, thank you so much for joining me, allowing me to celebrate just before leaving for Europe.[1] I am full, thank you again. I have a little secret: I planned this one just yesterday, and for me. Is that too selfish? I think this little health lila is giving me the opportunity to develop and cultivate just a little bit of humility. So, on to tonight's readings.

Between myself and my body of students, we have produced both a marvelous and prodigious body of Dharma work—I mean in written form, not in the domain of being, although that too, and without that, the body of Dharma work would be neither marvelous nor prodigious and nothing but empty flash, "lookin' good and goin' nowhere." And to what end? As the lead character in the movie *Iron Man 2* (a most excellent little trifle of entertainment) said, "It is about legacy."

You and I, all of us, will pass away, perhaps to be sentimentally enshrined by some few of our loved ones, but nonetheless to leave this world of illusion, confusion, suffering, and its rare moments of true beauty and joy, hopefully less rare and more common as our lives move inexorably toward their extinction. And what will remain? The Work, the Path, the Teaching—Legacy, if we have been so fortunate to have left something Real, something authentic, something of Objective value and, perhaps more importantly, utility.

---

1 Lee cooked an opulent feast for his devotees and served it at brunch on this Work Weekend Sunday.

When we are "disparu"—have dissolved into the "great sea of oatmeal" as the storyteller Gene Shepard used to call his live audiences during his occasional gigs in Greenwich Village in Manhattan in the seventies, and as I am now calling the endless, eternal, undifferentiated (maybe) Absolute—what will remain that indissolubly ties us to the Work, and more importantly, ties the Work to us? For it is our necessity that ties us to the Work, and the Work's necessity, when met by human effort, contribution, and worthiness, that ties the Work to us. And the Work does not betray or abandon Its own.

Legacy. Can we create such a "leaving"—such refuse (trash) of the mortal coil—by an effort of personal will or by the exercise of egoic brilliance, genius, or personal power? No, puppies, no. To produce even "great" works out of our own self-centered and self-referenced illusions, out of that which is false, may create a roaring buzz in the world of the primate (the life of Princess Di, et cetera) but will be of no practical value to a serious practitioner of any Path of Transformation or Alchemy. We are considering Legacy, not just something that people remember in their sentimental and idol-worshipping dream.

Legacy: something of lasting effect, perhaps even a *terma*, to use the Tibetan Buddhist word—a treasure hidden in plain sight, waiting for the perfect time and place to be rediscovered by the appropriate "reader." Something that does not rot as most things do in their mortality and their illusory foundation.

So how does one leave Legacy? Only the Divine can produce that which feeds and nurtures Itself. And only we—disgraceful and laughable creatures that we are—can be the vehicle through which this divine product can manifest, fulfill itself, and meet or even exceed its potential and its possibility. Yes, this, despite the magnificence of a perfect sunset, the vastness of the oceans and mountains, the mystery of space and its endless suns, stars, solar systems, galaxies, and universes, the amazing awesomeness of so much of the natural world. Yes, for better or worse, it is Man who is the vehicle of Return—of God meeting Itself face to face and gasping, confessing at last that yes, His Creation is Good.

Legacy is only created by getting out of our way, by sidestepping the traps and pathologies, the tragic illusions of our identification with the unquestioned separate self, the unreal, the delusory, the fantasy of independent and discrete existence. Yes, only in the Way of Faith and Surrender (and in the Way of Faith and Surrender, there is no such thing as sacrifice because there is no one and nothing to be sacrificed—good news indeed to finally have relaxed the strangling grip we maintain on all that we think is "ours") does Legacy arise, get actually produced into matter, into substantiality, and take on a Life of its own.

So, don't fart around. We have a limited amount of time and energy (this time) and cannot afford to procrastinate, to deliberate too long, to get lost in mind-numbing and Life-fucking philosophizing. (Back to "lookin' good, goin' nowhere—Marshall McLuhan anyone? Peter Max, anyone? Danielle Steele, anyone? And so on . . .) We need to *get on it, stay on it,* and ride that sucker like a fury (sparing the whip and spurs, of course).

As I have probably said too often lately: Can we? Of course. Will we? Well, if recent and ancient history is any indication, probably not, but that is entirely up to us. And, "Hey, baby," as Charles Bukowski and any other number of Legacy leavers might have said, your name will still be associated with such Legacy, though *you* won't give a good Goddamn (or a "flying fuck," courtesy of Kurt Vonnegut) about *that* little ego perk. (Baudelaire anyone? Bach anyone? Rodin anyone? Jesus Christ, anyone? And so on . . .)

So, don't forget to Remember God, don't "reach" for it, don't panic, and as Lao Tsu is reputed to have said in his Tao Te Ching: "Let things settle themselves."

राम राम

Doing the Best We Can

May 28, 2010

Good morning, friends and fellow humans. Yes, and being human means that we may never "get it perfect," so we might well adjust to getting it as good as we get it. I was very pleased to see y'all greedy for the Dharma at tea last evening—being greedy for the Buddha, or the Guru, as you wish, is pretty much a given. Now how about Sangha?

We is who we got, my dears. It is true that in *this* world, friends, family, even complete strangers can be quite reliable, loving, generous, compassionate—and our Refuge in Buddha, Dharma, Sangha touches other realms above, beyond, and untouchable relative to *this* world. So, we is who we got, like it or not, want it or not, understand it or not.

There is no need to "get it perfect," the desire for which is mostly neurotic or misplaced anyhow (or anyway, if you prefer). What we're looking for is doing the best we can, under the circumstances and all things considered, like karmas, genetics, bio-everythings, the planets, and so on. At the same time, understand that we are looking for doing the best we can, not the best our psychological script tells us we can, not the best our friends, family, society, and culture tells us we can, not the best our wild subjectivity tells us we can, and not the best our mind-body limitations tells us we can. We are looking for doing the actual, Real, Objective, Divine best we can.

I also want to thank you, most of you, for adjusting to the "new" Lee Lozowick. I have no time for sentimental politesse. I am driven by Yogi Ramsuratkumar's Blessings, and, as it seems, by my own frustrations, irritations, struggles, and attempts to adjust—there's that word again, "adjust"—to the limitations encountered through this little health lila. So I am driven to get to the point(s) quickly and decisively.

This drive often appears and manifests as a harsh, surgical stab rather than a sweet and gentle feather brush. I have no patience for subtle hints anymore—I've gotta see some *action*! So, forgive me, truly, if I have, do, or will offend you. It's tough times all over and in many domains. But at the same time I'm quite pleased, so far, with the evident results. As the American song goes, "Love is in the air," and it truly is showering its sweet perfume far and wide.

So forgive me, if you must forgive instead of gush with gratitude, wonder, and even awe, but it's sort of like this: get joyous or suffer with even more acute sensitivity than before. I, for one (and it's always been for One), being quite a bit more blown open than ever before, am supercharged with enthusiasm and melting in the majesty of this whole amazing Process—thanks be to Yogi Ramsuratkumar, of course and obviously (hopefully to everyone).

So as you've heard me say many times (but rarely with such intensity or demand), get with the program or feel left really far out and way behind, because we aren't just snailing along here; we're flying! Well, short but sweet—thanks for listening, and let's keep on tearing into it.

राम राम

Field Attention

June 2, 2010

Field attention. Sure, it's a nice concept, but how few of us have it. One of my dear devotees is so desperate to please everyone, and yes, *desperate* is an apt description, that when someone asks how far someplace is, or how long it takes to get to where we are going, this otherwise highly intelligent person *always* tells them what they want to hear (to avoid disturbing them and causing them suffering) regardless, or irregardless, of the facts. Of course such a strategy *inevitably* falls short when a child is told that a one-hour ride will only take forty minutes, not only because after forty minutes the child is really all het up but because very soon the child learns that the loved adult is a liar. Yes, that's right, a *liar* (not a pleasant way to be seen by a child who is attempting to trust one).

Of course to perceive a "field," one must be turned to the other, whether that other is a person or people, an environment or a "chamber," we could say. Since for the usual person, life is by their own commitment "all about me (me, me, me, and I)," how could they—and why would they—even consider anyone or anything else except peripherally and superficially? Of course the person storied above really wants, by moral principle and social conditioning, to serve others and really believes that they are—with about a zero recognition of the littered path they leave behind them (like the typical movie comedy scene of the bumbling idiot, who drops a match in a pool of gasoline as he gets in his car, and blissfully and ignorantly drives away while an entire block goes up in flames and explosions behind him).

I wanted to play bridge the other night in Paris, so I asked the sangha, by way of a public announcement, whether anyone played *well*. A precocious young man, a teenager, answered with great assurance, "Yes, I do." As he sat down across from me, he demonstrated a rudimentary knowledge of the rules, and then as the evening wore on, continued to manifest the evidence that he did not know how to play very well at all; he was just stumbling along (and hanging in admirably, even pleased and smiling as I won hand after hand, having bullied my way into winning the bid). When his obvious exaggeration was pointed out to him, he said "yes," in agreement. He admitted that he just wanted to "play," to which I commented, "Obviously, people believe that because I am the spiritual master I don't care whether I win or lose." Lots of Work in *that one* for you all! Of course his youth and arrogance are good excuses for his lack of "field attention," but at the end of the day, even such valid excuses fail to float.

This point, this subject of "field attention," is not a new consideration; it is, as ever, a most important element in being able to read spaces, to read people, in being able to understand the spiritual master and his needs and wishes (for the Work, of course). We all want to be useful, as Yogi Ramsuratkumar asked of me so many times, and to optimize that usefulness, to allow it to be practically effective, not simply inspiring in a "mental" sense. We would do well, quite well in fact, to cultivate a sensitivity (trained at first but later innate or tacit) to all the various elements—both physical, psychic and backward and forward in time—that are in relationship with each other and make up the holistic space or chamber that is encompassed in the particular field that can be of value or of service in any given moment. It can save someone newly approaching the Work literally years if our response to them is spacious, generous, and intuitive, rather than if we are reactive, brusque, too blunt, or blindly lacking in a "feeling into" their situation.

In order to facilitate this training, this cultivation, we must have stepped out of and left behind our solidity—that hard, rigid mindset of projections and expectations, ever-editorializing, judging and interpreting everything, literally everything, that interfaces with our sense awareness: sight, taste, smell and so on. In immediate terms, we have to cease being no more than our psychological script—the cultural, social, religious and childhood relational data that we have mashed together and identified with as if it were actually who we are in total. We have to be out from under this stultifying domination of our opinions and biases—in short, our *unexamined* mechanical functioning.

Besides what we have already noted, we need to be spacious and generous, relaxed, fluid, open to unexpected and especially unknown stimuli, and ready and willing to move in directions that may not make rational or linear sense to us in the moment and on the spur of the moment. As Devaki Ma said to Yogi Ramsuratkumar under exactly such happenstances, "God works in strange ways, Bhagawan." Yes, strange for us perhaps, but never strange for God!

Have you ever been turned off by being oversold by either a zealous or an unconscious salesman? Sure, and you probably found yourself wishing that this maddening boor, this mindless sales machine, had this "field attention," although you most likely would not have used that exact phrase. The examples are truly countless (or numberless, or endless, or infinite, yada, yada, yada). If you don't want to be one of "those" people, even at the most mundane level, the development of "field attention" is your answer, huckleberry.

People who judge by appearances, assuming some flashy chrome and mahogany fern bar is a fabulous place only because of externals; people who give me various gifts with no thought of what on earth I'm supposed to do with them (utility, space, and ugly considerations); people who judge restaurants by their "rep," wines by their labels, and art only by its dominance of the space have no "field attention." The list is almost endless. We are so convinced of our infallibility that we overrule our eyes, our noses, our tongues and stomachs and our better sense. This is no way to Work.

"Field attention" is a vital and essential ingredient in the practice stew. This "field attention" is a way to read into what actually is so, overriding our grossly superficial worldviews and our fantastic subjectivity. Sooner or later we must come to this because if (or rather when) we don't, our heartbreak, sorrow, anguish and disassociation keep increasing, often to the point of just a shade shy of unbearable. Of course that rawness can be an especially powerful impetus to Work, but on the other hand, who needs it if it isn't really necessary? So get on with it and profit mightily, both spiritually and materially.

राम राम

Ferme de Jutreau, France

Know Yourself

June 8, 2010

We went into a *very* high-end Asian art shop to check out a large Milarepa that was in the window—it was repoussé, seventeenth century, Tibetan . . . and 45,000 euros! One of the people with me, a man of quite masterful knowledge about artifacts, styles, repairs, and those artifacts that have been "monkeyed with," started telling me about the piece. For instance, the main body was bolted onto a base that wasn't the original, the base was empty (no reliquary items, prayers, and so on . . .), and the gold was electroplate, not gilt. By the time he handed the piece back, the shop owner's generous, charming, smiling demeanor had turned to a curt and snarling reaction. When we got out of the shop, my friend said, "What does it mean if the piece is electroplated, considering that technology wasn't invented back then?"

Oh yes. Fakes *abound* here, even in the best places—well, if not out-and-out fakes, pieces that are not entirely what they are claimed to be. Now without a thorough education, none of us would ever guess. And yet without a thorough education about people (which education is best and most fully acquired by knowing ourselves—self-observation, anyone?), we leap into relationships, parenthood, various healing professions and so on, and often, though mercifully not always, the consequences are unprofitable, to say the least. Without a thorough education in money and its uses, we also leap into financial dealings that more often than not leave us smelling like the shit we have leapt into and not the imagined roses.

So it seems to me that if you are going to really get into something, it would not only make sense but be necessary, not always in the short run but definitely over the long run (as in a hit Broadway show—"it's had a long run"), to be as fully knowledgeable in your subject as is possible. One of my suppliers of artifacts here knows stone almost masterfully, but not bronze at all, so he only deals in stone and leaves the other areas to his wife—the bronze, wood and so on.

What subject is more immediate, consuming, ever-present and relative to existence than our humanness, our existence itself? True, we didn't choose this field of endeavor, sort of, but nonetheless it is a given, and it's not like we can just change careers, professions, or go back to school and learn a new subject—although some benignly misguided individuals actually think they can (starpeople, Martians, cat in a human body, anyone?). So everyone knows the truth of this; at least all of *you* who are listening to or reading this know the truth of it. Yet we throw ourselves into diversions and distractions of every size, shape, and color (creative writing, H-O trains, tropical fish, philately or numismacy, astrology, tarot, et cetera . . . anyone?) with far greater and more enthusiastic energy than we do in studying *ourselves*: our minds, our mechanicality, our habits (bad as well as good), and our relationship to Reality as-it-is, the Divine, God, Absolute, Truth.

Yes of course, by being here in the school, on the Path, in the Work, at whatever level and to whatever degree, this demand to know ourselves is always tacit in the background, underlying and permeating every element of our lives. Still, without a conscious or specifically directed *attention* and a fairly sophisticated or trained way of going about this most precious and most profitable study, this subtle, under-the-surface hum does not get efficiently and optimally expressed or manifest. Yes, it is also true that we need to earn a living, support our families, pay rent and insurance and taxes, and we need not allow these pursuits and concerns to overcome and overwhelm us to the point that our real and *most important* aim is obscured—the aim of self-discovery, which is ultimately other-discovery, the other being inclusive of our selves, the True Other being not less nor more than One.

It should be obvious by now that one of the primary, if not the singularly most effective, forms of self-study is self-observation, as Mr. Gurdjieff taught. If we are even minimally intelligent, in fact if we are not totally cretinous, the information gathered in objective self-observation will produce all the necessary connections, all the "aha's," or "eurekas," to the inherence in a knowledge that encompasses relationship, social and political realities, and a profound appreciation and perhaps eventually living practice of intrinsic dignity and intrinsic nobility.

In any event, or in any case, even anyway or anyhow if you wish, the *principle* is clear (although oftimes the principal is far from clear, which would be useful to remember when dealing with him, her or it): the need for education, hopefully leading to knowledge, or at least to a thirst or hunger for knowledge. We surely wouldn't want any of y'all to end up your lives with nothing but a collection of questionable gatherings from your arduous journey—you know, the fabulous spiritual resumé without any substantial or actual value.

As a fun addendum to the opening story, we passed the same shop two days later and the Milarepa was gone. Sold? Retired? Returned to its consignee? Who knows? Perhaps we were of some small use, in my version of the unknown, saving some earnest and perhaps even honest artifact lover from a very expensive mistake. And perhaps again, in your own accumulation of knowledge relative to the important aspect of life, which is Truth or Reality, your willingness to share this knowledge will—even under somewhat tense or politically incorrect circumstances, probably quite unbeknownst to your surface consciousness—save some difficulty or even tragic error for a well-intentioned but as yet naïve spiritual aspirant. One rarely knows the vast distances and wide territories that a seed may cover, planted or simply set to drift on the current of the wind or stream, to finally take root in a welcome and receptive field. So, use discrimination, tact and sensitivity on the one hand, but on the other hand do not be overly self-censoring or chronically insecure when the time to make the teaching available is ripe (or is it rife, whatever that means?).

I'm sure those of you in any profession, from art to *chefferie* to astro-physics, to any New Age pursuit (aura cleansing or astral travel anyone?) know full well that probably the vast majority of the practitioners of that profession are either sloppy, uncaring, and inefficient (all the way to just downright wrong) due to ignorance, believing either that they know it all already or believing in some kind of "free expression" or spontaneity, or perhaps believing that they are "channeling" the Arcane Wisdom of some spirit guide, alien, or past ascended master. And then there are those who are unconcerned with quality, exactitude, or integrity of action, and couldn't care less how the job got done as long as it somehow resembled completion and they got their paycheck or compensation.

So too does this apply to the study of self. Most people do not have the discipline, the tenacity, or the fortitude to persist in the "search for excellence." They will compromise out of fear, laziness, boredom, desperation or whenever the "heat" becomes a bit too uncomfortable. I would like to assume that the select group of individuals hearing, listening to, or reading this small missile of hope, light, and transmission would have a more demanding possibility for themselves than the average pond scum and the wherewithal to follow through.

There are those so-called "antique dealers" who will sell copies or new pieces with full awareness and call them antiques. I would also like to assume that no one receiving this petite sermon would go to such extreme lengths of thievery, lying, and cheating when the one most suffering said abuse is themselves (although the peripheral pain caused to others can be widespread and even extreme). There are those for whom "cutting off their noses to spite their faces" is a modus operandi, but such stupidity—unexcused by ignorance, which as you know from your time in "law school" is no excuse—is really beneath your station (or your plateau, if you are stuck on one).

Now as you can glean from what we have considered so far, clearly there are levels and layers upon levels and layers, shades upon shades. So it doesn't pay to be rigid and dogmatic, assuming you are too pure for a touch of the devil in yer. We're all functioning in many spaces that include a great variety of different influences. What could be useful in our discussion is to realize that you can place your attention and intention on those aspects of this great mélange, olio, stew, that you wish to reinforce, strengthen, and cultivate, and you can ignore or keep your attention and intention off those aspects that are counterproductive, subjective, aberrant or irrelevant—in short, unprofitable.

One of the things you can take from this tirade is the data necessary to make such choices. So please *use* this, not just as grist for the mind, not just as a reflection-prompting catalyst, but actually *use* it to feed, to serve, to intensify, to deepen and to fuel your Work. That certainly is my purpose for it, and should you fail in these efforts, there is always another spark coming next week, not to mention four volumes of the Study Manual, two books of Poetry and essays, eight Journals, and about (I didn't stop to count) twenty other books, forty CDs of music, a number of DVDs and so on, all designed and executed (produced, not ritually slain) with the same aim. Ah yes. Have a delicious, wonderful, bright, and productive week.

राम राम

Good Enough is Good Enough

June 17, 2010

As y'all know (as I have mentioned this many times), much of what I would prefer—in some cases highly prefer—to do for myself, I give, offer, or allow others to do for me. The profit of service well-rendered is great and in a few instances even inestimable (on the great side). The vast majority of the service provided is quite adequate; the job gets done relatively competently and in a timely fashion, and on we go to grandmother's house, following the yellow brick road, or to further adventures of other sorts. Sometimes the service is useless at best, irritating or annoying, and at other times it is excellent—a very satisfying state of affairs for me, I must say.

In any event, there is no lack of enthusiasm on the part of devotees to offer themselves to this process, and no lack of pretension on the part of devotees to believe that what they are doing is what I want and that how they are doing it is how I want it done. There is no lack of skill on the part of devotees relative to their potential to serve, and at the same time, there is no lack of interference from those devotees' psychological scripts, rendering what could be excellent service to merely adequate service.

Well, I'm glad to have the job done, happy for the "good works" that benefit the Path, as well as the karmic and merit-gaining accumulation of devotees, and at the same moment more and more impatient with only adequacy in the place of excellence. Adequate is, well, adequate, but at this stage of the process, in this inning of the game, it is becoming less and less acceptable. I have said, and still affirm with definite agreement, that "good enough is good enough." Yes, as a statement and as a manifestation this is absolutely true. But "adequate" is *not* good enough. It falls short of—in some cases quite far short of—"good enough."

"Good enough is good enough" is a principle of my Teaching. "Good enough" refers to the holistic field of its expression. "Good enough" is a completion relative to elements of a process in which what could be called excellence is unnecessary—an exaggerated or overdone effort that often not only complicates or obscures but even ruins or destroys the most effective or useful results, sort of like turning a perfectly contextualized "spirit of the law" event (or work of art) into no more than a flawless, technical "letter of the law" paean to heartlessness and cool intellectualism, something pleasing to brains with no comprehension of the body's play of existence.

Adequacy is actually a failure to meet the mark: a striking lack of understanding of what is "wanted and needed," just getting the job done to get the job done without any deeper insight into the various ingredients of the whole multidimensional, multifaceted system that is being served, worked with, or within. Simply put, to do a job adequately fills the hole but does not fully accomplish the necessary demand. And, as I mentioned briefly earlier in this essay, most of what comes down the pike passing for competency is merely adequate, meaning that even though the job gets done, so to speak, the results are still disappointing.

This consideration is intimately tied in with the whole ball of wax (and why is that phrase always used and not "ball of string" or "wad of gum" and so on?) that we call "tasks" in the Work. Anything done "adequately" cannot truly be called a task well done. When we are given a task within the context of the Work, whether it be a quick single event or a short period of function, like some specific form of movement or the learning of a particular piece of music or poem—or a more long-term project as in a business, a theater piece or whatever—one of the elements of such an offering is the tacit understanding that the task will be effected with particularly one-pointed attention, with exacting integrity and diligence, and with no less than all the excellence that we can bring to it, all things considered—"all things" including Grace and karmic demands. To take a "task" in the manner in which we take most things, bringing to them adequacy but not a more highly integral fulfillment, is to have failed the task in one very real sense, even if the end result manifests what appears to be a successful completion.

As you all know, the common comprehension factor for those listening to me and trying to understand what I am mumbling or yelling about is fairly low. So I have asked a few people who have a somewhat higher comprehension to "stick to me like glue" and repeat everything I say, for the ease of those struggling to make sense of my garbled attempts at communication. Nonetheless, there are times, not uncommon, when I am left, even in a small crowd, without one of my four—yes folks, count 'em, *four*—translators. The work does get done adequately, even quite adequately, and yet, and yet . . . When someone is *there,* on the spot, of course the work is done very effectively. But being totally on top of it, so that there is *always* someone there, is not done with the same efficiency. This is a task that has not yet been embraced in the spirit of a genuine Work Task. The intention is present, the wish is strong, all well and good. But at the end of the day, it is the functional manifestation that carries the weight and scores the points—or not, as the case may be.

A task in the context of the Work is very different than any usual responsibility, commitment, or process. By its very nature, a "Work Task" requires a whole different level of responsibility and commitment than the usual person ever brings to anything in their lives—due to their being quite effectively dominated by their psychological script. Again, in terms of the Work, every task does not need a "super effort" (although a few particular and short ones might) but certainly begs for an uncharacteristic approach—for a "higher" function. The usual (and therefore mechanical) play of events that is called "adequate" is not enough, as adequate as it might well be. For a Work Task, "good enough is good enough" only because good enough is contextually defined by excellence, even by extraordinary measures, even if not necessarily by what we might term impeccability.

So, good enough is good enough. This phrase does not refer to what any individual ego or any specific personal psychological script defines relative to *its* own definition of "good enough" or in relation to *its* subjective labyrinth. It is "good enough" in direct synchronicity to the circumstance or situation; the elements of what is "good enough" will naturally change depending on the demands or criteria of the needs of what is manifest at any given time. "Good enough is good enough" relative to an outing with one's children would likely be quite different than "good enough is good enough" relative to leading a group of tourists through India, or relative to a marketing presentation to one's professional colleagues, and so on.

As with all "dharma" proclamations, we do not want to fall into the error of interpreting objective language through the wildly distorted lens of our lopsided and fantastically biased worldview—our life story, which is defined by confusion, lack of clarity, and ego or separative projections, expectations, editorializing and self-referenced defense systems and survival strategies. Such errors can never be Work productive or anything but divisive and false, in many cases leading only to disillusion and aggression toward the Path and the Teacher.

As with many of our key verbal "mantras," "good enough is good enough" is not a dogmatic, rigid overlay on the fluidity and infinitely variable manifestation of life unfolding as it is, here and now, but is a floating—although absolutely accurate—overview of what and how to serve any given possibility or opportunity. Yes. I hope this helps clarify various issues surrounding this most exceptional gift of phrase.

राम राम

Ferme de Jutreau, France

Enlightened Community

June 24, 2010

The Enlightened Community. What is that? First of all, I rarely use the word "enlightened" anymore, except to deny such a thing is even possible to define or recognize, especially from the platform of ego, of the mind, of any given psychological script, all of which limit any Objective View based on their completely self-defined autonomy and domineering, dominating stranglehold on the clarity of Reality as it is, here and now. Alternatively, I may use the word "enlightened" loosely in conversation, most often tinged with a bit of sarcasm or condemnation. My perception of that word has radically altered over the years, to some degree due to my own maturation and to some degree due to the astounding and glaring degree to which it has been misrepresented by fools, charlatans, and innocently confused, ignorant and dangerous people who have defined themselves as "enlightened" in various ways

On the other hand, my obvious shift has not seemed to stop my students from using that word in all seriousness, albeit with enthusiastic naïveté. A bit sad I would say, and hardly a good sign where attention is concerned. I'd like to imagine that my efforts, as small as they may be, are seen, recognized and embraced instead of resoundingly ignored. Well, since we have used it to title our Guru Purnima Celebration, and assuming it isn't simply a marketing ploy (a wee bit of advertising don't ya know?), what can be said about "Enlightened Community"?

Let's begin with communication. As a sangha, as a body of ostensible individuals, if we are not able to communicate clearly, articulately, and effectively, how can the word "community" apply to us, except in the most general or generic terms? We need to *hear* one another, not just listen to the gross words that are spoken. We need to understand what the other is saying, reading not only between the lines, but deeply at the heart of any given matter. We need to *hear* and respond with sensitivity, tact, or diplomacy if necessary, with understanding, compassion, generosity, and certainly with patience and tolerance, not to mention spaciousness and a willingness to respond and serve as called for, even at the price of some personal discomfort or extra effort on our part. We need to "do unto others as we would wish others do unto us," which includes honoring and respecting their gross needs as well as their Work needs.

And it begins there (here) with communication, not only receiving from others but giving. Say what we *actually* mean—there is no need to be cryptic, secretive, teasing, confusing, pessimistic, shaming, tyrannical, or poking our envious or bigoted or zealous noses in others' business. Say it clearly, audibly, and with efficiency. There is no need for lots of "fluff"—extraneous, unnecessary, and irrelevant (not to mention uninteresting and useless) information. When we are able to truly manifest all of that, even with those with whom we don't entirely resonate (to put it kindly), what's left except to follow the obvious, to walk through the many doors that must inevitably open based on self-honesty and alignment to a key law of the Work?

Clearly it wouldn't hurt to consider the laws of hospitality as well as those of communication. Of course we are not talking about "idiot hospitality," where we open the school—its resources and ourselves as well—to every psychotic, spoiler, faux spiritual aspirant, troublemaker, braggart, thief and criminal (psychopath or sociopath) on the planet.[1] We, however, might wish to consider, in the broader consideration of "Enlightened Community," the ideas of refuge and/or sanctuary.

When someone finds their way here and is appropriately in relationship to our teaching, protocols, and forms (guru and sangha in particular, within the fairly strong Eastern context),

1 Lee uses the phrase "idiot hospitality" as a play on Chögyam Trungpa Rinpoche's teaching on "idiot compassion."

and the offering is extended to a more visceral experience than merely through books, CDs, DVDs and gossip (hearsay or the recommendations or even peripheral references that they might have heard or overheard), and someone is invited to participate in our daily (or Celebratory) lives, then it behooves (and should dehoove but not rehoove) us to be spacious, generous and accepting of the fact that each individual is unique within their own eccentricities, idiosyncrasies, and level of maturity. In other words, we can allow such distinctions without being trod upon or allowing the space to be trashed, maligned (unnecessarily), broken or desacralized.

To include someone in our schedule of worship and work is a part of our offering of hospitality, as long as we aren't overly forceful or dogmatic, especially if they are scared, resistant, or outright belligerent. It is probably quite obvious already that some people take to this Path and School with ease, delight, gratitude, and empathy, while for others it is somewhat difficult, bizarre, uncomfortable, embarrassing—at least at first, or until they adjust to it—or in extreme cases even toxic.

Along with communication skills, we also need to have the skills of a good host; we will want to be flexible, flowing, and forbearing, while still "holding context" and maintaining maturity and a definite consciousness of boundaries and sensitivities. This can be trying, even quite stressful, when the person or persons whom you are "hosting" are the source of friction or in extreme cases offensive to you. It is one of the tasks of a devotee to abide by the law until the "law" is so obvious and so engrained in us that it is not only easeful and non-problematical but actually joyous.

It should go without saying that a part of the formula is service. Much of that subject is already covered within or under the umbrella of communication and hospitality, and still it might be worth a few words, especially if the words are well chosen and properly delivered. I cannot promise all of that, but let's see what develops, shall we? It also goes without saying that there are times in which we are quite happy to serve and other times in which to serve is an imposition, an annoyance, a great interruption of our "special" plans—even if those plans are no more than washing clothes we don't really need to wear or having a snack of crackers and peanut butter. It is difficult to put oneself in a situation in which "private lives" are not given what ego assumes is their due. We all need a bit of solitude, "alone time," time to wind down, relax, collect ourselves and stabilize (or restabilize). Yes, and, the demands of service are notoriously unconcerned with the personal wishes of any individual who happens to be the point man or woman on the front line—by virtue of timing, chaos, or circumstance—in just the exact position to provide what is "wanted and needed" in terms of service.

Forward, brave Bauls! Forward into the maw of struggle, perhaps doubt, pushing or nudging up against ingrained tendencies, habits of body and mind, and mistaken or illusory views of reality—*our* reality over and against Reality itself, as it is, here and now! If the consideration of "Enlightened Community" touches a chord in us (or even rings a bell, hits the swish shot from center court, or hammers on our thumb), we will want to begin to set the context that as luxurious, even necessary, as our "private lives" may seem, these "private lives" are secondary or peripheral to the ever-present possibility or opportunity to serve when needed.

Obviously there are times when someone else who wants to indulge his or her "private life" will ask us to replace them in a task of service that is their responsibility. Yes, this is the human realm after all. And even if we know that, we will have to choose between selfless service (or "as if" selfless) and insulted outrage or peeved annoyance (and therefore refusal of their request) at their obvious and inappropriate attempts to manipulate us. I have no advice to offer you; there is no hard-and-fast rule, as every situation is different, unique unto its own exact circumstance, factors, and implications. What I can say is that it never hurts to accumulate merit, as the Buddhists might say, or to earn a bit of good karma. I'll leave you to work out the details, moment to moment and event by event.

राम राम

Enlightened Duality

June 27, 2010

Good evening and thank you for staying for Darshan. And thank you for the Celebration—it was a mighty potent few days. We often use this word "chamber" in English.[1] I've been told it is difficult to translate from English to French; it is difficult to define, in any language. A chamber is invoked or evoked, whether purposefully or spontaneously. When a chamber descends, we all *feel* it; we know by direct visceral sensation that something is happening or has happened. A chamber causes wonderment, awe, joy, and even euphoric ecstasy at times, even if we don't know how or what it is that we are joyful or ecstatic about.

We had a small gathering in London just a few days ago, before returning to France, and a profound and extremely useful chamber arose, as it turned out after the fact. As the evening wore on, the fact that this space was a "chamber" was mentioned, and I had the thought that these types of spaces are both imperceptible and immeasurable at the same time. This may sound confusing, for if something is "imperceptible," how could the idea of measurability apply anyhow? The imperceptibleness does not refer to the common experience of a *felt* resonance, of some kind of higher or other-knowing; it refers to the often untraceable effects of the chamber—many of which occur long after the demise of our current physical vehicle or on levels of such subtlety that we're simply not trained to perceive accurately in those dimensions. Immeasurability refers to the nature of

[1] "Chambers" is a term originally coined by E.J. Gold.

"chamber work," which may reflect upon a vast multitude of aspects of our existence at the same time, but in various ways and with various effects.

This is good news. In fact this is excellent news! Simply to be "in" a chamber is an always positive and profitable affair, in spite of the mind's desperate attempts—or needs—to dominate, control, or co-opt all and everything pertaining to what it believes to be its territory or its possession. Of course we know—even if we don't live on the basis of that knowledge—that all of the ownership and identification business is not only pure illusion but self-defeating foolishness; yet still, the mind is a sophisticated and complex adversary and has its ways, as we also know.

I hesitate to even consider such subjects, but I feel that every little bit of education is helpful in some way, even if its demonstration is not immediate or obvious. So, it is said in the Eastern traditions, most of them at least, and in a variety of ways, that the best thing we can do for our transformation is to spend time in the company of the Guru. One of the reasons for this is that the Guru is a chamber-generating force—the more chambers, the more chamber work we engage, the stronger and more tangible (if it ever is tangible) all of this reinforcement becomes and the more tangible the effects or results become, even in their clear immeasurability and imperceptibility. You all will find, as most of you already have, that over time (meaning many years, not weeks or months) many, many things become clear that were confusing or nonsensical or completely lost on you in the moment. Often when a student reads *any* of our dharma books that they haven't read in several years, they are stunned by how much more they comprehend than the first time they read it—even when they felt they had understood it and resonated to it with great clarity and sympathy.

Every so often it is useful to consider the more "esoteric" ideas of the Work, because somewhere in us we hear and store these ideas away for a time and/or place in which the information will be more practically relevant to our level of maturity on the Path—to our degree of capacity to do something with the information (other than to have congratulated ourselves for our profound insight and grasp of deep ideas when we first heard it)—because we have the skillful means to appreciate the Wisdom of the Great Work and the vast dimensions of the Divine within the context of Enlightened Duality.

So, this raises many questions and motives for those questions, which, as sincere as they seem to us, are based on false inner reasoning and identification. The answers to our questions—maybe even all of them, but more immediately those about chambers and the specific use and context of that word in our own practice and transformation—are found in both the appreciation of and the tacit knowing of what I mean by the short but potent phrase, "Enlightened Duality." To fully grasp this Reality on all levels of our existence is to have the usual underlying motives of our questions completely transcended in the perception of what is always and ever true in all dimensions and Universes—even right here, right now, in the midst of neurosis, struggle, effort and, as the Buddhists say, "false view."

So in one sense, given what we have just considered about education, we need not freak out and concentrate too hard on this Enlightened Duality business (nor read the book seven times, one after the other, in the hopes that will pierce our armor and light up our dull philosophical obsessions). As Werner Erhard said many years ago, to simply "sit with it like a brick" (a heavy one, I would add) and let the nature of Reality essentially and spaciously draw us to Itself is a much more efficacious, productive, and relaxed way to go about this and most other things as well.

Enlightened Duality. Give it a chance to ripen. There is no need to pursue it, as if it could possibly disappear if we didn't grab it fast enough and hard enough. We don't need to trap knowledge or wisdom, and the more we try, the more mysterious and frustrating this whole spiritual business seems. It would not be out of the domain of possibility to apply this principle to other both similar and dissimilar matters, using discrimination and common sense, of course. Being too impulsive and zealous, not to mention dogmatic, about exciting new discoveries has led to some tragic spiritual errors, as well as many disastrous relationships.

Well. I want to thank you for your grand participation in the Sacred Bazaar—it has touched me, and more importantly, fed me. And thank you for your hard work, both physically and in dealing with my "paradoxical" behavior (although questionable might be a better word than paradoxical). It is a great Blessing to be in the Field of Yogi Ramsuratkumar and His Father in Heaven, and it is possibly as great a Blessing to be in your field as well, as Sangha and as individuals. Certainly it is a pleasure, though I don't always appear to manifest that, to be with all of you. Have a most wonderful chamber until we meet again.

राम राम

Ferme de Jutreau, France

We Are at War

July 18, 2010

Most of us are busy as little bees, always asking irrelevant questions, prying into things, ostensibly out of curiosity or actually believing that the answers are valuable, even necessary, or that they clarify some issue or point. In fact this is rarely the case. Often it is no more than habitual "blah, blah, blah"—our deep love of hearing the sonorous tones of our own voice, or the blathering, babbling mechanicality of what we are under the delusion is "social grease," or just ordinary human interaction niceties.

Are we attempting to Work or not? If not, okay, hang around, be sloppy, inattentive, and blatantly disrespectful to those who are here to Work. If we are here to Work, details such as these are not merely peripheral or minor ingredients but vital issues that bear our respect and our serious consideration. If we are here to Work, which I assume is true of most of you listening to this tonight, at some point it becomes imperative that we question all the usual assumptions about life; once again, the dull, uninvestigated sleep that we assume is normal waking and intelligent awareness must be fought with every ounce of energy at our command.

Listen! I hope it becomes clear that we are at war: at war with sleep, with illusion, with the lie, the false. There can be no truce, no compromise, no pandering or catering to the enemy. There is only one winner: either Reality or Truth wins, or mechanicality and the psychological script wins. The enemy has no human feelings, no subtleties, no sensitivities; the enemy is pure survival, and this enemy takes no prisoners—it is all or nothing.

Yes, I know this sounds very dramatic! Without an absolute commitment to ruthless self-honesty, to objective clarity, and to realization of Truth (recognition, comprehension, integration or digestion and animation of Truth), to submission to the higher laws, to God, to the One, the Absolute, to Father in Heaven, one cannot wage war against an enemy that knows no ethic, has no rules except win at any cost, has no honor or regret. Please verify this through study of the great Realizers of any and all traditions: Milarepa, Thérèse of Avila or John of the Cross, Meister Eckhart, Swami Nityananda, Jnaneshwar, the Baal Shem Tov, Rumi or Shams-i-Tabriz, Rabia, and so on and so on.

How does one come to such devotion to Ruin? To the dissolution of the separative identification, to the delusion of I, me, mine? Usually slowly, one step (or occasionally two) at a time, often by being tricked into it or seduced into it, finding oneself on the front line, in the trenches, and having no options or alternatives but to protect one's self, to carry on and struggle against this despicable, unacceptable, common enemy of mankind. And bear in mind that much of this war is fought inside, both at the level of the sub- or unconscious and also in the multi-dimensional complex, in the field that is above, beyond, prior to, yet completely integrated with what and who we are in fact.

There are vast sophistications, many vectors of "battle," and the behind-the-scenes strategies of countless factors at play; to try to comprehend or grasp all this at an intelligent, conscious level of outer awareness is not only a hopeless task bound to be frustrated but also a colossal waste of time and energy, a confused misinterpretation of the battlefield and of this war itself. Yes, we are at war, whether we know it or not and whether we want or wish to be or not. If we are not actively engaged, we will be—if not in this lifetime, then in another. Even so, there is no time like the present; urgency is ever an issue.

So, how to mobilize our force, attention, intention? How to gain any advantage, no matter how small? Pay Attention and Remember, Enquire, treat others with kindness, generosity and compassion, "Draw no conclusions mind." Work against sloth, greed, pride, vanity—all of the spies and saboteurs of the enemy. You get the picture: practice. Be relentless in an unwillingness to sell out your army's secrets to comfort, ease, distractions, fascinations, the false glitter of fame, power, arrogance, hubris, and all the "idiot" forms of useful and profitable efforts—all the pathological sides of our integrity. It is so, so easy to fall into any and all of this just a wee bit at a time, almost invisibly and so gently that before we know it, it is too late—we've been captured and re-imprisoned.

Look, old hippies, it doesn't do any good to put flowers in the guns of the enemy or to festoon its headquarters with ribbons and joys. This enemy will not be teased or tempted to meet you in reason or delight. It is intent only upon victory, upon maintaining its own assumed territory, and will not bow even to love.

Is this enemy an illusion? Yes, of course, totally. And the total dissolution, the piercing of the knot of illusion—not momentarily or temporarily, not many times, but finally, once and for all—is the final battle out of which the sun rises and happiness rules. Then, acceptance of what is, as it is, here and now (as a tacit relationship to all there is, not as a technique to be superimposed upon or on top of all there is) becomes the doorway to selfless service, which is itself the destiny of all good Marines.

Ah well, have a great week, a good night's sleep, and a most excellent Faith.

राम राम

The Guru's Blessing

July 25, 2010

There we were, sitting at lunch, and I was being my recently acidic, maddening, ugly, intrusive self, when I commented on someone's seeming contradiction of behavior: saying that she loved the salad I had made, while making disturbed faces as she ate. Assuming of course—and why not?—that I completely misunderstood her process, she patiently, kindly, and gently explained (justified) her ostensible difference of physical manifestation and inner response to me. And a very reasonable explanation it was.

Here's the thing, puppies and kits, goslings and chicks: You are speaking on one level and I on another. I am pointing at the deep unconscious, and you are defending what in you is conscious, as much as you know that. So what can I do? Apologize when I hear your brilliant and lucid, not to mention rational and sensible, description of your reasons for demonstrating what I have just poked at? I suppose that would be the reasonable, polite, well-mannered thing to do. Yes.

Unfortunately, these days (and I for one hope it changes for the sleeping-world better, as my distaste of my personal manifestation is reaching epic proportions . . .) this is not the response that comes forth, leading you to confirm, as you suspect that I am wrong and you are correct, right, superior and accurate, authentic to the core in your assertion of innocence. If I had a personal intention, my drive in these awful confrontations would be to suggest that you look at the deeper, hidden—*well* hidden—motives of your behavior instead of simply accepting the superficial and obvious dimensions of your behavior as if it were the be-all and end-all of your psychological and personal manifestations.

In other words, I am (albeit, yes, in an unpleasant and shamelessly unconscionable way) pointing out that there is more to our gestures and function than meets the eye—the eye of awareness and the eye of the lack of objective self-observation. This is the distinction between sleep and wakefulness, between the chronic habitual mechanicality of our script—our accepted beliefs and worldview, defined by our childhood decisions and by a stunning, blatant refusal to accept what is, as it is, here and now—and clarity or a perception of Reality or Truth, deep down to their core.

So please allow my provocations (as unfair as they may seem to your outer levels of self-knowledge) to thrust you, or at least point you, to more probable inner stimuli and don't be so quick to defend, excuse, justify or explain what you truly believe to be your actual experience. Thank you, and not just thank you, but so many, so many thanks and so much gratitude for those of you who will follow this discipline.

Wait, wait! Is it possible that I am wrong? Is it possible that I am needlessly disparaging your inner motives? That my sense, instinct, intuition is merely my own misguided inner motivation? Well, given the conviction and certitude, not to mention consistency, with which many of you believe you are right and I am wrong, perhaps I should look more closely at it all. Of course, that is what your ego wants—an apology, a red carpet to reign freely with no possibility of exposure, with no threat and with no demand to be worked on; yes, carte blanche to do its own thing without the need to fear exposure. Shall I capitulate? For I may well come to that in favor of carrying and sustaining this burden of representing Reality at all costs, most of those costs being my own personal misery, unhappiness, and physical stress, discomfort and breakdown.

If you continue to urge me in that direction, in fact to order me to cow tow to your neurotic commands through your categorical unwillingness to "be different," to follow the hints, clues, and out-and-out articulate instructions that I offer you on an almost constant basis, you may win out. And if you're willing to consider—right now, tonight—that I might be wrong in my assessments of your behavioral gestures and functions, be my guest. That is a chance I'm willing to have you take, if that is a chance you are willing to take.

If consequences be damned and the massive "investment" you have made to be here and study with me in this spiritual school are not worth a look at your own drives to power, authority, and superiority—in short, to winning—then by all means consider me wrong, off base, just an old sour, disillusioned, impatient, intolerant, cranky, rage-aholic, weak, ignorant, confused, muddled stick-in-the-mud. I must add, you do so at your own risk—a temporary risk, of course, as lifetimes and therefore new opportunities are endless. But it is a risk nonetheless, and if in fact I am wrong, then we're all going "to hell in a handbasket"—but together, if that is comforting to anyone!

On a more pleasant note, hopefully, I can barely express the wonder and mercy of the fact that y'all are loving and sustaining me here through this, as whatever copious amounts of self-love I had have been strewn to the wind, scattered to the far reaches of the Universe, diluted to homeopathic proportions. To not only put up with me (as I'm sure is true of some of you, with equally copious prayers that this is a phase which will pass, and soon!) in this demonstration of abusive, explosive, sword-swinging bravado, but also to actually be making use of it all, both in understanding and in more transformational ways (which I'm also sure is true of many of you) is a demonstration of magnanimity, dignity, and nobility that I appreciate from the tips of my toes to the top of my head, and way beyond, higher, and deep into the very cellular existence of my being. Without exaggeration and without a single grain of sarcasm, I am in awe.

May we, all beings, be happy and fulfilled in Dharma, Buddha, Sangha, and Guru (even the Guru!), and may the joy and power of the Blessings of Yogi Ramsuratkumar flow unimpeded like the Ganges in monsoon, and may the opulence, the *pushti* of our service to Krishna, and therefore to Self, never wane, never waver, never be in doubt or conflict. May we abandon ourselves to ourselves, Realizing only God, the other, and "Just This," and may all Divine beings celebrate our Guru Yoga and pour their Benediction upon us and ours like honey gushing from an over-full hive. And may we live lives of fulfillment, creativity, deep satisfaction and profound value and profit to the Work. And may every child, adult, and elder smile at you, knowing and seeing your transcendental and your emanent beauty, delight, and perfection. In fact, may delight and joy plague you unavoidably and may you never suffer unnecessarily, having embodied fully all of this, my wishes for you. I bow to you with hands folded, forehead to the ground and eternity before us.

राम राम

Sacred Objects

July 25, 2010

Hello and welcome. I'm terribly sorry that I can't speak to you, but my current garbled mumbling would be a great effort for me and would definitely fail to communicate what I wish to say. Even though I am not quite able to demonstrate my sublime verbal eloquence and startlingly radiant personal charisma (that's bit of humor, please!), I have brought something very precious, quite holy and inestimably valuable, in spite of a few hefty price tags. I'm talking about the Sacred Bazaar you see all around you, but at the same time I am talking about wisdom and an understanding of Reality that is at core, at heart, what we all are seeking for, even if that search is not conscious.

As most of you are probably aware, the difficulty of true, lasting change from self-reference to other-reference—or we could say from I, me, mine, to God—is a slow, often painful and difficult process, though in actual fact it need not be. I have spent the last forty or so years delving into the issues of consciousness and have made a few discoveries. One of the things I have discerned through hard-learned experience is that there is a time to push, to reach (though rarely), and a time not to, even when ego—or our personal habitual desires, our psychological script—is screaming at us to go for it, get tough, be aggressive and push, push, push.

Usually when we follow such urges, it is a big mistake, even tragic at times. The Universe is—how shall we call it?—not a definable object but an existence that is, of its very nature, ultimately intelligent. When we, in our selfish and presumed separative illusion, try to outwit this Universe, or twist or mold it to our own mechanical and suffering views, we must lose, for compared to the Universe and its great almighty Everythingness, we are no more than a microscopic bit of dust, if even that.

So relax. That should be good news if you can actually do it! Allow the Universe—or Reality, Truth or God if you prefer those terms—to point the way and send the limousine and simply let it carry you to the effective, optimum, and most profitable end result. And when, in those very few instances, to push is what is needed, the Universe will clearly indicate that. No doubt or confusion is necessary, though we tend to produce both in great quantities and with passionate urgency.

Another thing I have learned in this journey of most of my lifetime is that we, as organic creatures, are quite stubbornly attached to our status quo, even when that status quo is failure, pain, misery, fear or any other deeply unhealthy and unwholesome state. Isn't that bizarre? We are, in every moment, waking and sleeping, offered freedom, so to speak, and what we cling to, many times desperately and defensively, is imprisonment. Whether I can speak with you or not, what I bring is the possibility—and not only that, the literal opportunity—to consider freedom and walk its path to full realization. I can't tell you *how* I am doing this; I can only tell you that it is a certainty that it is so.

So, back to the Sacred Bazaar for a moment: This whole process is a most treasured gift to me and to you all, if you choose to participate—to play through my mediation (which I highly recommend, obviously). The objects displayed will, sometimes very dramatically and at other times subtly but *always* effectively, turn any space into a sacred chamber, a refuge, a Sanctuary. Yes, they are rare and beautiful, but their real value is in the extraordinary Blessing Force that they convey. When we are resistant, lazy, skeptical or (even worse) cynical on the surface, these objects take no notice and are not stopped in their inexorable mission to touch us with the Breath and Caress of the Divine—pure, pristine, and uncomplicated by the vast and sophisticated machinery that is mind and ego and all of its devious and toxic tentacles. So please do not be insulted by my obsessive delight and encouragement to throw yourselves in. Times are tough. Yes. Would you rather be surrounded by beauty and sanctity, holiness, or . . . . ? Thank you.

I want to thank those of you who appreciate and are making use of the Tibetan artifacts, the lamps and offering bowls. I know that thousands of monks and nuns—some living in monasteries and convents, some in Chinese "re-education" centers and many, many who are now dead—are grateful that their beloved and sacred artifacts continue to be used in heartful and serious worship and attention to practice. For all of them, my pranams and countless heart-tears and gratitude to you. Over the past year or two, I have become so passionate about these things that, if I could I talk, I would discourse for hours upon hours. I cannot appreciate you enough for your embrace of this, one of my great loves and devotions. A thousand, no a million, praises to you.

Sacred objects are always already free. They demonstrate and role model for us. A human master role models as well and is inextricably enmeshed in the interactive world of individuals, a world that is a glaring fantasy of mere imagination, yet if we are identified with our ostensible individuality, the Master, *even* the Master, has to deal with that entire and extreme context. This is not who I *am* (or not who Arnaud Desjardins *is*) but what I do, and it is a complex field of interplay.

Yet here I am in Madrid, truly happy—even thrilled I could say—to be here and ever willing to wrestle some more in the hopes, in the always possible chance, that someone, anyone, will get the arrow straight to the essence of the issue and never be able to go backwards. The Sacred Bazaar is one of my tools toward that possibility, and a brilliant one without question. This is our task, to confront our delusion, to see ourselves with objective clarity, to allow the scales to drop from our eyes so to speak, and allow this vision, perhaps a bit tentative (and perhaps not) at first, to become stronger and stronger until it is more prevalent in our attention than the myriad of distractions and seductions that are always pulling us away from Truth and keeping us from the Embrace of God.

So, the Sacred Bazaar is open, and I wish your homes to be well-populated by these most exceptionally holy works of art and surrender. And if there are any questions, I offer myself and those extensions of mine in service, love, and obedience to my own Guru, Yogi Ramsuratkumar, and wish you all a most productive practice and a life of joy and Faith.

राम राम

Do Your Part

August 1, 2010

Good evening. Hi, hello. Everyone, more or less, wants to know how to "progress" on the Path. As evidenced beyond a doubt by the vast majority of letters I have and do and surely will receive, much of this desire to "progress" is just a wish to be relieved of immediate suffering, struggle, or crisis, so that life will run more smoothly. We want to be free of the annoying and personally insulting manifestations caused by difficulties with mates, children, co-workers or bosses, job environments, poor money management, and so on—most of those difficulties due to our own unwillingness to grow up and relax, and the rest due to our bullheaded stubbornness in refusing the other his or her uniqueness.

Let me offer some help by shining a light on this dilemma. I am certainly not suggesting (as if that suggestion, were I to make it, would make the slightest difference at all) that any of you stop writing me or asking questions, but I am suggesting that you look closely and, more importantly, accurately at your ongoing mechanical and unexamined behavior. I have in the past and will in the future tell you what you need to know in order to take the next step, so to speak. I am tired, so tired, of being people's alter egos and consciences. I have patiently answered letters for years with detailed feedback, and at a certain point I've had quite enough of giving the same answer to the same question over and over, without seeing any active change in my erstwhile correspondent's willingness to actually *do* or implement what it is that I am providing input about.

During Bridge or in the kitchen or at the Sacred Bazaar or the tea space or wherever, I have been more than willing (though not gleeful or too enthusiastic) to give clues, hints, or even exact precision about areas needing work or clarification and about asked or unasked questions that are begging to be resolved. So I have, do, and will continue to provide the information you need at a time and in a place in which such information can be valuable and most profitable. If you aren't "getting it," it certainly is not because I am not giving it! So you really need not ask, at least more than once or twice.

You need to *listen,* to pay attention, and to apply my direct answers to your difficulties instead of ignoring it all and repeating the same questions over and over and suffering the same personal problems over and over, "like a broken record," as my exalted mother used to say. I have frequently pointed out people's "cramp" without having to be asked. Sometimes the question is the Universe speaking according to its own criteria for just circumstance, and when the Universe speaks, I (the guru) listen, respond, and become the Universe's mouthpiece.

So you need not worry that I will ignore you or that you won't get the necessary data you need to "know thyself." You have, you do, and you will continue to be given what you need. I do my part, and if this reciprocal process is to be effective beyond a mere philosophical platform, you need to do your part. Your part is to hear the feedback, take it to heart and body, act on it, and show up differently, transformed, altered by living life unburdened by your usual concerns. If you follow these considerations and apply my recommendations, your usual concerns will no longer be present; therefore they will no longer be relevant, and don't you dare be nostalgic about your old misery!

So there you have it. So *here* you have it. And all those letters people write to me, "Oh, you told me, and you were right but I didn't listen and now . . . " Blah, blah, blah! That shit is extremely unpleasant to me. I like the rare letters that say, "I did exactly what you told me to and everything worked out like magic. Thank you so much. Is there anything I can do for *you*?" Yes, those I enjoy. But they are few and far between.

If you don't do what you *know* you should do because of weakness, sloth, greed, arrogance, doubt, self-hatred, pride, fear, whatever, well . . . you deserve the consequences you get. Don't come crying or whining to me, because *I have done my part*. When you have indulged your genital imperative of running like a cheap whore after comfort or fame, don't complain to me ("No shit, Sherlock!") when it hasn't worked out.

I've been telling you the truth forever. If you want to swallow the lie (and I suspect that most of you know *full well* when you are doing that, but you just hope against hope that it will all work out fine), don't bring it to me when it doesn't work out. Especially when I've already given you explicit instructions to do something else, or more commonly not to do (sleep with, invest in, et cetera) what it is that your psychological script is urging you to do come hell or high water—and hell is most often the result, though it may take a few years to fully arrive.

I am doing my part. I am advising you according to wisdom, the Work, and the Universe's Will. To ignore that advice is fine as long as you do it at your own peril and leave me out of the swamp of your own dark motives when the "chickens come home to roost." I am *so* tired of doing my part, with sincerity and loving concern, only to have so many people do exactly the contradictory and therefore counterproductive things. So . . . be my guest, please, but don't try to force me to pay for your blatant denials and errors due to the clear rejection of my ever-present counsel.

Are we clear about that? Thank you. And have a truly glorious week full of delight, laughter, worship, praise and communion. I await.

राम राम

Graceful Benediction

August 8, 2010

Good evening, and I mean that. In fact I hope and pray that it is already an excellent evening, following a wonderful day, and soon to get better. Yes . . . And hello to those of you I'm looking at with my physical eyes and to those of you who I'm looking at in other ways, and to all of you, all categories included, as I'm always "lookin' at ya, kids." So . . . "Here's lookin' at ya!"

I was contemplating the quite amazing and extraordinary children, small and already grown up, in, around, even peripheral to this school, and I was catapulted into an internal consideration—which I am herewith externalizing—relative to the distinctions between karma and genes. Given the massive mistakes we have made, and many of us continue to make—and the idiotic things we have said to our own and others' children—it should be clearly obvious, beyond a shadow of a doubt, that our parenting alone surely cannot be entirely responsible for the magnificence of those children. Genes? Of course there is an effect, and in many cases a noticeable one or ones, but that alone does not explain it.

What then? Good karma, folks. Good karma. Of course the implication is that in order for us to be glorious people in other lifetimes, and in order to have such glorious children in other lifetimes (and we will be our children's children at some point), we would be well advised to mind our practice, mind our service, and especially, to mind our minds.

In *vastu* and other aspects of the Indian traditions, there are specific actions to take to insure that the karmic consequences we will experience will be beneficial, specifically producing physical beauty, health, and honorable, loving children. We need not make a science of this, for God knows too many of us are already stuck in the "letter of the law." Instead, we seem genuinely unable to grow up enough to apply even a minimum of maturity or common sense to our lives so that the "spirit of the law" is the rule by which we operate. Let us simply say that *all* of the practices of this school are designed to produce just such good karma—when those practices are actually integrated and animated, not merely discussed and intended. (As Tom Cruise's character said in the movie *Knight and Day*, "You know what 'someday' means? It means '*never*.' ")

And how do we know that the practices are designed that way? Because they are infused with, sourced from, and contextualized by Divine Influence and the ever-present Blessings of Yogi Ramsuratkumar and the Lineage, right back or down to His Father in Heaven. As we have heard so many times, it's always a return to the practices: kindness, generosity and compassion as dominant moods and forms of behavior, the Heart Breath, Enquiry, "Draw no conclusions mind," "Be that which nothing can take root in," and of course the Big Daddy of 'em all—Assertion, or "Just This," as well as many others. And lest we forget, the repetition of the sacred Name of Yogi Ramsuratkumar always reinforces all of them.

Even though the daily recommendations (or Conditions) aren't strictly practices like the others, to follow them with ease and intelligence (spirit of the law, not letter of the law) helps to enhance all of the practices, because these recommendations come through the suggestion of and with the Blessings of the spiritual Master, and carry, as do all the elements and aspects of our lives together, the guru's holy, efficacious and extremely potent Regard.

This is our advantage. This is our "ace in the hole," so to speak: the mystic, magical, and mysterious Alchemy that is the Guru's Attention, that ever-present Gaze, whether the person of the Guru is aware of it or not, that always pours its Graceful Benediction towards us once we have "connected"—plugged into the socket, become a part of the circulatory system. This is the distinction between the devotee and anyone else who may just practice out of good sense, purpose and ethic.

We are lucky enough to have discovered this Influence, and we have our part to do. The Guru has already done his part, is already ongoingly doing his part, and will eternally do his part. Yogi Ramsuratkumar called me to Him, watched over and Guided me all this life, continues to watch over and Guide me even though He has left His body, and will, lifetime after lifetime. The Guru's part is tacit, reliable and tangible at times, intangible at others.

Still, we have a part in all of this awe-inspiring wonderfield. We must be open, receptive (not necessarily consciously or even with ego-agreement, thank God!), and available; we must be willing to obey the Will of the Intelligence of the Universe, the "Word" of God. It is our involvement and trust in practice that softens, tills the ground, sows the seeds, fertilizes, waters, and suns the growing plant and ultimately provides the *full* possibility—for certainly, faulty and even no practice doesn't entirely eliminate the rays of Blessing as they shine on us.

Well, there you have it, my friends. Of course I could go on and on, and on and on, and undoubtedly would if I were not so adverse to the massive amounts of time it takes to write these missiles of love and Teaching, hopefully of education and instruction. And no, I will not start to do them on computer. Ah well, such is my stubbornness and unwillingness to embrace "progress."

Have a productive and profitable week until we meet in this sanctum sanctorum again, in this secret enclave of opportunity and potential. And please be happy and accepting but not lazy, procrastinating or aggressive, particularly where our refuges, Guru, Dharma, Sangha, are concerned.

Jai Guru, Jai Guru,
Jaya Guru Raya

राम राम

Holy Help

August 15, 2010

I received a good question this week. Oh, good evening, by the way. And a fully heartjoy welcome, for as cranky, impatient, hair-trigger-temper critical as I have been, you are my heartjoy—Buddha, Dharma, Sangha. These are what I love, what feeds and sustains me. So when I welcome you, singly and as a group, it is not just a social convention. It is a supreme, even cosmic pleasure to see you, even those individuals amongst you whom I seem most harsh towards or most hard on. Well, enough gushing, for after all, I am a Teacher, not an oil well, and thank God, for I certainly have better sense than to despoil Mother as is happening in the Gulf of Mexico and other places, here, now, as we gather to celebrate our lives together and the very really possibility of the True Work.

So the question: "In the process of self-observation, where do I go deeper and where do I recognize that which is meaningless? How do I make that distinction?" Well, I believe that this applies to all of us, and as should be clearly evidenced by the deep work-on-self that has gone on recently, especially for two of the women, the answer is quite simple: *You* do not make that, or any, distinction. You continue to observe with ruthless self-honesty until there is no "deeper" to go—you are out of the "corridor of madness" and there is only Light. Or we could say there is only "what is, as it is, here and now."

There is, of course, a certain discrimination involved in this whole process. It is fairly important to recognize whether one (you) is actually paying attention in an objective way—that is, without judgment of *any* kind. Judgment includes both negative and positive reactions, such as editorializing, self-criticism, displeasure, delight over the "successes," appreciation for your skill and progress, projections, comparisons to others or to your own previous efforts, and so on and on. After all, in the practice of Paying Attention and Remembering, to even make the distinction that this is useful and that is meaningless, as the question implies, and not only implies but literally states, is to already be entering into the practice from the wrong context, from a judgmental point of view.

So one merely practices with intention and diligence and notices the results, what arises in mind and body, and as a response to practice from the environment, human and otherwise. And one responds as needed through internal considering or external action. For example, if the Universe provides a deep *need* to move forward in your alchemical or transformational process, as was the case in the tea space for a couple of nights last week, then you jump on the opportunity, grab the window while it is open, with no hesitation or procrastination, even in the face of fear, even in the throes of great fear, sorrow, panic, and you *ACT*!

Notice that I said a *need* to move forward, not a wish to move forward. Most of us, maybe even all of us, have a desire to "win" at this game, but that desire is hardly equal to the kind of need that pierces, divides the "Red Sea" of our resistances, neuroses, momentous sloth, pride and all of that, and leaps at any chance to receive the Benediction, the Blessings of the Holy Help that we know the spiritual Master, as Transparent to his Guru and Lineage, is capable of providing. And this is how we must approach it.

Such doorways do not open all the time and most usually don't stay open for very long. We must jump, not impulsively but instinctually. There may never be a more important circumstance—not even "enlightenment," whatever that is! As should be obvious by the tragic "fall" from grace that is so evident in so many who could have been outstanding teachers—or perhaps not so bad but equally wasteful, the stagnation of so many in a state which they believe is "ultimate"—work-on-self is the vital link (in most cases the "missing link") between the Realization of Just This and the illusion, the "spiritual pride" or "spiritual by-passing" phenomena, the co-opting of Truth by an ego (all of ours) that can mimic so well that it can confuse and fool just about anyone, even sophisticated therapists and so-called spiritual teachers and metaphysicians as well.

So we dig, dig, dig, deeper and deeper until we dig through *all* the layers of veils that obscure the perfect, seamless, pure, joyous One, God the Absolute. We do not judge whether we are being "competent" or not. We simply "hammer on it" and trust, have Faith, in the total infallibility of the flow of Blessings and the Work. For this is at source for it all—and we need to embrace that mystic and magical reality and stop questioning it, second-guessing it and thinking we can stay three steps ahead of it by figuring it out and relegating all of this into nice neat little boxes, stored away for use wherever we need a justification for our failure to practice up to the mark.

So . . . Pay Attention and Remember. Only that. No definition is needed because when you are doing it, everyone will know, and when you aren't, you will know if you are truly self-honest, though you probably won't like it or want to know that you're not actually objective in your self-view. And when you are not, everyone else is not wrong (because they refuse to see what outstanding practice you are doing), although this is our usual frustrated reaction to our environment when the expected response is not forthcoming. So trusting the process includes trusting the sangha, as unconsciously moved by that very process, as a clear and accurate bellweather for our own on or off sadhana. Regardless of what people say, whether their words are useful or not, hitting the point or wide off the point, it is the unspoken *group* response that is always telling, and were we truly interested or invested in objective Paying Attention and Remembering, incredibly revealing.

Well, I'm off shopping for the Sacred Bazaar this weekend, having written this on Thursday, so wish me "happy hunting," in retrospect of course, for my discoveries and treasures become yours, and I don't live in the usual line or time frame anyhow, so I'll get it while I travel even though it looks like I'm back home at Ferme de Jutreau and it's all over. Have a fabulous week, please.

राप राप

It's All One

August 20, 2010

"It's all One." What on earth does *that* mean? Maybe we should have titled the seminar, "It's all One, and . . . " Yes, that really touches on it. It *is* all One, and unless we are willing make proper—meaning objective—distinctions, the Truth is absolutely and completely and totally and fully and comprehensively useless, to us and more importantly, to Itself. The Truth is only of value to Itself. This is at the crux of the issue. Why? Because, "It's all One," folks.

This may bring up the question, "Well then, if the Truth is useless to me, who am I and why is so much effort exerted to realize the Truth?" As Werner Erhard might have said (but he didn't, I did): You're a distinction-making machine. Yes, and not only that, based on being a reliable distinction-making machine, you are an "acting from intrinsic dignity and intrinsic nobility" machine. For if the distinctions you make are indeed objective—meaning an accurate recognition of "what is, as it is, here and now"—then your action will always be a natural impulse to the distinction you have made, a response and not a reaction, *or* a chronically habitual manifestation of your psychological script. Yes, your action must be automatic and precise, designed on the spot, in that moment, by the Universe in relationship to exactly that unique circumstance or situation.

Wow! That was a mouthful—is your brain all heated up from trying to figure it out? Too bad, what a waste of transformational energy, of alchemical fire, because you can't figure it out. You can know that it is so, both instinctually and in the domain of being it, doing it, acting in such a way. Let us not forget or be distracted from this important point made earlier: Truth is only of value to

Itself. I said that also, and I'm proud of it because it is not only true but wise, profound, and brilliant as well. It is one of those statements that can only be made from the state of distinction making in its authenticity.

When one makes distinctions from an inauthentic place, even words that may be accurate in their description of Reality are quite false and leave a bitter taste in the mouth of the hearer, if and when the hearer is authentic in his or her distinction making.

Truth is only useful to Itself. When truth is used to make a point, assert authority, justify one's "enlightenment," or to reinforce a point of view defined by one's life script or life story, it isn't true anymore even if it appears to be. Beware of the false façade that is so expertly designed that without looking behind it, it looks flawless—exactly what it is supposed to do. Be careful not to judge too impulsively without pausing for the Real to bleed through the false, which it always will if you are patient, willing to give it a chance, clear-visioned and undominated by your wish to see things in a way that supports your personal strategies, underlying motives and illusory worldview.

In fact, why judge at all? See "what is, as it is, here and now," free of all projections, expectations, seductive and fascinating implications, self-indulgent promises. Allow Truth to serve Itself. In fact, Truth will inevitably serve Itself anyway, so why not jump on the horse and ride it in the direction it's going, instead of being defined by confusion, doubt, falsity, lies, and delusions, and suffering unnecessarily as a result of all that?

"It's all One" does not mean that everything is equal, although that implication can easily be taken. It is true that in India various masters have literally ingested shit or mud as a testimony to "It's all One," and yet it is evidently obvious that shit is not chocolate mousse and mud is not tiramisu and tree bark is not filet mignon. Isn't it? Equality is a dream, a dream of one who misunderstands Truth, of one who believes oneself to have realized nonduality.

But look at such people's lives—what colossal hypocrisy, inconsistency, and hubris!

The belief that all is equal is a gigantic miscalculation, a radically distorted perspective. All is not equal on any level except the ultimate level, except the level of God Absolute. So what? That has nothing to do with *us*, "as we are, here and now." Bach and Boy George are not equal, as talented as Boy George might be (or whatever he is called these days) and as much of a fan of his as you might be. Dostoyevsky and Danielle Steele are not equal, as much as you might distract yourself with Ms. Steele's novels. And so on and so on. And yes, it *is* all One. It is, it is, it is, it is.

What to do? What to make of all of this? It is not a paradox. It is not a dichotomy. It is not a metaphor. It *is* all One. And we, each of us, are a part of a continuum, an inseparable field, a seamless Unity; each of us is also distinct, unique, and singular as well, and, if we are True, we exist only to serve that Unity.

Many believe that God exists to serve us—His Creation—or that Truth exists to provide meaning to existence. Nope. Guess again. God exists solely to serve Itself, as Truth is useful to Itself and *only* to Itself. Wow again! Bummer. Yes, and it's only a bummer to ego, to identification with the separate self, to our sense of justice, propriety, love, meaning, purpose, and on and on and on. In fact, it isn't anything—bummer, wonder, or otherwise. It is simply True.

It is all One. It is all One, and whatever we or I mean by "It" is void, empty, and at the same time, infinite in Its fullness, Its rich multiplicity. Let me remind you: this is *not* a paradox, a dichotomy. This is *not* a koan, a challenge, or a dare thrown down. This is not some mind-blowing affirmation. It is Just This, Truth, Reality.

Yes, my friends: It's all One.

राम राम

Be True to Your Word

22 Aug 2010

Hello. Good evening. How positively lovely to see you all here in this Blessing Field of Yogi Ramsuratkumar, surrounded by precious artifacts, outstanding good company, and True Benediction and Mercy. Hallelujah! On to tonight's consideration, which starts out somewhat darkly, but hopefully (and I say hopefully because I really do not know, I only have the beginning and as I write, it unfolds and goes wherever and however it wants) we will run head-on into the Light.

I loaned someone a substantial sum of money, based on the *promise* of repayment at a certain time. That was over a year ago, and I have not seen one penny yet. At the time the loan was made, the person did not say, "If the court case that I am involved in is successfully concluded in my favor, and I win the financial judgment that I expect, I will be able to repay you." In a similar case, another person did not say: "If my divorce is finalized when and as I expect it to be, I will be able to pay you such and such." The commitment was simply to repay at a specified time.

This is the thing: we are cheats and liars and we *know it.* We strategically orient ourselves to create advantages that we imagine will fulfill or further our desires, wishes, hopes, and dreams. We lie and cheat, knowing *full well* that we are risking failure to meet our *word,* our *promise.* We blindly believe that everything will work out as we plan, except that we aren't really blind. We simply do not consider what the *consequences* are, should we not complete our agreements.

None of these sincere and decent people to whom I am referring think of themselves as liars and cheats, but the "sins of omission" are obvious. Using language in a way to manipulate someone (namely me) into doing something by leaving out vital facts that might negatively affect the outcome of the agreement is without a doubt the sign of a liar and a cheat. I would like to suggest that you all take these examples seriously so as not to make (or it is probably more realistic to say *continue* to make) the same erroneous judgments.

We should consider this deeply. I am not talking about karma here; it's not that karma isn't a consequence, but it is on a different level and in a different dimension. I am talking about the immediate consequences when we jump to concretize some immediate situation, failing to "see the forest for the trees." The obvious disadvantages don't seem to have any mitigating effect.

The consequences of such errors can be extremely severe, although in the two examples used those consequences are merely my annoyance and the loss of my trust. To the Universe such behavior is a sign as evident as an exploding Roman candle: a sign of sloppiness, a lack of integrity, a willingness to be selfish and insincere and, ultimately, an unwillingness to work as deeply we imagine or fantasize ourselves to be already working. When the Universe's doors are closed, it doesn't matter how much *you* think you are working, 'cause you *ain't.*

If God is tentative towards you, that tentativeness is an absolute handicap on your actual opportunity to Work, on the very real possibility of the Help you not only need but count on to be there—*here*—when it is needed and timely. (Oh yes, now we're getting somewhere, my gaggle of geese, my pod of whales, my heard of ovine or bovine beings, hopefully one day to be a true band of humans, a sangha of bards, artists, practitioners, adorants, and gopis in fact!) Werner Erhard says, "You are your word." And then there is, "In the beginning was the Word."

To be sloppy in one's language is to disparage the word. Not a good idea. There is no way not to be a cheat and a liar except not to be. In reading Albert Camus, D.H. Lawrence, F. Dostoyevsky, Camille Paglia, James Joyce and others, one may not agree with everything they say but may still be impressed and even awed by their brilliant and magnificent use of language—by their mastery of the word. Let me reiterate what I have said about myself, and especially about all of my journals, the last two being exemplary in this regard: language is exacting and I use it very particularly and for very specific results.

As practitioners, each one of you is called to and expected to use language in a precise and *authentic* way. The view of a school such as this one is easily diminished for others who might belong here, but whose view is obstructed by a proliferation of liars and cheats; furthermore, such lack of integrity effects the willingness of the Work to confer responsibility, knowledge, and ultimately obligation. Please pay closer attention to your use of language and to your tendency to be haphazard and willing to compromise your integrity to achieve some temporary and meaningless but immediate advantage or gratification. And please don't bring me your moans, complaints and tears—your empty and insincere remorse—when you are suffering the consequences of your lying and cheating. I thank you for what should and could be (though most likely will not be) discrimination and discretion.

As a serious body of spiritual students, it is time that we stop assuming—without question, investigation, or inquiry—that our "sins," our cheating and lying, are innocent and aren't hurting *that* much, aren't doing *that* much damage. In the small picture this may be true, but given the longevity and maturity of this sangha, dharma, and community, it is time that we begin to view *all* things from the base, the platform, the foundation, the viewpoint of the big picture: how the Work and God are affected by our indiscretions, procrastinations, and laziness to bring impeccability to our lives. In fact it is our glib egoism that simply overlooks the discomfort, pain, and frustration our actions cause in the dream, in the world of mortality, temporality, and illusion.

Most of us are up to the task. It is obvious by the sheer extraordinariness of so many of the ashram tea spaces this summer that we are up to the task—to cease cheating and lying and all that implies. As ever, the question is not can you, but will you?

Well, my dear heart-companions of the Path, thank you again for your profound consideration of these ideas. You have my gratitude as well as my Help. I am leaving early tomorrow morning: *Road trip!* I will see you everywhere and in every way, and until our next physical meeting, have a most joyous and exciting and especially useful and profitable (in the Work sense) time of it, at it, and for it. My love goes with you.

Jai Guru, Jai Guru, Jaya Baulo, Jaya Krishna!

राम राम

Radical Change

August 28, 2010

Radical change? Yes! Oh, first of all, I would like to welcome you all to this auspicious weekend. We can celebrate and delight in what is absolutely, certainly, without a doubt, sure to be a weekend of profound teachings, good company, and maybe even a bit of transformational breakthrough, for the seeds are being sown for such events just as surely, even now as we listen and consider these ideas.

It is auspicious for several reasons, not the least of which is your good karma, but that aside, it is auspicious because I am working in a way that is different than before and in a way that many of you have not seen. It is also auspicious because the Blessing Force of Yogi Ramsuratkumar is pouring through stronger than ever, and because the sublimity of this rarefied atmosphere is highly prized by those who know. It is also extremely scarce in the world these days in its genuine form and essence, which this is!

Again, I will be aided and abetted in our considerations together by my Valkyries, whose collective experience (when they are "on" that is, which to all of our great fortune, especially mine, is much of the time) is an invaluable, inestimable gift to anyone who is not just willing to listen to their words and nod in sage agreement but to actually make use of their input, insights and very hard-earned wisdom. And I suppose I won't be able to resist throwing in a comment here and there, despite the frustrating, annoying, and maddening inefficiency of my vocal skills these days.

Radical change. Try it, you'll like it! But remember, as my friend Werner Erhard says, "There is no breakthrough without breakdown." You cannot change—I repeat, *cannot* change, not even at all, let alone radically—from where you are. Where are you? Besides in Emmendingen, Germany, in a seminar with Lee Lozowick, who I hope you won't curse and revile when you leave Sunday evening or Monday morning, if you have never met me before. Yes. Thank you for that small favor.

As I just asked, where are you? You are identified with a psychological script that is the result of conclusions drawn by a small child—the child you once were, not only physically but emotionally and mentally, and should be no more. You are a mechanical being, chronically habitual and dynamically committed to suffering, illusion, confusion, ignorance, and mightily resistant to every kind of change whatsoever, except the horizontal shifts that are a function of that psychological script (such as the willingness to try new foods you've never tasted before, and such and like).

So you have found the Path, possibly me as your guide; you feel the Truth of it all and have deeply committed to it and sacrificed for it, and here you are, unable to change as you are. What to do, what to do? You must prepare yourself for radical change by developing, cultivating, a field of softness, a willingness to consider your abject spiritual poverty and the lies you have labored under all your adult life (and most of your childhood life), and an unshakable confidence in your guide—*an unshakeable confidence* in your guide, whether you call it faith, trust, love, gratitude, or even obedience, devotion or dedication.

If you don't have a guide, you will *need* one, sooner or later, so throw yourself into the Sacred Bazaar game, for these empowered artifacts are all charged with the Benediction that will lead you to your guide if you aren't already there. And if you are already there, play with even greater vigor and joy, for this Benediction will help you surrender to the benign and selfless Influence that desires only one thing: your submission to Reality as it is, here and now, which is itself happiness, purpose, direction, and service to God, or the Almighty, Life or the Universe—whatever you would like to call It. After all, It doesn't mind what you call It as long as you know It as It Is in Truth, without the usual distortions of the Great Dream that is our normal perspective.

Radical change! You deserve it, and . . . you will have to earn it. I am sorry I can't just pour it into you like water into a glass, but things don't work that way. First you must empty the "glass" that you are, which as we've already said is full to the brim with biases, false ideas, and worldviews: a life story defined by neurosis and self-reference, self-obsession and mistaken beliefs. Then you have to make sure that the "glass" is in good condition—no cracks, no leaks, no dirt or germs that could easily contaminate the pristine, pure Divine Water that *will* fill it if you "play your cards right."

I am as transparent to Yogi Ramsuratkumar as you are ready, able, and willing to receive His Father in Heaven's Grace. If you are choked with filth, I ain't that transparent *to you.* At the very exact same time, if for whatever reason, known or unknown, you are just at the edge of breakthrough—inviolable and irrepressible breakthrough that will never allow you to return to your lethargy and sleep—I am not only fully transparent, but literally *I am* that Force of Radical Change, the catalyst for your own personal shift of context. How about them apples, Granny? Are you up to it, up for it? I am. That's pretty much all I'm up to and up for, even though in the outer world I have many pleasures and many treasures . . . .

राम राम

Freiburg, Germany

This Tender and Sweet Alchemy

August 29, 2010

Isn't it a miracle? In spite of the impatience, intolerance, anger, bitterness and all the rest of lee's manifestations of recent times, the Blessings of Yogi Ramsuratkumar have not diminished but are positively shining forth, bursting forth with evident power! He demonstrates His Benediction and His Benevolence even through the veils of His Son and Heir's (that's me again) unconscionably un-guru-like behavior. Well, un-guru-like for the West. In India, of course, as all of you know who have studied the traditions both ancient and recent, I am only being in a way that many great masters have been, some of them for their entire lives, some for periods of time as needed.

I dislike this current form—dislike it immensely and intensely—but alas, here it is, as it is, with all its ugliness. I must say that many of you are embracing this "what is, as it is, here and now" and actually making profitable use of my little lilas. Although I must say, I would like y'all to be careful around the temptation—the sweet seductive pull—to succumb to the "herd mentality" in relation to the Landmark Forum programs; in these I have offered you an extremely valuable tool, but many of you have turned it into a "golden calf."

Anyway, or in any event, I am pleased and awed and extremely grateful for your willingness to take what could be confusing and disturbing—the piercing scalpel of these times of my outspoken surgery on your egos—with faith and devotion (those of you who have and are). The point is that Yogi Ramsuratkumar is pulling the strings of lee—His Heretic and Poet (in the old court sense of it). It is His Influence, His by the Grace of Father in Heaven, that is most assuredly running the show. Hallelujah! Or as Aleister Crowley might have said, "Blessed be!" Now that I'm reminded of "the Beast" (the notorious Mr. Crowley), one of his other favorite phrases was "Christians to the lions!" It's a reference to old Rome and a metaphor for "ego to the fire of transformation!" Implying that if you are dogmatic and at war with the flow of Blessings, you will get transformed if you're willing to drop the judgment that keeps you at war. And hey, my friends, we aren't all Androcles (who pulled the thorn out of the lion's paw), meaning, don't make glib assumptions that Yogi Ramsuratkumar will take care of everything if *we* aren't doing *our* part, which, thank the Heavens, most of us are to varying degrees, inwardly and outwardly.

Praise. It is a rare, rare human being who can handle and manage praise. Many of us manage praise fairly well on the surface; it is under the surface, in the unconscious, where compliments tend to have their insidious effects, such as sabotaging our projects or plans—and more commonly, those of others—or starting to take more initiative than we have earned, and so on and so on. I have made a business of *not* praising people, but for the last year or so especially I have been positively *lavishing* praise on both individuals and the sangha, at least compared to my usual rare compliment. Too bad.

I made the mistake of complimenting the serving staff yesterday. Big mistake. My salad-making efforts for dinner seemed to be relatively ignored, though not entirely, thankfully. It isn't that they weren't hustling; they were just sort of . . . numb. We had a fabulous object lesson when I said, "Bring all the beets," and then later, "Where are the beets?" Apparently that was not clear, as a *large* portion of beets were left sitting on the serving table. Hello! Is anyone listening? Is anyone paying attention? Yes, we all work hard and with plenty of love and devotion; our hearts are sweet and generous. And, we need to think, look into situations, and handle the details as well.

Okay. Enough of that chirping and quacking. By my estimation, we had a fabulous seminar this weekend. Some excellent questions were asked and some good answers were offered and some tough issues may have been dislodged from their entrenched positions. We can only hope so. You all did some good work, for as we considered on Saturday, when any one person "works," everyone does their own work along with that person. Our task is to make a profit from the opportunities we have been given. We walked, stumbled, or crawled through a few doors this weekend, and it is our job, our responsibility, to keep moving forward, so to speak—and actually, more than a single directional movement forward, it is an all-directional radiance that we are called to animate. Anyway, we need to use the tools we have added to our "workshop" during these juicy few days.

As the world turns, a few people were having an intense interaction this morning, in which feedback was being offered to one person. I could hear loud voices in the next room in exchange, but it wasn't the heat of the conversation, of which there was plenty, but the clear urgency in the voices. We are called now—*right now*—to a higher, more mature level of work. Our care and concern for one another is deep, great, and extraordinary. We are bonded in a very uncommon way, like elements in the Mystical Body of Christ, or common feathers on an Angel's wings. So, even in the midst of anger, irritation, frustration, and impatience, the urgency of our desire to see and feel and profit from one another's breakthroughs is strong. And it is *urgent*; we don't have time to procrastinate or rest on our laurels, even if those laurels are woven from leaves of the Punnai Tree.[1]

As was also evident this weekend during the seminar as well as throughout the summer, as magnificent as the help offered by others may be, we aren't yet well-honed enough to do without my input. I am not planning to die, and at the same time, my manifestation has and is evolving to such a degree that . . . well, things just ain't what they used to be and most likely will not be again. I am not planning to go into seclusion, and at the same time, to many it certainly may *seem* that way. My vision—*Vision*—for the new Ashram in Arizona has so radically altered from my initial

---

1 "Punnai Tree" is a reference to Krishna's lilas with the gopis.

naïve and enthusiastic picture that I'm sure it will be misunderstood by some and even resented by a few. And yet, this Help is more necessary than ever. The closer we get to some kind of upscale, both individual and community (and for a greater number of individuals than in previous upscales), the more important, in fact crucial, the skillful means of the Guide becomes.

So, this urgency is not just some hysteria. It is a very pragmatic demand of the Work. We require the experience of the Guide and the Blessings of the Guide's transparency to his Guide and the Lineage in order to fine-tune and carry out the extremely delicate surgery that is before us. In the beginning we could just ram into the fortress door and shake the structure; as much as that may appear to be what is going on these days with my fierceness and fire—as my loving and generous supporters call it—it isn't just a crude assault. We are digging deep into previously inaccessible levels to cleanse the rot and bacteria. Thank God you all are able to work this way, because the veils have become thinner and the obstacles less formidable. Yes, there are those few who cannot and more truthfully will not understand, but that is one of the prices of this tender and sweet Alchemy. As they say in America, "If you can't take the heat, get out of the kitchen."

Well, my good friends, delightful company, and hard-working, generous and loving devotees, time has run out. Not wishing to be late to Darshan, I must end here. Thank you so, so much for being willing to "stand up and be counted" this weekend. You did some fine work, made a stab at super efforts, and I hope learned something from those who were not able to make the leap. My heart is ever with you, even if my body is in another location. And as every year, our time here was and still is miraculous, feeding, profitable, and invaluable. Seeing you is one of life's great pleasures . . . even those of you who I yelled at!

Until we meet again . . .

Jai Guru, Jai Guru, Jaya Guru Raya

राम राम

Ferme de Jutreau, France

"Delicate Impartial Love"

September 3, 2010

I've welcomed you to the seminar on Friday morning, and now I welcome you to Darshan, a closure of a sort on this lovely Sunday evening. I say closure "of a sort," because in a very real sense there is never closure. The Work goes on, whatever the situation, circumstance, or environment. The Work goes on whether I am physically present or not, whether it appears that my attention is fully on you or that I am ignoring you and unaware that you even exist. I am always offering help regardless of your perceptions, projections, fantasies, or biases.

In the salon the other day we had a short but sharp consideration, which was: "Why, when someone is asked a yes or no question, do they not simply answer yes or no?" There is always a story that must be told, a "But, well, I . . . " or some variety of defense, a clarification, and so on. I said, if and when I want information, I can and will ask for it. And I added that people think they are coming here to progress on the Path, to grow spiritually, to discover transcendental realms. Very nice. But first we need to build a reliable and mature foundation. One element of that, which almost no one has learned or embodied in thirty-five years, is to be able to answer a yes or no question with a direct and simple yes or no—and nothing more.

We have vast, truly extraordinary spiritual gifts, and for most of us, for the most part, those gifts are inaccessible due to our unwillingness to come down to earth, grow up as human beings, and apply our intelligence to our lives. This is something that is foreign to many of us, except within the very small confines of our specific or particular métier. So listen, chicks, pups, kittens, and snails, I'm too frustrated just scratching the surface and brushing people with feathers. What I'm learning now is surgery, deep surgery. I'm so tired of dealing with symptomatic expressions. I want to get down to the base, the core, and cut out the entire disease—eliminate it.

Of course I can't do this without your help and active, willing, enthusiastic and supportive participation. I've done a lot of operations this summer, and there has been some true participation. There have also been many instances in which the "patient" has not allowed my special brand of surgery to have any effect or useful results. At this juncture, I'd like to read a letter I just received from a treasured dharma brother, one of those rare beings who shares my view: Traktung Dorje Rinpoche, the Tibetan Buddhist who wrote introductions to my last two amazing journals—which, by the way, no one who considers themselves a student or even a friend or admirer, and who reads English even with mediocrity, should not own and study! Well . . . on to Traktung:

Dear Lee,

I hope you did not find the roses overly maudlin, like the expression of a school-girl crush. Three times in the last year you have interrupted my despondence with brightness: 1. The note you sent via mail. 2. A friend showing me an internet mock ad where you were making fun of some euro lady spiritualista. (I laughed with joy for weeks.) 3. The message delivered this last week. Each time you interrupted the smog laden, grilled fat, dirty diaper, sour mayonnaise smelling heat of this overly long afternoon family picnic called "human realm" with delicate impartial love.

The Al Jerrari Sufi order says: "If your friend has a need and they have to ask, you have already brought shame on yourself. You should meet this need before they even know they have it." So-called "spiritual seekers'" narcissistic self-aggrandizement precludes even common courtesy let alone such dignified behavior. It takes a true *beggar to display such qualities; you display this.*

These days oppressive disgust for falsity has me nursing a dark melancholy. I find myself unable to "get along with others" as their view of life sickens me and my view of life bores them. I am unable to remember how one "finds students" or what one would do with them. I am overly harsh with my friends—their proclamations of "wanting to go all the way" combined with ceaseless fixation on the "shit of shit" is tediously boring. To "want to live as Love" *but have* "What about me?" *tattooed on your every act wears thin after a time.*

My Beloved Guru says, "Traktung Rinpoche, you must have multi-lifetime view." But I don't. I seem only capable of "Get the fuck out of my way if you have no interest in real work" view. And though I keep being vicious, ugly, and mean to those around me, most of them will neither produce the "coin of the realm" nor leave. At the same time I have a small group of true, dedicated friends . . . so I should shut the fuck up and stop whining.

You, my dear friend, are a treasure in a ruin. I do not sound like cheery company, but come visit if you can. Bring however many you want for companionship—in case we turn out to be truly gross company . . . .
With love (actual love),

t.

P.S. A so-called "student" just wrote an email to ask: 1. "Can't I just be selfish for a little bit?" And two sentences later: 2. "I just want to feel loved." Ah, the black humor of it all. And after I kicked all "students" out!

Hey, how's that for someone who is on the same wavelength, eh? Now listen: none of you—well, very few of you—need to languish is such a horrid and unenlightened state. You can truly *be different* in any moment. You have the basic essence. And, if you can't even learn to answer a yes or no question with a yes or no, no more and no less, short of being silent, then it just won't happen. I have developed or created a comprehensive and intense training environment here—"here" being the entire field of this Divine Influence of Yogi Ramsuratkumar's Blessing Force, His Umbrella of Benediction, the context of the Mission that He generously entrusted to me, His True Heart-Son and Heir.

I am profoundly interested in an equally comprehensive and intense positive response from those who have been drawn here, however that magnetism has manifested. After thirty-five years of teaching, I'm ready for radical results. Yes, I have seen very satisfying progress, but . . . too little (in most cases, not all) and too slow. It's surgery time, folks. And unfortunately, in this Emergency Room, there ain't no anesthesia for you or for me. Believe me, there are times when I need it more than you!

So, that seems to fairly well cover the current state of affairs in this here Alchemical Lab. And how was your weekend? As you run, stride, walk, or crawl out of here, I wish you love, happiness, health, and beyond that, success in all that serves the Great Work, the sweetness of devotion, the sublimity of Adoration, and true Joy.

Jai Guru, Jai Guru, Jai Guru

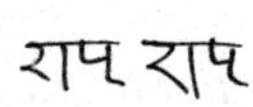

An Alchemy of Consciousness

September 11, 2010

Good morning! Welcome to this second seminar at the *vraiment belle* Belle Chasse. I won't be talking as much this year as last, but on the other hand, *à l'autre coté,* the Teaching seems to be richer, more potent, deeper and more incisive than ever. Imagine that! In fact, why just imagine, why not embrace it, use it, and profit from it? You have only you to benefit.

It is good to see you here, by the way. All of you. A few years ago I wouldn't have believed I'd ever say such a thing and mean it, but here it is and I do. Ain't that curious and amazing? As last year, we will entertain questions, which I will either answer in writing, *comme notre cher ami,* Chandra Swami, or they will be answered with the help of my aides, with coaching and kibitzing from *moi.* The more real the question, the more valuable, useful and profitable will be the answer. This is the way the Work is, not by any choice or definition or will of mine or yours, but by Its own essential Lawfulness and Justice. Bravo to the Work!

What is the Work? Many things, of course, one of which is a process of transformation, both inner and outer; if transformation isn't visible, noticeable, recognizable, it is questionable. The Work is an alchemy of consciousness that turns the base metal of illusion—the world of dreams, the tin and iron of lies, denial, fantasy and myth—into the pure and priceless gold of Surrender and Obedience to the Will of God. In other words, it is the conscious recognition of Reality, Truth, Grace, Mercy and Benediction and the alignment of our lives, passively and actively, inner and outer, with that Blessing Force and Wisdom.

In fact this could, and perhaps should, be our only aim, our only goal, our only wish and hope in and for our lives. This is what my Father Yogi Ramsuratkumar stood for, and I am His True Heart-Son and Heir. Based on the degree to which I am transparent to Him (that "I" not being lee lozowick but being His reagent, His Influence, so to speak), I represent Him and convey the opulent Gifts of His Father in Heaven. Well, enough of such highfalutin' blah, blah, blah. Any questions?

राम राम

Live and Learn

September 12, 2010

Good evening all, friends, supporters, devotees, disciples, tentative and not. It is somewhat bittersweet every year to be at the last Darshan in France—that is, at least the last personal bodily Darshan—until we return next summer. Although it may not have been so evident to some of you this year (due to my acidic and invasive not to mention almost constant criticism of ego and its insidious and vicious plays to sustain its dominance), my delight in being here is still a very real and deep essential mood for me.

Delight . . . I am always so happy to be here, as I am always so happy to be in Arizona when I am there. How amazing! I have the new Ashram and my new home to anticipate upon my return to Arizona, so of course that is a big pull and a situation for which I seem to have immeasurable enthusiasm. My plans for this new circumstance are thrilling to me, awesome in their sacred power of transmission, and just plain damn exciting—full of all forms of art, Blessing and Teaching Chambers.

On the other hand, I do believe we all had the best, the most successful, and the most profitable summer yet. The heat of the Teaching seems to have reached a scalding level . . . Bravo! We have had so many extraordinary teaching spaces and alchemical ovens; there has been such immediate potential and possibility and opportunity for real change, for cleaving more truly and profoundly to the Work and shaking loose the rigid and crystallized identifications with our psychological scripts. I hope y'all *use* it, and use it well for your own profit. Please, please, please do not simply bury all these gifts and leave them impotent, just more stories and philosophy.

And the Sacred Bazaar was spectacular this year. Thank you, thank you. This feeds me to an indescribable degree. Thank you, thank you again. I'm still somewhat abashed and embarrassed by my ugly and rude behavior, and yet it seems to have had extremely positive effects, at least in most cases. Bravo again! Good for you! We surely don't want to creep along at a snail's pace forever, with the Work threatening to retreat into benign obscurity, do we?

I also appreciate, perhaps more than mere words can say, your willingness, even your joy, in indulging my "days of salad and excess."[1] It has been quite a pleasure to whip up all of these concoctions, inventions, and occasional feasts for such a participatory bunch of *gourmands*. My compliments to you and my hat off to you as well.

We've seen a small surge of new interest in the community this summer as well, so my training on serving and hospitality such as it is and was, could actually be taken seriously, embraced, and activated in practical ways. Now wouldn't *that* be something! And remember, hospitality begins at home, so don't neglect your family and housemates in your virtuous service of others.

The lessons around food seem to have fallen on barren ground, though I simply cannot imagine how. I still have trouble believing that, even though all the facts seem to point to it. I have Faith in you, in spite of my peaked impatience and my ostensible intolerance for the gaping holes in practice and clearly evident, vast spaces of insensitivity.

We have made innumerable and dramatic teaching communications all summer. These manifestations are not just my "idiosyncrasies and eccentricities," so please do not shrug them all off as meaningless behavior quirks. I have been teaching, *teaching*, from

---

1 Throughout the summer and fall of 2010 Lee handmade sumptuous salads and huge sandwiches that he personally served to his devotees and friends.

the second I arrived in Europe, from breath to breath, moment to moment, day and night, present and not. Please, please, please show me you've learned something, many things in fact, and confirm my Faith in you, relieve my frustrations a bit and soften my intolerance. Bless you.

My friends, it is all about the Teaching—not just learning it in our heads, which most of us do quite well, but embodying it so the practice is the *first* thing to arise inwardly and outwardly, in thought, feeling and *action*, in every moment, prior to the lightning-speed reaction of the psychological script. That is our Work. In order for that to come to pass, we cannot afford to be lazy, laid back or lacking in passion about, around, and for this Teaching.

We must constantly be studying, in the context of the Teaching, using *every* life situation and circumstance to reflect back to us directly in relation to the Teaching, always self-observing, considering, looking for that opportunity, that possibility for Work, for breakthrough, for transformation, to be given a task, for another piece of the puzzle that is our labyrinth, both the labyrinth of the dream, the lie of illusion, and the labyrinth of Truth, the Real, of Being. There is no time to rest, except in the obvious ways that conserve energy and keep us healthy and sharp so we can actually be passionate instead of exhausted and worn out.

Okay. There is an English phrase that's used when one makes a miscalculation, an error of judgment, a foolish mistake, and one is trying to recover or just excuse the failures. This phrase is usually said somewhat cavalierly: "Live and learn." I'm sure there is a parallel in French. "Live and learn" is how we accomplish everything: walking, talking, developing skills in any area of expertise, driving, doing dance or martial arts with any degree of competence, mixing colors and using them effectively in painting, choosing what foods to combine and what foods not to and how to prepare them when we are working in the kitchen, and on and on. "Live and learn." As human creatures, this imperative is designed within us: live and learn. All of us do this selectively and refuse to do it or deny it, even outright reject it, in other areas

I'm sure you all know those who have one disastrous—or is it catastrophic?—relationship after another and never seem to learn anything from their messes. It is exactly the same in certain strategic areas of our individual lives: no matter how severe the consequences of our actions may be to ourselves or others, we just do not live and learn. We are stagnant, rigid, and invulnerable, stuck in a loop of misery and inauthenticity. As I've said a few sentences previous, we are *designed* to live and learn. The question is: What is it that keeps us from fulfilling this design? Anyone can answer: "Well, it's my psychological script, my life story, the traumas of the past that I am locked into . . . " Blah, blah, blah.

Having the intellectually correct answer is often one of the very things that stands between us and true self-knowledge, between having the factual data and real wisdom. When we already assume we know something, why would we pursue an investigation of that domain? Self-observation, objective and ruthless self-honesty, is about a genuine perception of what is, exactly as it is, free of our beliefs, our philosophies, and especially our certainty that we understand.

When we learn to walk or talk, living and learning is automatic. It requires no thought or conscious effort of will. It happens very naturally by instinct and survival, merely in the process of development. This is why to learn several languages as a child is quite easy. I'm sure you all also know adults who attempt to learn another language—spoken or movement—and never quite seem to progress effectively, to get the accents properly, to master the nuances. It is because their live-and-learn mechanism is already dominated by "It's all about *me.*" (And my biased, stilted, mechanical, dogmatic, illusory view of life and reality.)

On the Path, maybe even *especially* on the Path, this is what we are called to Remember: to live and learn. We are created to live and learn; to fail to fulfill this aspect of our being is to insult God, to spit in the face of Divine Intelligence, to stop the creative impulse in its evolutionary tracks.

So come on folks, let's get with the program: live and learn! Are you up to it? Much of the stunning irritability I've expressed this summer—and without a grain of elegance, charm, dignity, nobility or class, I might add—could certainly be attributed to the *ache* of a massive wall of what looks like a plain stubborn unwillingness on the part of so many even long, long time students to live and learn.

We stumble along in our chronic patterns, maintaining our habits, indulging our desires, burping, farting, breathing and suffering, but appear to be relatively uninterested in learning at all. Of course we vocalize plenty of sincere wishes to learn but, my friends, as is also said in English, I believe in England itself, in fact: "The proof is in the pudding." I see a lot of pretty flashy but tasteless "pudding."

Well, I'm writing this between 1:30 and 2:17 in the morning, uncharacteristically unable to sleep, so I'm going to "throw in the towel," another English saying that refers to the arena of the so-called sport of boxing, "give sleep a chance," a not-very-veiled reference to a John Lennon lyric, and hope that this little sermon has touched you—pierced you actually—deeply enough to make a difference.

Until we meet again in Darshan, I leave you with love, with my Faith in you, with the ever-present and ongoing Blessings of Yogi Ramsuratkumar and the Lineage, and with a wish to see "the heat of suffering become the fire of joy, surrender and ecstatic communion."

Jai Guru, Jai Guru, Jaya Guru Raya

राम राम

Live and Learn II

September 19, 2010

Good evening. Welcome. I am writing this eight days ago, so I assume I had a good week. And yours? I'm in Paris, well, no actually I'm in Brussels visiting my son and his girlfriend, both of whom are attending university there, well actually here, if we call tonight tonight. I am writing this the same fine morning I wrote the second half of last week's address, though it is 5:12 and I slept very well, thank you. Since the two o'clock-plus time I ended the last entry, I woke up, had another hour to sleep before I needed to rise to prepare for the one day seminar at the lovely Belle Chasse, but this entry was knocking loudly on the inside of my skull, so to speak, and so here it is.

I'd like to continue in the vein, the "mother lode," at least in this here mine, of our consideration of last week. To "Live and learn" should not and need not be a painstaking, tooth-pulling, snail's pace, turtle-creeping process of struggle. It should be and can easily be a smooth process of miss the mark, adjust, miss the mark, adjust, miss the mark, adjust, respond. This is how it was with Yogi Ramsuratkumar and myself. I always knew when I was missing the mark, whether it was a sense of things or a result of His direct feedback. And I adjusted—not when I got back to America or the next year before I visited Him, but directly, immediately, right there on the spot. When He told me not to hesitate, that was it. I never hesitated again relative to His wish or demand, even if I was "sweating beneath the whip" or my mind was screaming to hesitate, or my psychological script was pulling the reins to "beat the band," another American colloquialism.

I did what was wanted and needed instantly, one reason being that I knew that Yogi Ramsuratkumar's wish or demand had no personal motive, no "edge," no excuse. It was always what was "wanted and needed," as an action in the moment or as a context for all time—what was wanted and needed by the Work, by the Universe, aligned with the Will of God and Life. I never allowed (and it is a choice, my friends) my mind, my psychology, to wrestle with Him. I knew He had my spiritual interests at heart, my "transformation," my relationship to Father in Heaven, as His moving force, as His urge to respond to me, direct me, instruct me or *order* me; I followed as exactly and implicitly as I could understand or grasp His inference or implication. And if I missed the mark, I adjusted again, immediately, without discussion, contemplation, or a "group," even if at times I didn't fully comprehend where something was headed or even what was going on fully. I knew *He* was clear and therefore I didn't need to be. Capiche?

So until "living and learning" is the natural design and flows unimpeded, as if we were innocent children, literally as effortlessly as if we were learning to walk (and in a sense we are learning to walk on the ground of Heaven, so to speak, learning to walk in a true way, having to slough off the burdens of our learned confusion and misidentifications); until to live and learn is tacit, we may need to apply our intelligence to it, to be conscious of this Law and to make the gesture with a degree of will. If that is so, it should not be problematical at all. What is most important to us—God, the Path, this Work, or the blatant lie we are dreaming and animating in each moment? Is our pain and anguish, our pride, vanity, greed, fear or anger worth more to us than happiness, joy, delight, service, communion?

It surely may seem so, from the massive complex of feelings and emotions that vie with one another to keep us rooted in our habitual mechanical states. But if we are honest, we want *out*! And to get out is very simple. Live and learn. Take last week's and this week's discussions and establish them in yourself, plant them, water them, protect them and care for them commensurate with the value that they actually are, to use the seed-and-plant metaphor again. And why not, as it fits so well in so many circumstances?

To me it was always obvious when my behavior pleased my Master and King, Yogi Ramsuratkumar. From a simple, subtle, yet unmistakable, no-matter-how-subtle gesture or acknowledgement to a beaming and radiant smile, He never "left me in the dark." I am no more inaccessible or obscure, in fact much less so, than Him. How do you know you've missed the mark? Pay attention to the Source of feedback, the One for whom you are wanting to, *needing* to in fact, meet the mark. The response is always telling. In fact I *cannot* hide approval or disapproval, even would I want to. Were my motives in this "training" personal, of course, I could fake it to a very convincing degree, but since it is only to the Work, to the Absolute, to Yogi Ramsuratkumar that I owe my allegiance, I *cannot* mask the information that tells you *clearly* whether adjustment is necessary or not.

So your excuses, justifications, crying and whining over continually missing the mark are unconvincing, and in fact are often comedic in their absurdity and desperation. You (your ego that is) may be convinced, but no one else is, except perhaps your enabler or enablers, who or whom you have chosen quite strategically exactly because they are willing to be fooled, to continue to turn a blind eye to truth and placate you and condescend—very passionately and with great dedication and devotion—to your neurotic commands and patterns. And you don't need to examine me under a microscope (or view me with a telescope when we are physically distant), for my indications of your on-the-markness or off-the-markness are quite evident, even dramatic or dynamic many times. You just need to pay attention, be alert, awake, eyes open, senses ready, willing and able and antennae up.

Well, and on that word, if I don't add anything in the ensuing week, plus a day . . . I miss your company, truly.

राम राम

Ferme de Jutreau, France

Be Different

September 26, 2010

I just got a glimmer of something. We don't "get it." We've either got it or we don't. We already have it and use it and demonstrate it—or not. But "getting it" just doesn't seem to be a human (at least an adult human) thang. What a *Catch-22*! Or is it *Stalag 17*?

Got it? One of the most significant changes I have seen, with some exception of course, from the Landmark Forum training is that most or many of the graduates begin their letters to me: "I'd like to acknowledge . . . " Screw that shit! To acknowledge is to *be* different.

So, how to be different if we don't get it—if we either have it already or don't? Good question. I've been answering it for over thirty-five years now. Got it yet? A few of you have stepped up to the plate, but most people are writing me the same letters year after year, asking me the same questions year after year, looking very sincere and thoughtful when faced with *my* feedback (though not necessarily that of my empowered, so to speak, emissaries) but with no real noticeable difference.

It's all about context, of course, for as you all know, a change in context may appear dramatic, but it is only an ego salve that convinces no one except enablers, suckers, naïve, starry-eyed idiot practitioners and ourselves—mostly ourselves. Can we get it? *Of course.* How? By being different.

The problem is we are *trying* to be different or *trying* to become different. Nope. Don't work that way. We either start on the spot, in the moment, to live from a different context, or we maintain the old one, which is our identification with the dream, the lie, illusion—in other words, a life of unnecessary suffering. Bummer, man!

So, there is no "getting it." We already have it or not. What is that? Karma? Good family? Fortuitous environment? I don't know. What I know is that I want—maybe even need—to rely on people who "have it" and are demonstrating "it." I need to be able to rely on people's responsible and integral action, on their skills, their creative inspirations, their maturity, their ability to make value judgments that match my own. And if they are not responsible (there's that word again) for all that, I need them to be responsible for having missed the mark, in which case responsibility means no guilty, heart-rending confessions or ten-page letters of apology. Simply live and learn, adjust and go on, as any mature adult would.

As y'all know, these days I've about run out of patience and tolerance for whining, cloying equivocation and a willingness to continue as we are. It is "be different" or suffer the torture of feeling as if you have lost me, which a number of our European brethren have expressed feeling this summer.

No, puppies, *you* haven't lost *me*—it is *I* who have lost *you*. And such failure really pisses me off, as I am quite attached to most of you. So get with the program and stop drifting away in your false (you *lie*, babies) confusion, doubt, and lethargy. Neither of us can afford such sleeping luxuries.

Well, I'm sorry for such a rambling, disjointed (Is it? I don't re-read what I write; it takes too much time and energy.) and short address tonight. Busy, busy, busy! Not like a bee or an ant but like a Work Monster (not ogre) that sees what needs to be given and won't (or maybe can't) back off, chill, and coast. So until next week, or . . .

Jai Guru, Jai Guru, Hari Bol and Jaya Baulo Guru

राप राप

A Chance to Move

September 30, 2010

Good morning! I hope you are all ready to rock and roll! I am. The Work can have unusual ways of forcing its employees to produce what it wants produced. Ah well. Here I am, ready to help, if help is truly wanted. I know y'all say you want help. That's easy to do. And I know most of y'all really believe that your word is honest. Your belief is sincere but your word is not. Most of you don't really want help, not where help is *received*. You only want help where the *idea* of help is conceived.

But I am here to help, and if you are willing to take it as I give it—in the ways the Work has redefined "my" style and approach—then much excellent progress will be made this weekend. And if you resist, as usual, outside and inside (which is more likely)? Well, you'll still have a few good stories to tell!

As I can't talk as I used to, though I expect my old facility to return, I have to communicate somewhat differently. One of the several ways this occurs is through the Sacred Bazaar. The Artifacts and Deities speak for me (and *with* me), and speak they surely do—often quite loudly and dynamically. So throw yourselves into the Sacred Bazaar. Play, play, play! It is one of the few things that really brings happiness to me these days.

This has been a stunning summer, both in people's willingness to take risks in the Sacred Bazaar—for what is money worth anyway, if not to buy beauty and *real* value?—and in people's unwillingness to do the Work necessary to grow up, become adults, and leave their misery, suffering, fears, problems and struggles behind. We are *so* in love—not just attached or addicted to, really in love with—our horrible, petty, ugly existences. That is not *drôle.* It is unbelievable to me.

So, today and tomorrow we have a chance to move—from a millimeter to a kilometer. The question is not "Can you?" but "*Will you?*" Any questions? Let's go!

London, UK

Who Is the Guru?

October 3, 2010

Good evening. Hello. Welcome. Well, my friends, I think I'm just too human for most of you. You persist in identifying this deteriorated, miserable physical form as Me, as the Guru, and you will not be dissuaded from the severity and fantasticality of your illusions. When I visited Yogi Ramsuratkumar for the last time, I saw a horribly suffering, chemotherapy catastrophe who should have been allowed to check out many months before, as He and His Father wished and designed. A wish and design, by the way, which was resoundingly ignored, even vilified, by His so-called "loving" devotees, with the exception of a small few—the same small few from whom the Guru can draw an equally small satisfaction in the midst of such ignorance and blindness.

It does not take a friggin' genius to notice that I can't even take one sip of water, let alone eat or drink anything, without serious difficulty. I guess y'all assume that being the guru, I love nothing better than sitting around for hours listening to my students' delightful and delighted conversations and watching them devour, with enthusiastic relish, amazing meals and desserts while commenting on how fantastic it all is, while I cannot even consider sampling one teaspoon of tea or soup. That's how *my* summer has been going. Yours? On the other hand, I recently commented that this seems to have been the best summer ever for the guru, though *not* for the guru's body. Yup.

I guess I'm just too human for most of you. Sure, miracles happen by the fistful, but is it this body that affects all of that? Please, get a grip, wake up and smell the coffee. As this body fades in and out of its usual radiance, you are devouring the body, assaulting it—or at least attempting to, most of which I'm able to deflect—and not entirely ignoring the guru but missing the point.

Who am I? Not who is lee lozowick, but who am *I,* the transparency to Yogi Ramsuratkumar? And who was He but the transparency to His Father in Heaven, though clearly to a far greater degree than I have yet realized. Who am *I,* your *guru*—this ailing, uncomfortable, frustrated physical form? Please, again, give me a friggin' break. I'm just too human for most of you. Now that I'm not the knight in shining white armor, the hero leading ya'll in this body to salvation, *who* am I? I think you'll need to get a bit transcendental to get through all of this with some degree of success, hmmm?

Please, cut this body a bit of slack. One day of observation will, could, and should give you all the information you need to know to serve as a devotee, not as a starry-eyed idiot-student, lost in your own subjectivity, in your own sad stories of "me, me, me" and grasping onto the Landmark Forum ideas as if they were gonna save you, when the thousand-time greater gifts that I have showered on you over thirty-five years have not been fully used. You wanna talk about a *racket*? Please remember that I only recommended that program, however excellent it is, to less than two handfuls of people, and all the rest of you sheep have just herded along, blind to your own ignorance and *unwilling* to respect the wise counsel of your elders in the Work. You can't or won't organize your time to be at all Work Weekends on the ashram, but you'll work your ass off for Landmark? That is almost a new low! That is worse than an insult to your work—it is blatant abuse.

Okay, enough ranting. I'll be back in America next week, full of spit and bile and thoroughly exhausted, so please give me a break from the dynamics that perpetrated your sending me so much mail in France the last two weeks—and sending books, CDs, and other objects, all of which I now have to carry back to America (is anyone out there *thinking*?)! Please give me a chance to recover before you inundate lee. Use the *Guru* more than ever but give this poor human fellow a little breathing room, will ya? I think I'm just too human for most of you dreamers.

Jai Guru, Jai Guru, Jai Guru

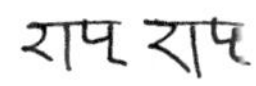

Something to Look Forward To

October 10, 2010

Good evening. I hope your fervent enthusiasm for the Work remains undimmed and unblocked, even though I am back, physically, with all my nasty habits of late and even nastier attitude. The trash can by my desk in the office has been so stuffed full since I have returned, I can see that your fervent enthusiasm to "not be uncharacteristic" remains undimmed and unblocked, in spite of the Landmark Forum "education," so called, that so many of you received, or claimed to have received.

Well . . . onwards. Visiting the new Ashram this week brought tears to my eyes. I am so eagerly awaiting and anticipating moving there to initiate this new phase in our Work and practice together. As I said to Bala, this new dimension will be "intimate" rather than more widely public, as I first imagined when the project commenced.

We've only had one consideration of the summer's wild teachings in After Dinner Talks so far, but I think that a clear context was set. I am no longer willing to "indulge fools gladly," except, of course, when that is the only option those "fools" can accept: to be "suffered" (indulged) gladly. It is or certainly should be obvious that your intelligence, all of you, is quite capable of "getting" the need, not just the luxury, of coming to a clear and definitive—dare I say objective?—self-clarity at the deepest of levels and leaving the superficiality of previous levels of awareness to the dust and ashes of the past. I have faith in you. You, most of you, *are* up to this demand—and it is a demand. From the gentle request it used to be, it has become a demand.

I had a private Sacred Bazaar salon this summer, and after I had set up, I announced as usual that "the game was on, the tables were open, and it was time to play." I was quite impressed and touched to be informed that everyone in the group had agreed to wait until everyone was there before beginning to select their pieces—very nice as a community ideal, sort of the "one for all and all for one" principle. I'm not suggesting we try to embody this exactly in everything, but I surely am illustrating that it is realistically possible to celebrate the joy of others—as Pema Chödrön's commentary on the bodhisattva vow suggested. As a community, we have worked long and hard together, and there are obvious positive results to show for it. It is time to amp it up and go for the next level, to "leap the octave" so to speak.

My health issues aside—and those issues are an "aside"—as a community we are called to hold a certain authority, and with me or without me (though I'm afraid to say it will most likely be with me for a while yet), y'all need to "get with the program." As I'm sure you will hear many times during the storytelling at ADTs, when asked or confronted this summer about certain modes of doing things, one of the things I said multiple times was: "Well, it isn't the way *we* do things, but it is definitely the way *you* do things."

When I say "we," I don't mean "*I*" exclusively—that is, lee lozowick's preferences, habits, personal choices. I meant that there is a Work principle way of doing things, a lawful expression of authentic objective practice, and there is the egoic, psychologically tainted, illusory, lie-identified, dream version way of doing things. It is up to each and every one of you, as individuals and as part and parcel of the sangha body (the "Corpus Christi" so to speak, and I ain't whistlin' Texas here!) to come to animate, know, understand, and embrace the "way *we* do things" and cease to stubbornly and rigidly do things the way *you* do and have always done things, as was so eloquently outlined Thursday evening at the ADT (that's After Dinner Talk, not Always Dumbfounded Talk).

Another principle that was exposed relentlessly this summer was to appreciate the "spirit of the law" rather than being a being a zealous, dogmatic, "letter of the law" fundamentalist. That is something else you will hear plenty about in the coming storm of stories from the summer in Europe. As to what twists and turns my manifestations will take here in Arizona, over and against all the things you will be introduced to from our overseas sojourn, who can say? But I feel I have pretty much had it with sycophantic gestures full of fear, denial, and an outright and categorical refusal to self-observe, to be ruthlessly self-honest. So, I imagine some of the summer's activity will be evident here as well. *That's* something to look forward to! It's something to look forward to if your work is truly important to you.

As you all know, especially here in this school, life is about an ongoing, sometimes moment-to-moment choice to work consciously as the alternative to sleep, laziness, procrastination defined by habit, comfort needs, sloppiness or pride, vanity, sloth and etc. (that's et cetera, not every technological candy). Do you email your mother? Or do you actually call her on the phone and make personal contact? (And the million-and-one ordinary choices that we so mechanically enact all the time.)

It is time to bring some consciousness—meaning adult maturity and integrity—to our activity rather than just blindly stumble or roll along just as we always have, just because we haven't gathered an undue quantity of moss. Well, ta ta for tonite, my dear, dear friends. Jai Guru, Jai Guru, Jai Guru

राम राम

Timing Is Everything

October 17, 2010

It was said that during one of the Landmark Forum Advanced Courses, the trainer commented on several of our community participants by saying that they were uncoachable. That is exactly how I heard it reported. I would say that the community member about whom that comment was spoken, is without question one of those "uncoachables." There are a few of you, a number of "uncoachables," here in this room tonight and a number in Europe.

I need not go into everything this implies except for two points. All of these "uncoachables" want—in some cases desperately, passionately, and heartbrokenly—to be coachable. In some cases this is based on having a small taste of the reality of their (so far) impenetrable armor; in other cases this is based on having no glimmer of awareness whatsoever, even believing themselves to be open, ready and able to be coached. They are not insensitive people, although I have on recent occasion called some of them "stones." They recognize the pain of this abject (I believe that is the appropriate word, though a bit strong) failure to "get with the program."

I have been giving instruction in becoming coachable for years, and it is thus: objective self-observation, or in our language, ruthless self-honesty. I believe in the Landmark Forum programs they call it "owning your racket." Yes? It seems to me that the first step to this state of clarity is the realization that you are not self-observing. Okay, enough on that point.

The second point is relative to the absolute wealth, the treasure, the cornucopia, the wish-fulfilling tree, the gem-spitting mongoose of story, of teaching, that will be spilling out, pouring, gushing like the Ganges in monsoon, at the After Dinner Talks for some time. This summer we hit another mother lode, and if you wish coaching, its value is incalculable. So, if you are not just passively occupying space, taking notes or not, but allowing yourselves to be an active element of the chamber, which in no way necessitates some kind of forced or efforted "participation," you may find the key to becoming "coachable" if you are now uncoachable. And if you are one of the coachable (to varying degrees, of course) majority, you will most certainly be filled to pleasant satiation (or saturation perhaps) with profound Holy Blessings and Sacred Help. So please take the ADTs as a resource of inestimable utility and of irreplaceable input. That, of course, means being there!

So, thank you for listening and hopefully engaging these issues . . . and next? How about timing? The most perfectly-designed input for someone—or shock, if you will—will be completely ineffective if delivered at the wrong moment, or at a "bad time," as in the timing scheme of the Universe or the Work. That is not what ego would call a bad time: "It's a bad time, I'm having my period," or "It's a bad time, I'm on the phone, in the shower, driving, making love, oops, having sex," and so on.

It's not like shock can work a little bit. It either has the necessary effect or not. There are no degrees. So of course most of us are always wanting to and frequently trying to push things along, being the impatient know-it-alls that we are. We assume that—given our obvious intelligence and our profound desire, not to mention the urgency of the situation these days and always—if we just had the key to our ignorance, to our blindness, all would be well. *Wrong*. The key is what irrevocably alters us forever, not just what occupies the mind and satisfied the intellect, answers the question in that way but leaves our activity, our being, completely unaltered.

Am I a master of timing? No. But That which moves me, through me, as me at times—call it God, Supreme Intelligence, Truth, Life, Reality, Yogi Ramsuratkumar—always knows exactly and precisely (and without redundancy) the perfect timing to provide or produce this miraculous shock—for it always is miraculous. And if we need to wait twenty years, well, "patience is a virtue," doncha know?

So I've heard it said and seen the truth of it as well, countless times in myself and equally countless times in others.

Not only must the timing be accurate in the sense of circumstance but also in the sense of our personal—both physical and psychological—capacity to receive, sustain, and (hopefully) use the shock. That may mean you need to raise your children first (and let them go when it is time, even if you have to kick them out of the nest, or rip yourself out of it!) or finish a certain cycle—financial, health-wise, artistically or whatever—to put certain things behind you before you have both the maturity of experience and the free attention to give to the shock, to appreciate it for what it is, to be undivided in your choice to embrace it and make value of it.

Ah yes, timing is everything.

And so, my patient, forbearing, and dear, dear friends and, hopefully, students—another Sunday Darshan program comes to a close. But oh, our tea space awaits, and being sentient as it is (the tea space, that is), and populated by untold numbers and dimensions of beings (subtle for the most part), it awaits eagerly, with great anticipation, hoping, above and beyond hope of course, for a meal of liquid gold, diamonds, and rubies, and hoping against hope that mere entertainment isn't tonight's fare. As y'all know, the menu is created on the spot, and when it works, by the wings and hearts of all those subtle beings, by God it really works!

And what luck! The tea space is open, freely available *every* night, right along with the very real possibility of feeding those beings with sublimity! Of course, if you are there, you get the "points." And if you're not? Oh well, join the club of passive lethargy and spiritual mediocrity. It *is* good enough just to get by, good enough for God, karma, evolution and life. But is it good enough for *you*?

Jai Guru, Jai Guru, Jaya Baulo Guru Raya

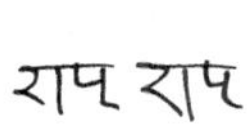

A Total Unknown

October 24, 2010

I've just finished reading Rose's sixty-page write-up of our time at Hauteville. Very impressive. Most of these teachings you will hear at the After Dinner Talks, as well as reading them at some point in *Tawagoto.* One of the things that really stands out in the exchanges is how people refuse to let go of their desire to hear the answer they want to hear. When my answer approximated this desire, they appeared satisfied; when it didn't, they acted confused, misunderstood, impatient with my answer and so on.

When you ask a question—if you are honest about being willing to really do something about what you consider to be problematical—it is important, maybe even imperative, that you allow yourself to be open to whatever the answer is and however it might come. We tend to ask questions as a gesture, kind of slipping our toe in the water but without a real, total commitment to *change,* to being lifted out of, above, and beyond our chronic mechanical behaviors, to being installed and established in a new, totally unknown position on a new, totally unknown foundation.

Yes, this is scary. Yes, it is like starting over. Yes. It can feel not only like we've lost everything but as if we've never been weaker, more ignorant, more helpless and hopeless. And from that unknown, that emptiness, that nothing, we can truly create something that is new and real and true to *now*—something uncomplicated, untainted and undefined by all of the child's assumptions, projections, false conclusions and misinterpretations, free of the effects of trauma and free of Mommy and Daddy. From this new base we can build a life of genuine clarity and objective function, undominated by the machine of the past, of the lies, of the dream, of the illusions of false beliefs and an untenable worldview.

So if you are not bottom-line willing to dismantle the structure that you so dearly hold on to in spite of immeasurable angst and suffering, tension and discomfort, your questions may be word-perfect, your ostensible motives may be at least pointed in the right direction, your heart may be in it, and you may, *as far as you are aware*, be honest, but the answer will do you *no* good, no good at all. Still the question may be useful, even particularly profitable, not for you (except through "backwash") but to others in the room who happen to be open and vulnerable, not because they want to be, necessarily, but because in their minds it isn't their question and they feel safe and relaxed, not being "on the hot seat."

Funny thing about human psychology—even though I am articulating something that could and would seem to create suspicion and defense, it can't and won't. Ain't that grand? Which means there need be no concern for those of you who are sincere in your intention to do this Work, to inhere in this Path, to be filled with Faith and taken by Surrender and, lest we forget, ravished by the Beloved. Not to worry, not to worry, there need be no concern. The guru's got it handled, covered, got your back.

Jankha Smith died yesterday. She dropped over with a stroke, was in a coma for a few hours, and then moved on (I gave her permission to go, and encouragement once she was in the coma). At times when someone dies it seems incomplete, like the whole timing is off; things are fuzzy and unclear. At other times it's just right. With Jankha it feels perfect. She was truly with Me. There's no dissonance to her passing, no disconnect. It's a smooth transition.

It's a funny thing about the practice body, isn't it? When I visited London, of course, Jankha was always there. I mean *there*, not just physically present but visibly. She wasn't one of the "movers and shakers." She didn't lead groups, make art, write books, contribute lots of time, money, or direct community service. What and how did she practice and participate? And yet there is no feeling in her death that something, anything, was left undone. How nice for her, and for Dave. As a couple they were a bright light in the sangha. Dave's amazing and inspiring commitment to her and his impeccable service—and as you all know, impeccable is not a word I use often—and their radiant mutual love.

Bravo! She is on about her natural karmic and evolutionary work freely and with the full Blessings and support of the guru and lineage. May we all have such extraordinary luck when it is our time, for as you know with sangha deaths, those we have witnessed, it isn't always like this—definitely not always like this—and sometimes it is even surprisingly problematical when it seems it shouldn't be, due to outer world (living) activity. Someone else we know died in Brazil last week, alone, found on the floor by his bed, chasing another miracle cure (psychic surgeon) as he has been doing for several years. His passing was not the celebration that Jankha's is, to make the previous point.

So . . . Three cheers for a "good" death, and if it's not, there is no one and nothing to hold responsible but ourselves. It is we who set context, handle business (family, parents, children, siblings and so on), define relationship within and without the sangha—both elements having effects on our clean or messy chalkboard—and establish and maintain contact of purity and innocence, or stain, projection, judgment and distrust with the guru. And Jankha, bless her heart and soul, had it all well-covered, some of it, like her relationship with her mother, which she handled literally a couple of weeks before she died!

So it doesn't take years of inherence and reinforcement; in fact it can all happen in a moment if that moment is authentic, totally without baggage, hidden or otherwise—without "attitude" in other words—and reliable over the rest of a lifetime. The Work knows when we are reliable and need not be tested over years and years, and that is good enough for the Universe, God, karma, and it all (and everything).

So lions, porcupines, armadillos, snails, clams, puppies and toads, be sharp, stay sharp, and don't do anything stupid like Romeo, unless Juliet is in on the plan. Communication, communication, communication!

Jai Guru, Jai Guru, Jaya Guru Raya

राम राम

Who Do You Say I Am?

November 7, 2010

Dr. Svoboda told us that prana follows attention. If you have no attention, if your attention is scattered, distracted . . . where does the prana go? I'm not going to tell you, but this is a vital question seriously worth consideration and perhaps contemplation. Let me repeat: If you have no attention, or if your attention is scattered, distracted . . . where does the prana go? Keep in mind that prana is vital to a life of clarity, health and work. You can't practice effectively if your prana isn't "right and bright."

Jesus asked James, "Who do they say I am?" And when James was done answering, Jesus said, "And who do *you* say I am?" This is the anchor, this is our hope. What anyone else says, maybe even including me, is not the criteria for lasting commitment; the criteria is: Who do *you* say I am? Who do you say I am in the waking "I," in the awakened "I"? All the other "I's" can go to hell and will if they aren't there already; they should never be what you base your decisions on about me, this Path, this school, this sangha and this mass of confusion.

I didn't say, "Who does your fractured, broken self (whenever it feels the least bit of fear, anger, recoil, resistance, tension) say I am?" Nope. Who do *you* say I am? You might only catch that once in a lifetime, or you might live there daily. What matters is what you allow to define your commitment and your attention. Is it the false, the unreliable, the constant-fluctuation mind: yes, no, if, maybe, (should I?!) and on and on ad infinitum. Or do you define your commitment in the heat of Reality, in the glimpse of Truth? And then *live* that commitment, even if you have to squeeze a truckload—hell, a damn planet!—of illusions into that life, the life of commitment, of practice, of right attention, of "doing the right thing."

If the commitment to a relationship changed with every shift of the wind, there would be no relationships lasting more than a *very* short time. For those lucky enough to feel devotion or more on a regular basis, God bless you, and I have a sneaking suspicion that anyone who persists and survives on the basis of the above will in the long run, in the maturing of their guru yoga, be in a state of heaven pretty much most of the time.

It is the survivors who survive in the Work. Those who leave too soon end up with a mass of pretentions and lives of lies and hubris, even if everything seems to be working beautifully well. Don't give up over a little gap in the intensity of your commitment; double your efforts, or even add ten percent to them, and be tenacious, stubborn, and unwilling to buckle under to every little voice that whispers in your brain or ear. Even some of the sangha have said such unconscionably stupid things to other sangha members! What is that all about? I know. I'm asking *you.* It's another question for consideration and contemplation. Well, already too many questions for one night, but what the hell . . . lest we falter while we're hot, let us forge on.

What do you expect to get from the Path, from me? Are your expectations realistic, in alignment with Dharma? (Study, study, study! Information isn't all there is to it, but no information—or worse, the wrong information—can be a real handicap.) Or are your expectations the result of some emotional weakness, at the effect of psychological aberrations? Remember: "A chain is only as strong as its weakest link." Bummer, since that applies to the sangha as well. Luckily there is a multi-level, multi-dimensional series of chains, but on the gross outside, we've got some pretty weak links—not weak minds, none of those here, just confused and undisciplined ones, and ones that assume certainty when doubt would be a much healthier assumption.

And, as sangha, it doesn't pay to ignore (entirely, but don't waste all your time and energy either) those weak links in the chain, but remember, you don't necessarily strengthen them by just wailing away on them, trying to pound them into strength. It's in the fire, out and cooled, in the fire again, out and cooled, in the fire again, et cetera. Too long in the fire weakens the metal; cool down too slow or too fast, it may crack, break or weaken the blade. If the crack is internal, therefore invisible, then your assumptions about your own "expertise" and "justice" can really be dangerous. And, too many times in the heat ruins the instrument.

This "work on self"—even when the self appears to be an other—is an exact and exacting science; it is only learned under the tutelage of a true master, with lots of trial and error. So you better be able to "afford" lots of materials, resources, and supplies, because there *will* be errors. Entire projects will have to be trashed, discarded. Remember, "Don't try to fix it." You can't turn a bad blade into a good blade; you can only create a new blade that is good from beginning to end. And such training both takes a lot of time and is time consuming as well (or not, again, if you are extremely fortunate), depending on the individual.

And yes, this is a Path of Grace, as the first volume of my biography will amply convey, and it is also a Path of Guru Yoga, and also a Path of the Work. Are these separate? Of course not, but then again they can certainly *seem* to appear to raise contradictions. How does that work? Oh dear, oh dear, still another important, very important, question for consideration and contemplation—and, to be really loose about it, let's say that consideration is a group process, like a group dharma grope, and contemplation is a solitary practice. So, both exterior and interior wrestling with important questions is not only useful but likely necessary. Not ultimately, of course, but the mind being what it is, and we being who we are—under illusion, lost in dreams and lies, identified with the false and at the whim of a vast multitude of "I's"—it is better to go the extra mile, so to speak, and cover as many bases as we can get to without being tagged out.

Whew! Tonight is just too sizzling to keep rambling on. Thank you so, so much for your enthusiastic engagement of the ADTs and recently the Bridge spaces and tea spaces. Such things really feed and inspire me. Keep up the good work, fight the good fight, and please guard against dogmatic zealousness, righteous indignation, and spiritual pride. My hat's off to you, my heart's open to you, and my Father's Blessings are raining down a storm.

Jai Guru, Jai Guru, Jai Guru

राम राम

There Is Always Another Chamber . . .

November 14, 2010

The Bridge space Wednesday had pretty much wound down and Sharana, who hadn't been playing at the table, was in the room the whole time. She asked if she could add something at this late time, when essentially I had gotten up and was on my way out of there. She said, "I have the feeling lately that the questions are just intellectual, information expressed, and asking for more information." No profit in that blind loop. So she went on to consider that the people bringing themselves, and possibly questions, to the space were unwilling to make the sacrifice necessary in the vulnerability (or context) of their question to spark and sustain a "chamber," the kind which we have seen with some regularity lately in the Bridge space.

On one hand, I agreed with her. The space was kind of dead, almost morbid, with a lot of sincere and deeply committed students and guests, but no "juice," no passion, no *fire*. I have a different view than Sharana. The questions, even the most mundane, had within them a seed of Reality, of the vast not only possibility but probability of igniting a forest fire of passionate consideration, discussion, and revelation. Even the absolutely most banal few words held a key, and *we*, not the questioners, who may be unaware of their mechanicality, were the parties to be held responsible to do something about it.

We could easily have raised the pristine dharma to sublime heights, but we were too lazy, too dull, too uninterested, too whatever. A chamber is a communion of forces acting in consonance, not a force applied from outside to make something happen. *We* failed that night, not the questioners, because we know better, or at least should have. So, it is never useful to lay down on the job. Is it? I was a little saddened by the windows that slammed shut and the opportunities that were lost by our simple procrastination. I flashed on a couple of outstanding possibilities, but was not speaking at all that night. Ah well, there is always another Bridge space, another Darshan, another ADT.

Sorry this is so short....

Jai Guru, Jai Guru, Jaya Guru Raya

राम राम

Afterword

Khepa Lee Lozowick (1943-2010) was an American-born spiritual teacher who, from the beginnings of his radical awakening to God in 1975, taught thousands of people in North America, Europe, and India. Contemporary prophet and poet, Western Baul guru, and spiritual heart son of his master, Yogi Ramsuratkumar, Lee left his body in November 2010, leaving a multifaceted legacy: a comprehensive teaching, several ashrams dedicated to his teaching and lineage, over twenty books of prose and poetry, forty CDs of original music, and a sangha or spiritual clan of dedicated students.

Although many aspects of Lee's teaching style were geared specifically for Westerners, the heart of his teaching—as he said many times—was rooted in the Indian tradition of his lineage. Lee's relationship with his master, Yogi Ramsuratkumar—the revered beggar saint of south India, who was himself the spiritual son of Swami Ramdas of Kerala—was a rare example of the traditional guru-devotee relationship, the mode in which Lee worked as well with his own students. While firmly established in the *parampara* (lineage) of his master, Lee's deep connection with the Bauls of Bengal was also blessed by Yogi Ramsuratkumar. For over thirty-five years, the practices, sadhana, and teachings instructed by Lee—so resonant with those of the five-hundred-year-old tradition of the Bauls, who encode the transmission of their esoteric practice in song and dance—have given rise to a *sampradaya* (spiritual clan or school) of Bauls in the West.

Grounding his teachings in lineage and tradition gave the path and practice a foundation or canvas on which Lee as *khepa* was the mad painter, using uncanny and sometimes wild hues, textures, and unexpected, exultant strokes.[1] While he called his students to live his teaching of Spiritual Slavery—radical surrender to the Will of God and reliance on guru and God—he also led them on path in which all aspects of life were integral to sadhana. Traditional dharma was seamlessly interwoven with tantric Baul *sahajiya* teachings that took Lee and his students on a road ranging wide and far, from ashram renunciation and disciplined practice to householder life to rock and roll tours across the U.S. and Europe.

Lee Lozowick was a poet, lyricist, and lead singer for an American rock band, *liars, gods & beggars*, a blues group, *SHRI*, and a European band, *The Lee Lozowick Project*. He was a prodigious writer, a connoisseur of art in all forms, a dealer in sacred artifacts, an advocate for children and conscious parenting, and a planetary citizen; his traveling schedule alone in the last twenty years of his life was daunting, as he began to actively teach in Europe during the late 1980s while he also made annual pilgrimages to India to spend time with his master in Tiruvannamalai. Beyond all appearances in form in his many different guises, activities, and functions, Lee eternally sat at the Feet of his Master, Yogi Ramsuratkumar.

Lee's many books have been translated and published around the world—in France, Germany, Romania, Spain, Mexico, India, and Brazil—and include: *In the Fire; Conscious Parenting; The Alchemy of Transformation; The Alchemy of Love and Sex; The Only*

---

1 The Baul term *khepa* is a term of respectful endearment referring to one who lives in the spontaneous, primordial state of *sahaj samadhi*, and as a result, is often experienced by the common conventional view as madcap, provocative, unpredictable, and even incendiary or insulting. Very few earn the appellation of khepa; such a one is inspired to the point of divine madness by a vision or a great *mahabhava*, (divine mood) that springs from an profound abiding insight into the Supreme Reality.

Grace is Loving God; and *Enlightened Duality* (with M. Young).[2] Several ashrams around the world are dedicated to the teachings and lineage of Khepa Lee Lozowick, making up the mandala of the Western Baul Sampradaya:

Triveni Ashram (Hohm Sahaj Mandir). Originally established in 1980 in Prescott, Arizona by Lee Lozowick, this ashram sanctuary is now located in the high desert mountains of Arizona near Chino Valley. Triveni Ashram is the location of the samadhi shrine or abode of Lee's body—a sacred place of tremendous spiritual presence, blessing, and peace and the center of the mandala of the Western Baul Sampradaya. Daily *puja, arati,* and chanting the *nama* of Yogi Ramsuratkumar, meditation, *seva* and other traditional rituals are observed along with a weekly Sunday *kirtan* and Darshan program with videos of Lee Lozowick. Formal teachings are given by Lee's core group, the Cadre, and other senior students four times a week as well as at other gatherings. Formal celebrations occur several times a year, including the Jayanthi (birthday) of Yogi Ramsuratkumar on December 1 and the birthday and *mahasamadhi* day of Lee Lozowick on November 16 and 18 respectively. For more information, call 928-778-9189.

Triveni Retreat Center. Located in the desert hills adjacent to Triveni Ashram, this retreat center was established by Lee Lozowick in 2000. The tradition of spiritually empowered solitary retreat initiated by Lee is carried on today by his students; the retreat center provides excellent vegetarian meals, an atmosphere of profound sanctuary, and the peace and power of a pristine natural environment in the high desert of central Arizona.

[2] The first volume of an extensive, authorized biography, titled *Spiritual Slavery, A Biography of Lee Lozowick*, was written by his long-time student M. Young and is available through Hohm Press.

Serious retreatants of all spiritual paths are welcome. For more information, call 928-499-0290 or 928-636-4627.

To contact Triveni Ashram or Triveni Retreat by mail:

Hohm Sahaj Mandir
P.O. Box 4410
Chino Valley, Arizona 86323

Ramji Association, France. Called "Ferme de Jutreau," this ashram in the countryside of central France was established by Lee Lozowick in 1995. Daily puja, arati, and chanting the *nama* of Yogi Ramsuratkumar, meditation, seva and other traditional rituals are observed along with a weekly Sunday Darshan program with videos of Lee Lozowick. Formal celebrations occur several times a year, including the Jayanthi (birthday) of Yogi Ramsuratkumar on December 1 and of Lee Lozowick on November 18. The summer schedule at Ferme de Jutreau includes monthly seminars, Guru Purnima, and other times of formal teachings given by the Cadre and other senior practitioners of the Hohm Community. For the annual schedule of events, contact:

Ferme de Jutreau
86260 Saint Pierre de Maille
France
011 33 5 49 84 57 28
011 33 5 49 91 01 43

Triveni II, Hohm Sahaj Trust, Tamil Nadu, India. Established by Lee Lozowick in 1999 at the request of his master, Yogi Ramsuratkumar, this ashram is located one block from the gate of the Yogi Ramsuratkumar Ashram in Tiruvannamalai. A regular schedule of puja, kirtan, meditation, seva, celebrations, charitable activities, and many other events can be obtained by contacting Volker and Ute Augustyniak.

Hohm Sahaj Trust
Triveni II
95 Chengam Road
Ramana Nagar
Tiruvannamalai, India 606603

Trimurti's Sat Loka Ashram. This ashram was established in 2000 near Bozeman, Montana by Purna Steinitz, a long-time student of Lee Lozowick. Daily meditation, arati puja, chanting, community and seva are observed. Regular satsang and teachings are given by Purna as well as weekly Darshan and kirtan programs.

Trimurti
P.O. Box 1952
Bozeman, Montana 59771

Kripa Mandir/Rasa Creek Sanctuary, British Columbia. This sanctuary was established in 2008 by Lalitha, a long-time student of Lee Lozowick. The daily schedule includes meditation, arati puja, chanting, and seva as well as a Sunday evening Darshan program. To contact Kripa Mandir:

Rasa Creek Sanctuary
1871 Trinity Valley Rd
Lumby, BC V0E 2G4

CPSIA information can be obtained
at www.ICGtesting.com
Printed in the USA
FSOW04n0130020816
23284FS

9 781935 387350